WHEN SURVIVAL IS KILLING YOU

Embracing the Protective Nature of Your Brain and Body

Esther Perry, LPC

pink umbrella books

Copyright © 2025 by Esther Perry

Cover Art by Emma Perry

Formatting by Pink Umbrella Books

Edited by Marnae Kelley

Softbound ISBN: 978-1-949598-31-5
Hardbound ISBN: 978-1-949598-32-2

No part of this publication may be reproduced, stored in a retrieval system, or transmitted in any form or by any means, electronic, mechanical, photocopying, recording, scanning, or otherwise, without the prior written permission of the author.

This publication is designed to provide accurate and authoritative information in regards to the subject matter covered. It is sold with the understanding that neither the author nor the publisher is engaged in rendering legal, investment, accounting, or other professional services. While the author has used their best efforts in preparing this book, they make no representations or warranties with respect to the accuracy or completeness of the contents of this book and specifically disclaim any implied warranties of merchantability or fitness for a particular purpose. No warranty may be created or extended by sales representatives or written sales materials. The advice and strategies contained herein may not be suitable for your situation. You should consult with a professional when appropriate. The author shall not be liable for any loss of profit or any other commercial damages, including but not limited to special, incidental, consequential, personal, or other damages.

To DZ for the sliding door that led me here. And to my earths for loving me and choosing me through every season.

CONTENTS

Preface - Exhausted	1
Chapter 1 - Surviving	3
Chapter 2 - Limits	5
Chapter 3 - Upgrading	6

UPGRADE 1.0 TAKING THE LEAD — 9

Chapter 4 - Communicating	11
Chapter 5 - Organizing	13
Chapter 6 - Defending	16
Chapter 7 - Battling	21
Chapter 8 - Failing	27
Chapter 9 - Pause	30

UPGRADE 2.0 RESPONDING TO THREATS — 35

Chapter 10 - Emergencies	37
Chapter 11 - Active	45
Chapter 12 - Passive	50
Chapter 13 - Combination	54
Chapter 14 - Unsafe	67
Chapter 15 - Safe	70
Chapter 16 - Recharging	76
Chapter 17 - Sleeping	79
Chapter 18 - Eating	86

UPGRADE 3.0 CREATING THE NETWORKS — 89

Chapter 19 - Developing	91
Chapter 20 - Expanding	94

Chapter 21 - Network	97
Chapter 22 - Memory	100
Chapter 23 - Example	107
Chapter 24 - Listening	114
Chapter 25 - Mindful	118
Chapter 26 - Interrupting	124
UPGRADE 4.0 STARTING TO SPIRAL	**129**
Chapter 27 - Cycle	131
Chapter 28 - Trauma	136
Chapter 29 - Stuck	140
Chapter 30 - Chronic	151
Chapter 31 - Gradual	158
Chapter 32 - Strengthen	164
Chapter 33 - Refresh	173
UPGRADE 5.0 SEARCHING FOR RELIEF	**177**
Chapter 34 - Rewards	179
Chapter 35 - Perspective	184
Chapter 36 - Fix	190
Chapter 37 - Harm	196
Chapter 38 - Hooked	202
Chapter 39 - Facing	209
Chapter 40 - Repeat	216
UPGRADE 6.0 DISCOVERING THE ROOTS	**217**
Chapter 41 - Connection	219
Chapter 42 - Foundation	224
Chapter 43 - Caregivers	228

Chapter 44 - Generations — 236
Chapter 45 - Relationships — 243
Chapter 46 - Trust — 248
Chapter 47 - Sex — 255
Chapter 48 - Reshape — 261
Chapter 49 - Secure — 266

UPGRADE 7.0 RESTORING THE SYSTEM — **271**
Chapter 50 - Parts — 273
Chapter 51 - Protectors — 282
Chapter 52 - Unravel — 292
Chapter 53 - Boundaries — 299
Chapter 54 - Repair — 305
Chapter 55 - Review — 312
Chapter 56 - Support — 314
Chapter 57 - Reassemble — 319

BONUS UPGRADE — **321**
Chapter A - Parents and Guardians — 323
Chapter B - Helpers and Professionals — 327
Chapter C - Teens and Youth — 333
Chapter D - Judgment and Discrimination — 340
Chapter E - Deterioration and Dying — 346
Chapter F - Neurodivergence and Schizophrenia — 348
Chapter G - Epigenetics and Methylation — 357

Appendix — **359**
Treatments and Modalities — 361
Bibliography — 367

PREFACE – EXHAUSTED

Have you noticed lately that you're losing control? That you seem to be falling apart the more you try to get it together?

Have you started to wonder why you seem to be the only person who can't unlock the secret to getting through life? You're so done with feeling stressed and frustrated and tired all the time.

Some part of you knows that life shouldn't have to be this hard, but you can't figure out how to break out of the cycle.

Maybe you just want a decent night's sleep.

Maybe you just want ten minutes with your family that don't end in yelling.

Maybe you just want to stop panicking.

Maybe you just want to stop the pain.

Maybe you just want to feel anything instead of nothing.

Or maybe you just want to feel like living is better than dying.

And you probably haven't given yourself much credit for how hard you've been fighting. And how many days you got up to face it all again. Even when you didn't want to.

You probably don't count all the hours and months and years that you worked on goals to change, or quit, or grow. Because you only count the days when you gave up, when life got too overwhelming and you couldn't do it all.

So you started to lecture yourself, hoping it would motivate you. But it didn't. At least not for long.

That's when you really started to beat up on yourself. Maybe even leaving real cuts and bruises.

But, in spite of everything you've tried, you're still stuck.

So, you figure there's something wrong with you. You've decided that you're not good enough, strong enough, or smart enough to handle life like everyone else.

At some point, you started believing that you're too broken to ever feel normal. And now you wonder if things will ever get better or if you'll be stuck like this forever.

I'm here to tell you that your problems are real. But it's not because you're weak. It's because you're in survival.

CHAPTER 1 – SURVIVING

Survival is brutal. It's kept humans and other animals alive since the beginning of time.

It's a system inside of you that kicks in when you're facing danger. It's the part that helps you run at top speed when the cops bust your party or gives you ninja reflexes when someone almost hits you on the freeway.

But survival isn't just about quick reflexes and defending yourself. It's also the part that keeps you from giving up when everything feels hopeless. It's what numbs you out when you just can't escape anymore.

Maybe it looks like eating a whole package of Oreos so you don't set the laundry on fire. Or using up all your sick days so you don't punch your boss in his arrogant face. Or lying in bed all day while your kids watch cartoons and eat popsicles because you can't stop crying.

Although these situations are not as interesting or exciting as saving a baby from a burning building, they're still part of survival. They're part of what keeps you going day after day.

And it's also why you feel so stuck.

You see, the survival part of your brain wasn't really built for the life you're living.

The human survival system developed for a very different world. A time when people had to worry about growing and hunting enough food every year, collecting water, losing loved ones to death or disease, and protecting against wild animals and "bad guys." Even though it could be tough living, the options were clear: live or die.

These days, your brain still has to worry about all the same things, *plus* worldwide disasters, corrupt politicians, hackers, nutrition facts, bullies, and credit scores. And paying for housing, medication, college, and retirement.

Every day you're surrounded by pressures that aren't exactly life or death, but, in some ways, they kind of are.

Money, work deadlines, staying healthy, building safe relationships, and standing up for your rights are all important parts of surviving. But if these things go wrong, they're not really going to kill you (well, at least not right away). So, you get to walk around dealing with a bunch of worries that are only *sort of* life or death.

Now, don't get me wrong, your great-great grandparents had a lot of the same challenges and plenty to deal with. But they didn't live with 24/7 media feeds and news outlets constantly updating them on violence, global warming, crime, how they're failing as parents, and the newest thing that's causing cancer.

It's no wonder that you're overwhelmed. Every day your survival system is so overloaded with unpredictable threats that your brain and body are almost always at 99% capacity. Which is why your whole day can melt down with a tiny, 2% problem. And why going off-grid or getting online can feel like such a relief.

All this time you thought you were failing, but you've just been operating with an out-of-date system.

What you need is an upgrade.

CHAPTER 2 – LIMITS

The first step to upgrading your survival system is to get to know how your brain and body work.

But here's the challenge: this is a *big* file to download.

Scientists have worked for thousands of years to figure out how the basic parts of your brain work, and they are still learning new things every day. And so far, it's complicated. Like, *really* complicated. Which means it takes a lot of time and energy to research and put together the bits we do know, let alone the stuff we still aren't sure about.

But your brain is already overloaded.

When you're in survival mode, the part of your brain that can download and learn new things is low on energy and space. So, even if you work really hard and focus all your energy, you're still going to fail. Your brain doesn't recharge on a can-do attitude or free up space by squeezing another goal onto your to-do list.

No wonder you've been feeling like the odds have been stacked against you: they have been. The information you need is too big for the space and energy that's available in your brain right now.

You are not the problem, and you are not a failure. You just have limits.

You can't stop your life and get a degree in brain science just to make it through another Monday.

CHAPTER 3 – UPGRADING

Now that you know what you're up against, let's talk about how we're going to get you upgraded.

Before we get started though, let me tell you that this book isn't magical. There is no one-size-fits-all recipe for everlasting happiness and perfect relationships.

One self-help book isn't going to change things overnight. You can't repair your mind and body like it's a piece of broken furniture or a leaky pipe.

True healing and growth will take time and patience. And it can be hard to find the space and energy to focus on these things.

So instead of offering a quick fix, I'm going to teach you some of the things you need to know about your body and brain so that you can work *with* yourself instead of *against* yourself.

To do this, I'm going to compare your brain and body to a high school. Since you already have some idea of how a school system works, this keeps us from having to start from scratch or get you that degree in brain science to understand everything.

Just like a high school, your body and brain are one giant system with different areas that are working on separate things but all at the same time.

Think about how a high school has a principal, librarian, custodian, teachers, students, tests, supplies, and *so* many more pieces. Because most people are used to how a school works, it doesn't seem too confusing. But if you really think about it, it's kind of amazing how many schools can keep all sorts of things running and students graduating, especially when the class sizes are big and the budgets are small.

Your brain and body are very similar. It's impressive how much they're doing, all day, every day, even when it feels like you're falling apart.

As you begin to learn about all the different ways your system has been working for you, I'm hoping you might ease up on the criticism and give yourself a little credit.

And now that you understand what we're trying to do, let's go over the plan. Brains, especially ones in survival, like to know what to expect.

So I'm going to let you know that this book is broken up into small sections or upgrades. This should be easier for your brain to download and understand, especially if it's low on energy and space.

Every upgrade is a complete lesson or idea so you can walk away after each upgrade with some useful information, even if you're not able to make it through the whole book.

Each upgrade will also build on the one before so that the complicated stuff will actually be easier to understand by the time you get there.

And, if you still get overloaded, take a break. Take a few days. Think on it or sleep on it. Your brain can only do so much, and the book will be waiting here for as long as it takes.

UPGRADE 1.0
TAKING THE LEAD

CHAPTER 4 – COMMUNICATING

Let's jump in by talking about communication.

Communication in your body is handled by a bunch of connecter cells called neurons.

They are tiny messengers that send and receive signals all the time. You have billions of them, and they run through your entire body. **When you string them together, they're called nerves.** And they communicate all sorts of things back and forth through your brain and body, such as thoughts, emotions, pain, pleasure, images, sounds, etc.

This will probably be easier to understand when we think about our high school analogy.

In a school, different kinds of messages keep everyone updated about what's going on, especially when there's a lot happening. Whether it's an email about fundraisers, a bell for lunch dismissal, or an overhead announcement about late buses, communication is happening everywhere, all the time.

Neurons are very similar. They send messages back and forth all day to handle everything in your body. Some neurons are in charge of forwarding signals, and some are in charge of stopping signals.

If a neuron passes a signal, it gets fired up and forwards the pulse to other neurons that will keep passing or stopping the signal until they deliver the message everywhere it needs to go.

Each neuron has a unique signal all by itself, but they can't communicate much on their own unless they combine together to form signal chains. We call these chains nerves, and they communicate specific meanings or ideas to other parts of your body based on how the signals have been grouped together.

A signal through one group of neurons might be saying you're hungry. Another group could be communicating that you're hearing your favorite song on the radio. And another group might be telling you that you're late.

In this way, neurons and nerves develop their own internal language.

It might help to think about neurons as letters in the alphabet and nerves as words.

Each letter has a unique identity, but it won't mean a lot unless that letter combines with other letters to form a word.

Similarly, neurons don't mean very much all by themselves, but when you combine them together to create a nerve, **each nerve holds a different meaning**.

And since each nerve takes on a unique meaning, they can combine into bigger groups called **nerve centers** that **coordinate all the individual nerves into really complex ideas**. This is like taking the words we build from the alphabet and turning them into sentences and full conversations.

It really starts to beef up the communication and allows your system to do complicated tasks. And because you have billions of connections, your brain and body are always handling an impressive amount of messages all at once.

This is why you can be late and hungry and still sing along to your favorite song. *And* still have other neurons signaling messages to keep your balance, manage your temperature, hold your bladder, and keep breathing.

CHAPTER 5 – ORGANIZING

Hopefully you have a better idea of how neurons work, but, if you're still lost, you're probably good to keep going. If all you can remember is that nerves and neurons send messages through your body, then you should still be okay to understand the next few chapters.

Right now, we're going to talk about two different nerve centers that are really important players in your brain. We can understand a lot about survival when we learn how these two nerve centers communicate together and work with your body.

The frontal cortex of your brain is the first nerve center we're going to talk about.

The **frontal cortex** is a big chunk of your brain right behind your forehead, and **it's where you do your on-purpose and big-picture thinking**.

This is one of the largest nerve centers in your whole body, and with good reason. This is the part that tries to solve important life problems, like who the Bachelor is going to pick in the finale or how you're going to get out of that BBQ with your pushy neighbors.

It's also the part of your brain that helps you focus on the things that are important to you. And talks you out of risky stuff, especially as you get older.

This part of your brain is pretty legit, actually. Even on your worst days, your cortex makes iPhone technology look like preschool math. (No offense to the hard-working preschoolers out there.)

The best way to understand your cortex is to think of it like the *principal* of your brain and body.

In a school, the principal's job is to think of the big picture. Her main job isn't to teach classes, serve food in the cafeteria, or sweep the hallways. *But* if the teaching is going poorly, or the food is always cold, or the hallways are sticky, she would be in charge of noticing these problems and working with other teams to fix them.

Just like the principal, your frontal cortex is all about the big picture. It doesn't control digestion, sweating, or your heartbeat, but if any of those things were acting weird, your frontal cortex would start doing a lot of on-purpose thinking to figure out how to deal with it.

A principal can also tune into the communication at pretty much any time she wants. She might make calls, send emails, or check in on security feeds so she can coordinate and give updates.

Your cortex works in a similar way. It's connected to a lot of the nerve groups communicating inside of you, and it can tune into different feelings or ideas when it needs to. Sometimes it's to notice that you need a jacket, sometimes it's to make a plan for dinner, and sometimes it's just to overthink the 27 ways you're going to fail that thing next week.

It's definitely an important nerve center in your system, and it's the part where you really have the most control of your thinking and your actions.

In a perfect world, your cortex is a brilliant leader with great authority and a lot of wisdom. A boss that keeps your system organized and running smoothly, even when times are tough.

But, if you end up in survival for too long, your cortex doesn't stand a chance. It will get completely overloaded and become overwhelmed, tired, and impatient because there's just more to do than it can possibly handle.

It will feel a lot like a broken school system where the principal is exhausted, grumpy, and worn out all the time. The staff won't get clear instructions on how to work together or get support when they need it. So even though classes will still be taught and credits earned, the whole place will feel disorganized and frustrating.

The same thing ends up happening between your cortex and your body.

Without a clear plan, all the other parts of your body and brain will switch to survival and do what they must to keep you alive. This means that there will be less time and energy for communication between your cortex and your body. If this goes on for too long, everything in your system will start to feel chaotic and sloppy.

It's really hard for your cortex to keep up when all your big picture, on-purpose thinking is spent just putting out fires and staying ahead of the chaos. Even basic things like showering, laundry, and eating will become difficult to fit in.

And, just like a school principal, your cortex can't just fix the whole system by barking orders and taking over all the jobs. And, *unlike* a principal, your cortex can't just fire parts of your brain and body and start over . . . no matter how dysfunctional they are.

So, as much as your cortex wants to take charge when everything is breaking down, it's probably going to burn out from all the effort it takes just to keep things afloat.

To help you fully understand how your cortex can get so broken down like this, we need to introduce you to another player.

CHAPTER 6 – DEFENDING

The next part of your system that we're going to review is called the amygdala (uh-mig-duh-luh).

You have an amygdala on both the left and right side of your brain, and they're about the size and shape of a bean.

Now, you might wonder why we're jumping from one of the largest chunks of your brain to one of the smaller ones. In spite of its size, your **amygdala has a really important job** in your system: **to keep you safe**.

Let's go back to our school setup. The best comparison for this part of your system would be a security team.

Since a security team's main job is to make sure everyone is safe, security guards will spend most of their time watching and listening to everything around them in case a threat shows up.

Because they are always watching and listening, they get a chance to know the system inside and out. Most of the time they're probably watching a bunch of security feeds or walking up and down hallways and stopping every so often to listen and respond to their radios.

From a distance, it might seem like they aren't doing all that much, but it's really important to understand that this *is* their job. It's critical that security guards are allowed to focus on their environment and be tuned in to every part of the school. That way they have time to get to know what's safe and what's not.

If a security guard spends time getting to know everyone and the regular patterns of the school (and they aren't getting distracted by other issues all the time), then they are in the best position to notice threats early *and* to defend the system whenever they have to.

In a perfect world, this means they'd be able to block out danger before it even happens or send out alarms with plenty of time to get everyone to safety.

Your amygdala does the same thing for your brain and body.

Your amygdala is in charge of security and spends a lot of time in the background, just paying attention to everything you're going through. In the same way security staff would use cameras and radios to scan the school, your amygdala uses your senses to review what's happening inside and outside of you at any given moment.

It does this by checking the nerves coming in from your senses like sights, sounds, smell, tastes, and touch. By staying in communication with all of these senses, your amygdala has a much better chance of detecting problems before they get out of hand.

In fact, our touch sense isn't just about what our bodies feel on the outside of us, but also about what's happening on the inside of us. Upset guts and high fevers can be just as dangerous as a hot stove. That's why it's important that your amygdala is communicating with all these parts of your body.

The amygdala is *very* different from your cortex. Instead of coordinating big projects and keeping track of the past, present and future, **your amygdala has to be constantly tapped into the live stream of your senses**. The amygdala has to stay in the present **so it can spot danger and sound the alarm** to keep you alive.

So, in order to keep focused on the present and not get stuck on complicated steps, it has to have really simple processes for handling danger. It does this through **matching**.

Here's how this works.

When you go through dangerous or scary things, **your amygdala records short snips of your senses** to save for later. Your amygdala then uses these recordings to look for any situations in the live feeds that match up. If you do end up in a situation that matches an old danger file, your amygdala will sound the alarm since it will assume that danger is about to surface again.

This might be a little clearer if we think about how a security team will probably have mugshots of people who might be dangerous.

For example, if a security guard discovers that someone has threatened their school, they will likely save a picture of that person and keep them on file in their security office. By doing this, they can quickly notice if someone on the security feed matches the picture and go into protection mode.

In a similar way, your amygdala will keep files on sights, sounds, tastes, smells, and body feelings that have been linked to dangerous situations in the past and **go into emergency mode when one of these matches comes through the live feeds**.

This is why you might get spooked in a crowd when someone looks like your 7th grade bully, or why you avoid the corner where you had that car accident last year.

Matching is a very important process for your amygdala, even if it's not perfect. It's better for your system to have a false alarm once in a while and protect itself than to miss danger completely.

Let's walk through a more detailed example of how this works so you can see what it might look like in real life.

Imagine that you're 8 years old and just showed up at your friend Jimmy's birthday party. You're super excited because you see he has a giant piñata in the backyard.

So, after you eat cake and play some party games, the piñata finally comes out. You get really excited when your turn arrives and run up to get blindfolded and be spun around.

Now, imagine that as you're swinging, a neighbor drives by and honks his horn at someone trying to cross the street. Well, since you're blindfolded, you get startled and confused. You forget what you're doing, and the piñata comes sailing back at your face and knocks you over. Sadly, this makes you hit your lip on the picnic table and start to bleed.

Luckily, Jimmy's dad is really nice and helps you out. So after you let out a few tears and get all cleaned up, you head back outside and have a lot of fun for the rest of the party.

From then on, you might not remember much about busting your lip since it didn't hurt too bad and you still got lots of candy. But your amygdala probably noticed that you got knocked over and might have decided to save some files on the situation so it's prepared for future piñata attacks.

The challenge here is that your amygdala isn't going to tell you what memory snips it ends up saving, and it might even save some matches that aren't really connected to danger.

For example, in this situation, it might save the sound of a horn so the next time you hear a car honking, you get spooked, jump out of your chair, and feel panicked without fully understanding why. Your amygdala could also file away the feeling of darkness because you were wearing a blindfold. So, tonight, when your mom goes to turn off your bedroom light (as she usually does), you get angry and yell at her to leave it on, even though you didn't really mean to be mad about it.

Sometimes these matches are helpful, and sometimes they are a little off, but you can't really blame your amygdala for saving these files when you ended up with a bloody lip. Your amygdala is doing its best to protect your system and trying to figure out every match that signals danger.

And like we reviewed at the beginning of this book, your poor amygdala can have a hard time with making correct matches in the modern world, where horror movies are safe, but tanning isn't.

Now, not to stress you out, but there's still more.

Your amygdala can really struggle to get things right when you're already living in survival.

Going back to the school comparison, I want you to imagine what it would be like if a security guard worked in a really dangerous school where things were unsafe or really stressful all the time.

In that situation, it's hard to keep track of all the files and matches. There's just too much going on all at once, and they don't get a chance to learn the difference between safe and dangerous because the school is dealing with tough things nearly every day.

The same thing can be true in your system. **If your life has been stressful** for a long time, **your amygdala can get pretty confused** about what is actually safe and what's dangerous.

Your amygdala might have a hard time knowing how to relax since it doesn't understand what being safe looks like or feels like. And, at the same time, your amygdala could also go so overboard on protection that you find yourself blowing up or freaking out over simple things.

If this is you, you probably get upset with yourself a lot for being so sensitive to things that don't seem to bother everyone else. And your friends and family might even criticize and tease you about it, thinking it will "toughen you up." Which only adds to the stress.

Even though your amygdala can help you survive a rough history, it might also mean that your body and brain never learn how to live any other way.

And a life of survival isn't really living.

This is why things like joy, peace, or even love sometimes feel out of reach. There isn't much room in survival for anything safe and calm.

I realize it might be upsetting to hear this. And to find out you're here because of danger or problems in your past. You probably didn't choose to be here, and now you're stuck, trying to find the motivation to dig yourself out of the mess.

It's definitely not fair, and you're allowed to be as hurt or as irritated as you need to be.

Learning about these systems can sometimes be rough. Even when the information is helpful, it doesn't mean it just fixes everything.

You can give yourself some credit though for making it to this point because we just got through some of the toughest pieces of this download. It's a lot to learn, and you made it.

The next chapter should be a little easier as we'll talk about how these pieces work together. And I'm hoping it will give you some validation that your system isn't as broken as you might have thought.

I'm sorry if this is a difficult process. Bring the mess along, and we'll get there.

CHAPTER 7 – BATTLING

We're now to the part of this upgrade where we tie a few pieces together, and I think you'll start to see how much of this applies to you.

We're still not to the part where we talk about the details of what happens to your body when your amygdala sounds the alarm, but we will in the next upgrade because that's important too.

Right now, I want to go back to the school comparison. We know that there are a lot of ways to respond in an emergency at a school, depending on what the threat is. Staying safe could look like leaving the building, moving locations, or finding cover.

What's interesting is that there is almost always one pattern that is the same for a school-wide emergency: the people in charge change.

At first, this might not be obvious, but you have probably watched it happen and didn't really notice with everything that was going on.

Remember how a principal is usually in charge of everything in a school, including the building and the people?

Well, one of her main goals will be to stay ahead of what's coming. And part of that will include making plans to stay safe and avoid danger. But, if the danger still happens anyway, that's when a principal will change from a leader to a follower.

When this happens, the security teams become the best option to handle the risk since they have prepared and trained for these exact situations.

They are in charge of noticing the threat and then managing everything until things are safe again. They will take over all the communications, give orders, follow up with everyone, and stay in charge until the threat passes.

During this time, the principal will probably still help, but she's no longer the person in charge. Her communication access will be shut down during the threat so that the emergency lines stay clear. That way the security team can easily take over the leadership of the school.

If you think about it, it's a brilliant system. If the principal had to be trained in security too, she'd always be battling between her big-picture principal duties and keeping her ear to the ground for danger.

Having one player in charge of the big picture and one in charge of danger is really smart. It allows the principal to not get distracted so she can do her job, and it allows the security team to be free from big-picture projects that will distract them from watching and listening to the feeds.

Your brain is just as brilliant, and it has the same setup.

Your frontal cortex is usually in charge, but, **during danger, your amygdala takes over** to make sure you stay protected.

Unfortunately, since the cortex is the only part where we have *on-purpose* control, the amygdala takeover doesn't always feel great. When your cortex loses communication with the rest of your body and can't control anything, it can make you feel pretty overwhelmed.

For many people, this isn't a big deal because the alerts don't turn on very often. And when the emergency response does take over, it's not too complicated. Your amygdala "security team" handles the danger and then gives the control back to your frontal cortex "principal" when all is safe again.

During the danger, it may be hard for your cortex and amygdala to be on the same page because your only goal is to stay safe, and you don't really have time to process all the details.

But, once the danger has passed, your cortex will reconnect and work with your amygdala to update the danger files based on what happened. That way, your security response will get better over time. Most of this happens in the background of your mind, so it won't be obvious what the updates are.

An easy way to see how this takeover can work is by thinking about horror movies. When you sit in a theater and watch something scary, your cortex is clearly aware of what you're getting yourself into. It knows that things are going to jump out and scare you, and it also knows that none of it is real. But most of the time, no matter how prepared you are for something to jump out or come crawling at you, your cortex still won't be able to stay in charge.

Your amygdala is going to start getting really nervous as it notices all sorts of scary matches coming through the live feed like squeaky doors or things moving in the shadows.

So, when something finally jumps out of the corner, your amygdala is going to take over. You might jerk in your chair, or scream bloody murder, or throw your hands up to protect yourself. Even though your cortex totally knows everything is fake, it can't stop your amygdala from taking over and sounding the alarm.

In this situation, it's usually pretty easy to get your cortex back in charge because it's obvious why you were scared and that you're not actually in danger. Your amygdala will get the message it was a false alarm and let the cortex step back up as the leader.

Your system is going to be able to walk out of the theater, review and update the files, and move on to the rest of your day. When your cortex and amygdala both do their jobs correctly, they make a pretty good team.

So, let's talk about why a survival system struggles to keep this all organized.

Let's think about the school again but one that has experienced a lot of dangerous stuff. We already talked about how the security team might get overwhelmed and have a hard time keeping up with the issues. They can also get so used to danger that they just assume everything is unsafe and call everything an emergency.

If this happens, then the rest of the folks at school are constantly responding to false alarms and won't be able to keep up with what they're supposed to be doing. Staff and students aren't usually going to keep writing essays and solving math problems while sirens are blasting.

On the other hand, if security doesn't notice or respond to threats correctly (or at all), then the rest of the school is getting regularly caught off guard by danger and definitely can't stay focused.

And in both situations, a principal couldn't focus on her duties either because of the constant threats. Obviously, keeping everyone safe will be way more important than planning assemblies or budgeting. She'll likely start focusing her big-picture skills on looking for danger and get distracted from doing her regular jobs.

With the whole system acting more stressed and on edge, it's also likely that things with the security team will continue to get worse. They will trigger the alarms more easily and respond badly. They might get mixed up and sound the alarm to leave when everyone should stay or to stay when everyone should leave. They might also get slower and slower to react as they run out of energy.

This usually leads to a lot more false alarms or missed alarms, which just keeps the whole school system in survival mode.

Your system can end up with similar problems.

If your body and brain become stuck in survival, it's hard to focus on anything but threats. Your amygdala might take over control a lot more often than it needs to or miss obvious signs of trouble.

As this starts to happen, your cortex will try to do what it can to help but won't be able to stop getting taken over all the time. This is usually the point where the cortex starts losing sight of the big picture and gets really focused on the danger.

It might get stuck in the past, replaying old memories to find out what went wrong and see what can be fixed. It could also start looking into the future to prepare for every little thing that might go wrong. The overthinking can get out of control!

And because your focus becomes obsessed with danger, you might also start forgetting important things, like your best friend's birthday or to pick up your kid from school.

The rest of your system might delay jobs it's supposed to be doing, like digesting food or sleeping. And it might have a hard time letting you relax even when things are actually okay.

As you can imagine, this doesn't really help the amygdala security team to cool down at all, and the whole system can get really overworked.

Because the current danger files aren't keeping you safe, your amygdala and cortex will spend all their energy trying to figure out what danger matches they are missing or need to fix. They don't know how to let go and move forward with so many unresolved threats hanging over you.

If they had the time to hold some system meetings and reorganize some of their files, they might actually get somewhere. But in the middle of survival mode, they're only going to be focused on dealing with danger. Over time, both **your cortex and amygdala** will start focusing on their own survival tasks and **struggle to cooperate or be on the same page.**

This might even feel like having two totally different people inside of you and not understanding how you can decide to act one way one minute and do the opposite the very next.

For example, your cortex might notice that your angry outbursts are getting out of hand. It'll probably try to fix things by telling you something like "Just control your anger. It's not that hard–just don't yell anymore." But then, less than 2 minutes later, your amygdala will take over and scream at your sister because she rolled her eyes and called you an idiot. When your cortex finally regains control, it will be upset that you weren't strong enough to hold back the yelling, and it might even tell you that you *are* an idiot.

Or your cortex might constantly tell you to stand up to your boss about not getting paid overtime. But then your body freezes every time she walks into your cubicle because your amygdala decides it's not safe when she's around.

It really stinks after a while because life is hard enough without having to manage a raging battle inside of you all the time.

Just so you know, this is *not* a sign of being crazy. This is a sign that your cortex and amygdala are both very strong and doing what they're supposed to, but they're not working well *together* and need some help.

Think about how a high school might look when the principal is overwhelmed and the security team is always under threat and the whole school is used to everything being interrupted by emergencies all the time.

It's going to be hard for everyone to get along and communicate well. Everyone will probably feel like they're not being heard or getting their needs met. And lots of problems will be swept under the rug. There will probably be a lot of blaming, anger, stress, avoidance, and regular threats to quit.

With your brain and body going through the same kinds of breakdowns, it's no wonder there haven't been any easy fixes. You're trying to organize a bunch of parts that have a mind of their own and cool down systems that are *supposed* to be sounding alarms and interrupting everything.

It wouldn't surprise me if you've got a lot of those same kinds of blame, anger, stress, avoidance, and give-up feelings going on inside of you too.

Hopefully you can see why it's not helpful when anyone expects you to fix all these complicated layers by saying stuff like "just snap out of it," or "just stop making excuses," or "just be more positive."

CHAPTER 8 – FAILING

If you've been dealing with survival for a long while, then your system is currently at max capacity. Asking your body and brain to work on another "fix it" plan isn't going to be that useful, and it's definitely going to feel overwhelming.

Plus, you've already tried those goals, right? Eating better, exercise, meditation, journaling, gratitude lists, and so on. Since you're here, reading this right now, they probably didn't work. Or you forgot to keep them up, or you just stopped caring.

It's not that these ideas are bad or that they don't work–it's that a survival system genuinely can't care about those things, even if it wanted to. Those are the things people can keep up with when they feel in control and believe they have a future. Survival doesn't come with those luxuries.

Your cortex is the only part of your brain that can understand, learn, and carry out goals. And self-improvement is a big-picture thing. So, **how is your cortex supposed to get back on track when your amygdala is hijacking everything** all the time? Not to mention that your cortex is already maxed out, trying to keep up with a million things.

In fact, there are a lot of coping skills that are supposed to help you *during* an emergency response, such as breathing, taking a timeout, or thinking before you speak. But let's be real about this. Now that you know how these nerve centers work, can you see that these kinds of skills are actually *more* likely to fail during a crisis?

If your cortex is the only place where you can understand and remember to use these big-picture skills, and you're supposed to apply them when your amygdala has taken over and your body is in the middle of an emergency, then how is that really supposed to work?

If you think of our school, that's about as useful as having the principal going from person to person to tell them that it's a false alarm and to go back to their seats. Since she's cut off from the communication systems, her messages can't get very far. If, by some miracle, anyone even listens to her over the sirens and distractions, they'll just ignore her and keep the evacuation going.

If you were at school that day, who would you decide to follow? I'm betting the security staff, just in case there really was danger.

Going back to your brain and body system, **this is why you can follow every step of a really useful self-improvement plan and still fail** when things get stressful. Your system is much more likely to hear and follow your amygdala when things are sketchy, even if your cortex has a wonderful plan.

So we need to be more realistic about improving things.

Although a journal or a new exercise plan might be steps you use in this healing process, they aren't going to be the whole process. You'll have to be willing to approach this in a totally new way.

We can do this by teaching your cortex how to become a better leader of your body and brain.

Now you might be confused since we just got done talking about how powerless your cortex can become, but your cortex *can* regain leadership of your system. It's just not in the way you'd expect.

Most examples of leaders in our world are so toxic that it's not surprising that we use the same dysfunctional techniques with our brain and body.

We don't motivate people or brains by yelling at them and criticizing them all the time. And we don't create healthy systems or bodies by expecting too much and making it feel like nothing is ever good enough.

Since that's probably how you have learned to deal with yourself when things are tough, we're going to work on unlearning this and replacing it with something different.

We're going to help your cortex become a supportive leader by teaching you how to better listen to and cooperate with your body system. We're going to help you recognize that your system is trying to get your attention because it's trying to communicate with you, not because it's weak or too sensitive. And we're going to help you slowly appreciate how much your system is *already* doing so you can better understand why you're exhausted.

Hopefully this will make it a little easier to find some patience for yourself as you work on becoming a better system boss.

But don't worry. We'll keep taking it one step at a time so you don't get more overloaded.

CHAPTER 9 – PAUSE

The first step for becoming a healthier boss is **taking a break**.

This probably sounds too simple, but it's a key step before we move on.

If there's a racket in your system all the time, it's going to be hard to communicate. You can't just yell over the alarms and expect something to happen. We need to **start by pausing and letting your system rest** a little before we can do anything else.

To do this, we're going to walk through an activity where you'll just follow along. It shouldn't be complicated or difficult, but feel free to skip it if it is.

You're allowed to take what you need from this book and leave the rest. Please don't force anything that isn't working. That's a toxic leader habit, and we're going to try to let go of some of those.

If this activity *does* seem to work for you and you like it, you can use it on your own. But it's okay if you don't remember to use it because that's normal. You're more likely to forget things when you're in survival. It's not a failure. It's just a fact.

So, I will be reminding you throughout this book to go back and run through the activities so you can practice them without having to pressure yourself into remembering (or beat yourself up if you forget).

It might take a few tries before any of them work. Your system may need some practice before it can let go a little. That's okay too.

The activity in this chapter is meant to help your whole system take a short break and relax. So, it's useful to start practicing it during times or in places where you already feel kind of safe or, at least, don't feel too threatened.

It will be hard to let your guard down and keep your amygdala from taking over if your kids are going to start screaming, your boss is going to walk in, or your spouse is going to flip on that TV show you hate. In time, these will be the perfect moments to use them, but not before you get some practice.

You don't need to do anything fancy, and you can jump right into the activity if you want. But you can also make it cozier by putting on some chill music, sitting in your favorite chair, or cuddling up with your pet.

Ready? . . . . Here we go.

This activity is called **Calm, Safe Space.**

First, I want you to start imagining a place where you believe you might feel safe.

(It's best if it's not a place from your past as reality has an annoying way of sneaking in the danger matches.)

As you think of a calm space, I want you to think about whether this place would be indoors, or outdoors, or both. It doesn't have to be a real place.

Now where would this place be located? Would it be a real place like a library, the mountains, on a beach, or in a giant skyscraper? Or would it be a fantasy place like under the ocean, in your favorite book, in the clouds, in a kingdom, or on another planet?

As you think about the location, start to imagine the things that you could add to help you feel more anchored or settled. Would you have people who feel safe and calming? These can be friends, family, angels, teachers, or even Bob Ross. (I'm sure he'd be happy to add some happy little trees.)

Would you add places to lie down or sit, like hammocks, bean bag chairs, or giant, comfy beds? Or would you add something for high energy like snowboards, speedboats, or ziplines? Would you bring your pet along? What would the weather be like? Would you have food or drinks, like tea, chocolate, or Hot Cheetos? Would you add any smells in the air? How about any sounds?

Once you have an idea of everything you want in your space, let's dive into the details to help you get a better sense of it.

Let's start with everything you see. I want you to keep adding what you need in your space to feel like you belong there. Then spend some time noticing how it feels to look at these wonderful things. This could be the open road, sunsets, the Milky Way, buildings, beaches, mermaids, dragons, etc.

Then I want you to notice the sounds around you and focus on them. Maybe this is a babbling brook, a thunderstorm, the wind in the trees, or your favorite music. Notice how your body starts to feel as you connect with these sounds.

Next, I want you to imagine how it feels to touch the things around you. Imagine your body getting cozy in a hammock or driving in the cockpit of a race car. Feel ocean waves pulling at your feet, or the weightlessness of your body in outer space, or the cushiness of sitting in a fluffy chair, or a cool breeze blowing across your body as you run through a meadow.

As you continue to feel your body settle, imagine if you'd be eating anything or tasting anything on your tongue. Maybe you sense sea water in the air, or enjoy the crunch of a perfect apple, or drink refreshing spring water, or savor the sweetness of a piece of chocolate.

Lastly, I want you to imagine what you'd be smelling. Maybe the scent of wildflowers in a meadow, the smell of baking cookies, a hint of a campfire, or fresh laundry.

As you notice and imagine all of these senses, I want you to think of what you'd like to name your space. It could be as simple as "My Calm Place" or "My Safe Space." But you can get creative and think of a name that would be special to you.

If the name doesn't come right away, don't stress. It might come to you as you spend more time there. But if you do find a name, just imagine saying that name to yourself as you keep your senses focused on what's around you.

Now, remember that your senses might have unsafe matches that pop up, so if something you've added into your space begins to feel funny, just erase it or ask it to leave and replace it with something else.

If you need to, you can create boundaries and barriers in your space that don't let in outside stress. You can hire robots or gorilla bouncers to kick out any unsafe judgments or criticism that might try to sneak in. You can even imagine that the rain in your world washes away anything stressful and install a magic button to make it rain whenever you need to reset.

Go ahead and sit for a bit with these boundaries and continue to notice your senses and see how you feel. This would be a perfect time to pause the book and take a moment to rest, but you get to do whatever feels good for you. If you'd rather go on, just fold down the corner of the page or stick a gum wrapper here and come back when the time is right.

Hopefully you were able to feel a bit more settled during this activity and allow your system to take a tiny vacation. If it worked a little bit, it might be helpful to keep practicing.

Repeating the activity can help your system get better at letting go and calming down a little more. But if you automatically feel stressed thinking about that, you can also wait for the book to remind you again.

Now, just a quick side note. You might struggle with this activity if you have something called **aphantasia**. This means it's **hard (or even impossible) to imagine pictures** in your mind. If that's you, this activity might have felt complicated and frustrating.

Not every activity or idea works for everyone. And that's perfectly fine. If this activity didn't help you, then go ahead and take a break and see if you can find something else that will help your body feel more calm or settled. We'll go through other activities during this book so you will have more options to choose from as we go.

Okay. You've officially made it through the first upgrade.

Even if it took you a long time to make it to this sentence, you are doing great.

Some of you might be ready to jump into the next download, and that's cool, but don't feel like you have to. Many people learn better when they take time to sit with ideas and process them. If that's you, go ahead and pause. We'll be here when you've got some space and energy for the next upgrade.

UPGRADE 2.0
RESPONDING TO THREATS

CHAPTER 10 – EMERGENCIES

Now that you have had a chance to take a break, I want to talk more about what emergencies look like in your body and not just in your brain.

By reviewing this information, you'll learn that your body is probably reacting the way it's meant to, even if it's frustrating and confusing. And, hopefully, you will begin to understand that you're not as broken as you might feel.

To do this, we're going to go over exactly what happens to different parts of your body as you go through an emergency response.

It can be really eye opening to understand that survival reactions are part of what's been going on with your body. And you can start to see just how much it's been impacting you.

So let's jump in by going back to our school analogy and putting together a few more connections.

When you think about how emergencies are handled in a school, you'll realize that the security team will sound different alarms and take different actions based on the situation. They are in charge of recognizing the threat and announcing which plan to follow so that everyone knows what to do.

The same thing is true for your body **while your amygdala is managing an emergency**. It's in charge of **choosing a crisis plan** and then **sounding the alarms**. This will tell your body what kind of action to take so it can handle what's going on.

This may not be obvious to you because the signals aren't really for your conscious brain (aka your frontal cortex). These messages are for your **organs and tissues and muscles**. Pretty much all your insides **get directions for carrying out the emergency plan**.

If your amygdala decides that **boosting your energy** is your best chance at survival, it will direct many of your organs and muscles to activate and turn up the energy. But it might also decide that **slowing down the energy** is the better option and send signals to shut down many parts of your body too.

In a crisis, **each organ or body part plays a different role in the plan**. These are generally based on the messages back and forth between the amygdala and your body. By keeping in touch with your body, your amygdala can update the system as the plan moves forward or changes.

Now, I haven't talked much about what happens in your body yet. And there's a reason. If you've been struggling with survival responses, just talking about those feelings can sometimes trigger your amygdala into thinking you're in trouble again.

Unfortunately, if you're someone with a really good imagination, and you can pull up clear images in your mind with sounds, smells, and body feelings, then you're at a much higher risk for developing a stressed-out amygdala and more likely to struggle with survival.

This is because your amygdala doesn't have a concept of time.

Remember that your amygdala is only built for being in the present. It has a hard time understanding that the vivid memories and worst-case scenarios you are pulling up in your mind aren't actually happening to you right this second.

So, when your brain starts getting full of old trauma clips or doomsday nightmares, your amygdala can mistake these sensations as a live-feed threat, especially if the images are realistic and detailed.

This can make it difficult for some of you to review these details about your body. It can bring up body sensations and memories that trick your amygdala into thinking you're under threat.

If you *do* have an active imagination and are worried this information might overload you, I have a couple tricks that might help.

As you read, go ahead and imagine that these reactions are happening to a cartoon character on a TV screen. That way it keeps the information a little distant and less realistic and gives your amygdala the idea that the danger isn't too real or too close.

If that doesn't work, you can also try to turn the images to black and white or ask your body to turn down the "volume" on difficult senses or feelings until you know how to handle them better. You can slowly tap your feet back and forth to stay focused. And you can even imagine putting any uncomfortable feelings into a safe or special container until you are more prepared to deal with them.

If things go off track, jump back to the Calm, Safe Space activity, listen to your favorite song, or watch a funny video clip. There's no downside to this since it will give you a chance to show your system that you're really trying to be a better boss by taking it safe and slow.

Now that you're a bit more ready, let's go over the way your body reacts when the signals are sent to **turn *up* energy**.

Go-Mode

When the emergency plan tells the body to activate and energize, your system is likely to go through the following changes:

Senses. Your senses can feel sharp and have a laser focus on anything and everything that could be dangerous. You might be able to focus on the tiniest details or hear the softest sounds while completely missing big things going on around you, especially if your amygdala decides they're not part of the threat.

Time. You might feel like time slows down in go-mode. The hyperfocus from your senses can keep you one step ahead of everything, and it might even feel like you're in a slow-motion fight scene in an action film.

Cortisol. Cortisol is a hormone that gets dumped into your bloodstream. This hormone tells your body to release glucose (or sugar energy) so that there's enough fuel to get through a crisis.

Adrenaline. Adrenaline is also dumped into your bloodstream. This hormone helps your body to increase the capacity and energy of your heart and lungs. This can make your body feel unstoppable because adrenaline helps many parts of your body work at their highest level.

Lungs. Your lungs will breathe harder and open wider to take in as much oxygen as possible. This happens so your body is prepared to take action. You need extra oxygen to make sure your muscles can keep up with the plan. You will also breathe more from your chest and less from your stomach since it will bring in oxygen more quickly. Strangely, this will sometimes feel like it's hard to breathe because your lungs get so full of oxygen.

Heart. Your heart will start beating really fast to deliver the adrenaline, oxygen, and sugar as quickly, and as often, as it can. That way your muscles are ready with all the materials they need to work at peak capacity. Your blood pressure may get really high to try and make sure that your body is getting plenty of blood flow.

Chest. Your chest can get really heavy and even experience pain as your lungs expand and your heart muscles pump harder.

Muscles and tissues. Muscles and tissue all over your body, especially in your arms and legs, will start to shake and tremble as they get full of energy from oxygen, sugar, and adrenaline. If your muscles and tissues are ready and fully supplied with energy, your body can immediately jump into whatever action is needed to stay safe.

Sweat. Your body will immediately start sweating to keep you cool so that all the energy and blood flow doesn't overheat you.

Temperature. Your body temperature may quickly change to hot or cold depending on the person. The sweat might chill you out or the energy might heat you up. Sometimes it'll switch back and forth.

Head. You might have a high amount of tension in your head as your blood pressure increases and your muscles tighten. Your jaw might clench to tighten the muscles in your face and neck. This is a natural instinct because it can reduce the amount of head and face damage you might experience from a blow or punch. You may also feel dizzy or have a sense of buzzing as your vision, senses, and body reactions are hijacked to focus on danger.

Shoulders. Your shoulders may automatically tighten and lift up to protect vulnerable areas like your head, chest, and neck.

Throat and mouth. Your throat and mouth will likely get dry as moisture is pulled away to be used by your sweat glands. You could also find yourself shouting or screaming to be intimidating, to get help, or to warn others.

Arms and hands. Your arms and hands might have the impulse to go over your head for protection. You can also find yourself clenching your fists as if you're about to throw punches.

Legs and feet. Your legs and feet get positioned to spring so you can move quickly and with force.

Digestion and bladder. Your digestion and bladder will actually shut down in go-mode. These systems take a ton of energy, so, if there's a crisis, your body will slow down or stop everything that's happening in your stomach, bladder, and intestines. This allows your system to borrow energy and send it to the muscles that are working overtime. Sometimes this quick change in your stomach can make you throw up or feel nauseous. Your guts can also get twisted or uncomfortable, or you may suddenly feel like you have to pee or poop.

Whole body. Your body may adjust positions like ducking down, turning sideways, or crouching to keep your eyes focused on danger while protecting more sensitive areas of your body.

As you read through all of these body changes, you might remember going through something like this when you faced a crisis in the past. You may not have noticed how activated your body was because it made sense at the time.

Maybe it helped you jump out of the way of a car that nearly hit you or made you run faster through a haunted corn maze. It might have even helped you stay focused during a test or get that project finished just in time. In these situations, it probably didn't upset you to have your body change into go-mode because it helped you feel safe or get through something hard.

Again, when the system is working right, it's a great setup. Your amygdala manages danger before your cortex even has a chance to understand what's going on.

But when the system is confused and disorganized, that's when things get uncomfortable and difficult.

We'll talk a little more about this in the next few chapters, but before we get there, let's talk about what the slow-mode or standby approach looks like in your body since it's quite a bit different.

The slow-mode information may not feel as overwhelming as go-mode, but you might find that it's more difficult to keep your brain online and stay focused as you read. So here are a few more tips to help you through this part.

As you read, you can tap your feet back and forth or stand up and dance. Or you can find something that smells strong to keep under your nose. You can also read the words out loud, or even sing or rap them to yourself. Just like the last tip, you can imagine these things happening to a cartoon character on TV, but make the cartoon overly dramatic or ridiculous this time. These ideas might sound silly, but that's kind of what we're going for. It's harder for your brain to go offline when things are funny.

Now that you're prepped, let's go through what happens inside your body when the signals are sent to **turn *down* energy**.

Slow-Mode

When the amygdala sends emergency directions to go standby or to slow down, your system is likely to go through the following changes:

Senses. Your senses may go numb and have a hard time focusing on anything in particular. You might see spots or feel like you're looking at bright lights. You might hear sounds around you that you can't understand or feel like your ears are buzzing. You might also get dizzy or feel like the room is out of focus or spinning.

In really scary situations, you might feel completely disconnected from your sense of touch (both inside and outside of you). You might have an out-of-body experience where you see yourself from a distance or from above, or you might get stuck in your imagination so completely that you fully block out everything around you.

Sometimes you can feel so disconnected that it seems like you're dreaming or that nothing is real at all.

Time. It can be really hard to measure time when your body slows down. In fact, while your body is in slow-mode, it can feel like time stops or even gets stuck.

The strange part about this is that once your body comes *out* of slow-mode, you can have a hard time remembering how stuck you felt just moments before. It will often feel like you're coming out of a dream. If you fainted or went unconscious, this makes a lot of sense, but losing time can just as easily happen while you're upright and awake.

Lungs. Your lungs may slow down, and you might feel like they are frozen or find it difficult to breathe.

Heart. Your heart might slow down and decrease blood flow through your whole body. It will beat just enough to get oxygen to your vital organs.

Muscles and tissues. Your muscles and tissues will likely go limp or freeze, making it difficult to move or take action. This allows your body to use as little energy as possible.

Temperature. Your body temperature is likely to go cold. The lowered energy in your system can make things feel chilly.

Head. Your head can get really fuzzy and confused and have a difficult time keeping thoughts together.

Face. The muscles in your face may lose energy and go flat. This can make it hard to express how you're feeling.

Throat and mouth. Like your other muscles, the ones in your throat and mouth can go limp and make it difficult, if not impossible, to say anything...even in situations where yelling or speaking up might help you.

Digestion and bladder. Just like go-mode, your digestion definitely turns off during slow-mode. Your body is trying to slow down and save energy, and turning off your stomach, bladder, and guts always helps with this. In fact, it's safe to assume that your digestion is interrupted during most stressful situations as it takes too much energy away from your survival systems.

In general, slow-mode is a signal to your body to save energy rather than use it. So you might end up with a really tired and unmotivated body, even when you haven't been doing much of anything. Slow-mode tells your body to use as little energy as possible and start saving what you have left. This means that a lot of body systems will shut down or go into standby.

This is a difficult reaction because it makes everything feel really foggy. It just seems like everything goes numb, including your brain. Which makes it pretty tough to remember things and stay focused since the point is to feel nothing and forget.

If this is one of your body reactions, try to be patient with yourself. It might take a while to recognize when your body has been numbing things out. Learning about these systems will start to give you more awareness of what's going on, even if it doesn't change anything right away.

Okay. You did it. We've now made it through the details about what kinds of things happen inside your body during stress.

How'd you do?

If you're still feeling tense or zoned out, you might want to take a slow breath or two before you move on. And if that's not enough, you can wiggle your body or get up and do a little 10-second dance before you keep going.

You can also go back to your Calm, Safe Space or just pause the book until you feel ready to come back. Remember, we're trying to work *with* your body, not against it. So there's no judgment if you have to take it slow.

CHAPTER 11 – ACTIVE

I'm now going to give you a little more information about how your body system uses these emergency responses to manage danger. It might seem like there would only be a few ways for go-mode and slow-mode to play out. But it will probably surprise you to learn how many different emergency reactions are possible.

Let's talk first about what behaviors can be part of your survival plan when your body switches into go-mode.

Fighting

One of the most common emergency plans for the body is to fight. When you sense danger from another human or an animal, you might end up fighting to defend yourself or your loved ones.

Go-mode will definitely help with this process. It will keep your muscles tight, your senses sharp, and your energy going for as long as possible.

This high energy helps a lot if your fight response actually involves **getting physical**, but it also just helps to make you look more **threatening and intimidating**.

If you've ever watched animal documentaries, you'll see that looking aggressive and getting loud is a really common way that animals protect themselves and scare each other away.

Humans do the same thing.

For a lot of people, getting stressed won't look or feel like being afraid. It will look like **anger and aggression.**

Protecting yourself with anger is something most everyone does to some degree. Anger keeps people at a distance. It covers up your fears and difficult emotions. And it might have helped you deal with, or get out of, tough situations in your past.

You might have blown up at your mom when she criticized your friends. Maybe you pounded your sister when she took the remote. Or you might have pulled over on the freeway to scream at your toddler who got out of his seat.

An angry or aggressive response is one of the oldest survival tricks.

In fact, anger is such a primal response that it can be hard to control your own fight response when someone around you gets mad. Your amygdala knows that anger in others can be threatening. This is especially true if you have grown up around a lot of anger and fighting.

If you were raised around bullies, gangs, violence, war zones, or abuse, you know that showing panic or fear can often make these situations worse. Being aggressive or fighting back might be a solid way to survive, even if it's not pretty.

Sadly, if you feel that the only way you can solve problems now is through fighting, intimidation, violence, or aggressive behavior, then you have probably noticed that it gets in the way of your relationships and life opportunities. In extreme cases, it might even land you in prison or a cemetery.

If this is your situation, it's really not fair that the way you have learned to survive is also the very thing that might rob you of actually living.

Running Away

Running away is also a pretty common way to escape from threats and danger. In fact, fighting and running away will sometimes happen together. A lot of animals and people will fight just long enough to get a chance to run away, especially when you're cornered.

This response is called **flight** in the mental health world since it's another word for running away.

It's probably obvious why your body would have a run-away plan for danger. Getting away from danger is just plain smart. Adrenaline and high energy clearly help support this escape plan. With all that energy, you can run really fast and for much longer than usual.

Running away will often happen when your system notices a threat and doesn't see a way to stay safe where you're at. Even fighters will run away when they know they're outmatched or outnumbered. And if you don't trust anyone around you to have your back, a quick exit can help you feel like you're in control and don't have to be a victim.

Now, not all flight responses include running. Sometimes this can look like **driving off** when you're stressed and need to regroup. It could also look like **rushing to leave** a dinner party that feels too crowded and overstimulating.

Unfortunately, if leaving difficult situations becomes your only survival tool, it might get challenging when you keep walking off the job instead of communicating with your boss. Or when you're stuck at home because you feel the need to flee every time you go out. This can lead to a lot of anxious feelings, especially when you run out of places to run.

Protecting Others

In some situations, go-mode pushes people to **rescue** and **protect** others instead of running away.

Parents are usually first on this list because their instincts are to protect their children. And it's not surprising that firefighters, police officers, soldiers, and paramedics generally seem to have these instincts too.

The intense energy of go-mode often helps first responders and soldiers run *toward* burning buildings and gunfire. It helps parents pull their kids out of earthquake rubble or fight off wild animals. And it can help bystanders pull strangers out of burning cars.

In crisis moments, go-mode can make your body so strong and full of energy that you will seem almost superhuman. This invincible feeling may lead you to **act like a hero** instead of running away.

This doesn't mean that protecting others always looks heroic, though. When rescue behavior is the *only* way you learn to deal with stress, it can very easily turn into controlling or dominating behavior, especially when you start to believe that you're the only one who can keep others safe.

This can be a messy place to end up. It can be hard to admit that your behavior has gotten out of hand and that your responses might be hurting others or pushing them away.

Staying Busy

Keeping your body busy can be a really common way for people to experience go-mode.

When go-mode is getting set off without a clear reason, it can be hard to figure out why your body is anxious or full of energy. And sometimes your system gets triggered by those high-stress moments that feel *sort of* life or death but don't have an easy fix. Things like money issues, or raising teenagers, or a toxic boss.

And if you can't fix what's stressing you out (or if you can't magically win the lottery or get your teenager to talk to you) then you might find your body randomly switching into go-mode a lot.

Because go-mode tells your body to get away from danger and find safety again, getting busy can be a way to trick yourself into calming down. In fact, this kind of busy-ness may not even feel stressful to you. It might just feel like your usual **get-it-done energy**.

Staying busy gives your body the chance to redirect the energy of go-mode *and* feel like it's taking care of something. It's true that piles of dirty laundry and a lawn full of weeds can really add to stress. So **taking care of chores** can make your brain feel like you "handled" the stress and allow your body to feel calm again.

There are many ways to stay busy and feel like you're getting things done. You might take on **extra projects** or new exercise routines. You can even find yourself shaking your leg or **fidgeting** a lot when you can't get up and move around to work off the go-mode energy.

It makes sense that some people get into the habit of busy-ness as their go-mode response.

The big challenge here is that it never really fixes the reason your system is getting triggered to begin with. Unfinished chores and projects can definitely add to stress, but they're not likely to be the core reason why your go-mode is always on. And staying busy might even be a way that your brain has learned to distract from the real stuff that you don't want to deal with.

Risk Taking

Risk taking can also be a way to deal with go-mode energy in your body. This response is pretty similar to the staying-busy one. It's likely to activate when you don't know what's triggering you or when your stress doesn't have an easy fix.

For risk takers though, the message from your go-mode probably won't feel like stress. It usually feels more like a signal to do something exciting because your body has **adrenaline to burn**. With high-risk experiences, you can easily use the high energy in your system to **jump into something intense or dangerous**.

These high-risk moments will usually create an amazing sense of **harmony between your body and mind** because what you're doing finally matches up with the go-mode energy that's been bottled up inside of you.

And when you're safe and back to regular life again, your brain feels like you've "handled" and lived through the danger, which will help your body feel more resolved.

Risk taking could include sudden urges to drive or ride anywhere fast, max out a credit card, have a fling with a stranger, hike up a mountain, or get into an extreme sport. As odd as it seems, high risk moments might be the only times you feel like yourself, especially if you don't have other ways to sit with the intense feelings.

Sometimes this response won't feel like a problem since the energy will work itself out of your body and you'll feel better. But things might get hard if this is the only way that you deal with stress.

Your constant need for an adrenaline rush can easily get in the way of important priorities and responsibilities. It may lead to manic episodes that push your limits and your energy further than you wanted. Unfortunately, it might also end in more serious consequences like injuries or even death.

CHAPTER 12 – PASSIVE

Now let's talk about the reactions you might have if your body gets the message to turn things *down* and use slow-mode.

Shutting Down

You probably wouldn't think of shutting down or slowing down as a way to deal with danger, but it's actually a common emergency plan.

Slow-mode usually happens when your system is running low on energy, or it realizes there may be no way to fight back or escape. It's kind of a wait-it-out emergency plan. It slows everything down to save your energy so that you have a chance of surviving as long as possible.

Sometimes this response is referred to as **flop** in the mental health world.

For example, if you are getting attacked by a bear, you will probably start off in go-mode and try to run away, fight, or find someone else to help you. But if these plans don't work, then your system will eventually run out of energy and won't be able to keep going.

The amygdala will then switch up the alarms to move your system from its first response to shutting down. If this happens, going into shutdown will turn down your breathing and heart rate, which then slows your bleeding and energy use. It will also **dull your senses**, **numb the pain**, and help you **dissociate**. And, if it needs to, it will send you into a full **blackout** where you don't have to deal with whatever comes next.

You might know this reaction as **playing dead**, and it can sometimes trick a predator into giving up. But it's also how your body handles a lot of damage if the attack doesn't stop or slow down.

It will allow your body to save the energy you have left and tune out the worst bits. This will increase how long you can survive in case the damage gets pretty brutal.

With everything running on low power and your senses numbed out, it gives your body a little more survival time. It might give you more time to be found or leave you with just enough energy to wake up and call an ambulance.

Just so we're clear, your amygdala realizes that this plan is not your best bet for surviving, and it doesn't really want to go here if it can help it. But life or death situations create some hard choices. So when the only option you have left is to shut everything off, go silent, and hope the danger passes, your body will do it. It rarely feels good or safe, but it might save your life, and keeping you alive is your amygdala's job.

Now, in modern times, shutdown will look a bit different since it's rare to get chased by a bear or stuck in the wilderness anymore.

For many people, shutdown is likely to come up during those *sort of* life-or-death moments. Sometimes this looks like your body going numb when your ex shows up at a party or passing out or fainting when you get your blood drawn. This can also look like zoning out or losing focus, feeling "lazy," having an out-of-body experience, or getting sleepy at confusing times. It might happen when you're taking an important test or when your significant other wants to talk about where the relationship is going.

It can also look like struggling to speak up, sleeping all the time, isolating yourself, or always forgetting what you were doing. It really just depends on your system and the danger matches that your amygdala has put together.

Unfortunately, shutting down is the most common response for kids and adults **stuck in abusive situations** where things really are life or death.

When you can't get away and you can't find protection, your body will shut down as a way of letting your mind escape when your body can't. Your system will go offline or dissociate to protect you from getting overwhelmed and will keep you from saving too many memories of the situation.

This can also happen during any kind of assault.

Going numb or limp *never* means that you consent or agree to the bad things that happen to you. Your body is just trying to protect you when it doesn't see another way to survive.

The problem is that shutdown can sometimes feel like you *decided* to give up or give in. You might think, "Whatever, I'll just let this happen and get it over with," especially in uncomfortable or dangerous sexual situations. But that's not really a choice. That's still your amygdala giving survival orders.

When your system feels like speaking up or fighting might make things worse, it will send signals to give up and numb out. This is all part of the shut down response.

In fact, if you've been through a lot of danger in the past, and your system used shutdown to survive, then your body is *more* likely to go back to that, even in a situation where you could easily escape or fight, or simply say "no."

Many people will feel ashamed or blame themselves for not doing more to protect themselves (or others) during these situations. Your amygdala learns from your past experiences, though. So it will keep using the survival plans that have kept you alive, even if they feel awful.

When you're in the moment, you really don't have much control over what your amygdala chooses to do when it gets triggered.

No matter how your body responds, it is still not your fault, and it doesn't mean you're okay with what happened.

Unfortunately, when your brain and body haven't had a lot of success with other survival plans, then shutdown can become your default plan. This can lead your body to fall into **episodes of depression** every time your amygdala is triggered or your body is low on energy.

When these depressive episodes come up, it will make it nearly impossible to keep up with work or school or relationships. It will make it hard to get out of bed or motivate yourself to eat and shower. And it can even trick your brain into thinking you don't have much longer to live.

Since you **lose all sense of time** during shutdown, your brain will have a hard time imagining a future that looks hopeful. Your senses will only be able to focus on the darkness and numbness you're feeling right now. This experience can make it feel like you will always be lost or that you're slowly dying.

And without any view of the future and everything feeling so bleak, it's obvious that it would be pretty hard to care about . . . well, anything.

How is grocery shopping, laundry, school, work, or taking care of your basic needs going to feel important when you feel sure that you're lost and dying and nothing you do seems to bring hope?

If this is you, you're not crazy. You're actually stuck. And there *are* ways to lift the darkness. But you don't have to believe that right now. Trust and hope are really hard to hold on to when you're trapped in the dark.

Please consider finding a professional who can help you hold on and who will be patient with you as you find your way. If you need help knowing how to do that, you can skip to Chapter 56 right now and come back when you're ready.

CHAPTER 13 – COMBINATION

I know this book is getting heavy. This is the last chapter about survival responses, and then we're going to talk about ways to take care of yourself in the next few chapters. As always, take your time if you need it.

This chapter will help you understand how some survival reactions use a **combination of go-mode and slow-mode**. Sometimes this is part of the plan, and sometimes it's because your system gets stuck between plans.

Finding a Protector

Finding a protector is an extremely important survival plan. In the mental health world, this is sometimes referred to as the **fawn** response, and it's the very first survival plan that we use as humans.

Because we all start out as babies and can't protect ourselves or keep ourselves alive, we need **help from someone else to survive**. Crying and screaming is a great way to let people know that you're in trouble, especially when you're little.

Go-mode will support this survival plan by giving you energy to **cry loud and throw a fit to get attention**. What's interesting though is that your system can also send **shutdown messages at the same time to make your body limp and floppy**.

This combo response is actually quite genius because adults are wired to protect tiny humans who are helpless and adorably pathetic.

So a baby that uses high energy to cry but also uses shutdown to fall into your arms and weakly sob can train your brain to care more about their tiny survival than yours. (This is usually where the protecting others emergency plan gets started in adults.)

Unfortunately, this is also why temper tantrums can be no joke. A very hungry and tired toddler can use this combo to high-energy punch you and low-energy deadweight you all at the same time.

As kids get older, they will still use this combo reaction when their body gets stressed. You've probably seen this when a child gets startled and will use high energy to run to a trusted adult only to collapse and even shake as someone holds them.

Another way you can see this is when kids (or even teens) throw a fit. This often happens when they get overwhelmed and don't know how to handle it. Their body will flip back to the original emergency response: yell, make demands, and then act helpless until someone takes pity on them.

Obviously, this can get really complicated with teens since they don't always want to be comforted or get advice. But it doesn't stop their body from going back to this survival plan.

And honestly, finding protection isn't just for kids and teens. Adults can still do this when they're caught off guard. Just go to a haunted house or a corn maze. You will see full-grown adults jump into each other's arms or hold up their friends as human shields when they get freaked out.

What's interesting is that this response can mature really well over time. If you grow up with parents or guardians who do a good enough job of helping you feel safe, then you will learn that you can feel better by asking for help. As your caregivers help you to understand what you're feeling and what you need, you will be able to identify what's going on and discover that words and questions are a much easier way to communicate than tantrums.

You'll also learn from their modeling what it takes to protect yourself and stay safe.

That way, you will learn how to **build and maintain relationships that you can depend on** when things get rough. Having a community where you can get (and give) support is one of the oldest survival tools.

But if your system never really gets experience with feeling safe, then your amygdala will struggle to understand the difference between safety and danger.

This will make it hard for your amygdala to develop and practice anything different. And it will struggle to move on to more independent emergency plans. You might find yourself still acting like a kid when you get overwhelmed. Maybe you throw tantrums, act really helpless, make up sob stories, or constantly want other people to bail you out.

You may notice that you are always looking for other people's approval and help. Without the protection you needed to develop your own sense of safety, it will be hard to feel stable on your own, no matter how much validation and support people try to give you.

Freezing

Freezing is a response that happens when **your body gets mixed signals to activate and shut down** all at the same time. This means that your system is full of go-mode energy, but also getting the message to switch to slow-mode.

In some cases, this happens because your system doesn't know how to turn off high energy without just shutting *everything* down.

When you haven't had great models for handling danger or you haven't really known what it's like to feel safe, your body struggles to let go of survival mode and feel calm again once the threat passes. This means that you have to find a way to stop the high energy so you're not always stuck in go-mode.

One of the ways this can happen is through freezing. By **clamping down and numbing out the high energy** buzzing inside of you, your system can quiet things down a bit.

Although this can help to mute out go-mode, it doesn't fully turn off the survival mode or allow you to relax. This frozen state ends up causing a lot of clenching and tightness and **traps the energy in your muscles and tissues** instead of working it out.

For most people, your body can only balance the intense feelings for so long before the energy comes out. This might look like freaking out or blowing up after you've been holding things down for too long.

But it can also look like feeling **exhausted all the time** because your body can't calm down enough to get good sleep, and can't wake up enough to feel motivated. This is why you can **sleep a ton and still not feel rested**.

Just like shutdown, freezing also happens a lot during moments where your body is getting the signal to run or fight but you are cornered or overpowered and can't get away. This is really common for abuse, assault, and unwelcome sexual situations.

These experiences are pretty overwhelming. Having both go-mode and slow-mode turned on all at once can feel like pure chaos. Your body will have a **hard time moving or taking action** while alarms and adrenaline are going off everywhere inside of you, telling you to do something.

You might feel ashamed if this has happened to you because you weren't able to respond the way you wanted. But when it comes to survival, freezing isn't a choice.

When your amygdala decides that go-mode isn't working, it will switch your system to shut down. And, unfortunately, there's not much you can do about it. Not to mention that you are never responsible for *other* people's negative actions. No matter what you were doing, or wearing, or saying (or not saying), or how your body responded.

Sometimes you don't even have to be in direct danger for this response to happen. Many people will freeze up when they're intimidated by authority figures. Their system will feel overpowered or helpless. Being questioned by a cop or lectured by your parents might trigger this. This can also happen with bullies, teachers, or bosses.

Sadly, a freeze response can sometimes make it seem like you're being defensive and disrespectful instead of feeling stressed out. Because your body gets locked up and has a hard time expressing anything, it might be **hard to speak up** or say the right things. It can feel like and/or look like you're being cold, distant, or stubborn or giving attitude. This is super frustrating when that wasn't how you meant to respond and it just makes everything worse.

In its most powerful mode, freezing can also show up as a **panic attack**. Panic attacks seem to happen when your system is sure there's a life-or-death threat but not really sure what to be afraid of.

Just because your amygdala spotted a match and sounded the alarms doesn't always guarantee that your system will be clear on the details. This means that your body will shift into go-mode but end up shutting down and freezing when it's not sure what the danger is or how to defend against it.

Because this one is messy, it doesn't look exactly the same for everyone. You might break down in tears, shake uncontrollably, get really stiff and frozen, or have a hard time breathing. You might freak out on everyone, or keep repeating yourself, or say things that don't make sense.

This is why many people call an ambulance and think they're dying the first time they have a panic attack. Every inch of **your body is getting the message that there's deadly danger around with no clear threat** in sight (except for what's happening inside of your body).

In **other extreme cases of freezing**, your body can also flip into full-on shutdown where your body goes **completely numb** and you **pass out**.

The difference between an extreme freeze response like this and a shutdown one is that the go-mode energy during freezing will usually make your body **stiffer instead of limp**. And in some cases, your mind will still be aware of everything going on around you instead of going offline.

If your body keeps getting stuck in freezing and panic responses, then you will face a lot of anxiety every day. Your system is going to feel like something bad is always coming, but it won't really know what to look for or how to prepare for it. So you'll just start getting **anxious about getting anxious** since your body freaking out has now become the clearest danger match.

Sadly, this means that any twinge of stress or nervousness can throw your system right back into panic.

Over time, your body will have to shut down more and more to turn off this anxiety. And just like a shutdown response, freezing can eventually turn into episodes of depression and low motivation but with a lot more muscle tension and anxiety thrown into the mix.

As your cortex tries to stay prepared, it will build up all sorts of fears about how much worse things might get. And, for most people, the fear of how bad it will get becomes the scariest part of this cycle.

But you should know that your body actually does have a limit on how much it can panic. You only have so much adrenaline and cortisol that can be pumped out all at the same time. It's likely that you've already faced the max amount of panic your body can throw at you. As bad as these attacks feel, it might be slightly relieving to know that you've survived the worst of it, and they probably won't get much worse than they are now.

And with some of the info and practice in this book, you can start to get a better handle on them.

But it's okay if that doesn't help you feel better right now. You're allowed to feel upset and frustrated with these cycles. They're seriously awful.

High-Level Functioning

Being highly functional can be another way your system copes with stress.

In this response, you're always **worrying about all the things that can go wrong** and **trying to stay ahead** of them. You might feel some stress in your body, but you might also numb a lot too.

This setup is much different from the others. Instead of having high energy go to your body, the emergency response will actually power up your cortex while your body is more likely to go into slow-mode.

This **gives a bunch of energy to your frontal cortex** to always make sure you're ahead of everything. And while **your body is numbed out or clamped down**, it's easier for your cortex to stay focused and not get distracted by "less important" things.

In our school analogy, this might look like the principal taking over all the security duties and making sure she's three steps ahead on every plan. She might send orders over the intercom all day while ignoring messages from the stressed out teachers and classrooms so they don't distract her. And when something does go down, she'll probably notice and start dealing with the situation long before the danger shows up in the live feed.

Your system can end up doing the same thing. Your cortex will actually stay in control and manage the situation with logic and planning. Your body may use slow-mode to keep your system quiet while your cortex handles everything.

Since your cortex spends most days running worst-case scenarios, it will detect problems at least 3 steps before your amygdala notices a match so **your body will rarely be caught off guard** or have to react.

Basically, your system learns to analyze your experiences instead of feeling them so you can **maintain control through logic and planning**.

This might encourage you to be driven and work after **high-achieving goals** so you can depend on yourself and always be prepared. It may also push you to be a rule follower so that you don't get off track with your plans.

From the outside, it may seem like being highly functional always brings you the perfect life, but, in reality, this "perfect life" can sometimes become a never-ending to-do list and a drain on your energy. If always being prepared and staying ahead is your only survival response, then it's going to be very difficult to keep up the energy you'll need to stay ahead forever.

After a while, it may feel like everything is your responsibility and that you're to blame when things don't work out as they should. This can lead to a constant sense of dread that makes you feel like something bad is always coming and you're never doing enough to be prepared.

Eventually this dread can get your brain feeling kind of paranoid and make it hard to rest or relax. **Racing thoughts and ruminations** can easily take over. Sometimes it can get so bad it becomes difficult to leave the house or go out in public. And you can even end up with **compulsive or controlling behaviors** as you try to find ways to be prepared and keep the chaos under control.

This also means that your cortex has to keep putting off other priorities, so there's never any time to take care of yourself. This can make it challenging to stay present and make time for your needs and relationships. Your family may also become resentful as you expect them to be just as high functioning as you are and do everything your way.

There's often a boiling point with behavior like this. Your body needs to be listened to and taken care of.

So, in spite of all your control and functioning, your body will start pushing for the attention it needs. You might blow up at confusing times, or cry a lot in the shower, or end up with addictions or closet behaviors that you're ashamed of.

This is why you can end up in a full blown breakdown after many years of seeming to have all the right answers. You probably didn't notice how overloaded your system was until it all began to fall apart.

Many times this can also be triggered when the people in your life make it clear that they're fed up and/or you start to realize that your relationships are in bad shape. This may really cause you to crumble when you discover that the people you have taken care of and protected have now become distant or don't want contact.

Caretaking

Caretaking is another response that often goes along with high-level functioning.

This usually starts because you notice that it's easier to feel calm when the people around you are also calm. So you learn how to take care of others and help them with their problems. That way life also becomes less stressful for you.

If you have spent a lot of time around people who freak out and blow up, then you are more likely to use this response. In these situations, caretaking is a more direct way of calming things down since the other person's behavior *is* the threat. And your system realizes that falling into your own emergency response will usually just make the situation more stressful.

This emergency response also uses the same energy combo that the high-functioning response uses. Your system will use slow-mode to numb out your body while your frontal cortex uses go-mode to

focus on the moods of the people around you and stay ahead of what's coming. That way, you can notice when a situation is getting tense and step in with some problem-solving skills long before your amygdala gets triggered.

This means that you will get pretty good at **handling sticky situations or difficult people**. You can keep their stress from spilling over onto you. It can also help you feel a little more secure that the people you care about will also want to stick around and support you. Who doesn't want to be around someone who makes them feel better?

This kind of reaction is also part of the **fawn** response. It goes along with finding a protector because making sure you have supportive people in your life helps your body and brain feel safer from threats. Plus, this can be part of what helps to build a safe community where you find comfort in giving and getting support.

The downside of this response, though, is that it can often cross over into extreme **people-pleasing** where you lose track of who you are and what you want for your own life.

Your system can end up getting wired to be more concerned about other people's emotions than your own. This overload of empathy can cause you to doubt and dismiss your own feelings and end up in a lot of one-sided relationships.

You may struggle to express how you feel due to constant shutdown. Your words, body language, and/or facial expressions can get so used to being flat that you don't seem to have emotions anymore. In fact, you might find it difficult to know your own feelings without a few hours or days to reflect.

Without a sense of your own needs, you may find yourself giving in to other people's demands and wishes a lot. You might be expected to be compliant and do things for others that they don't or won't do for themselves or for you.

It can also make it hard to tell the truth when it's easier to tell people what they want to hear. You can find that you're doing most of the work to keep your relationships going.

You may spend a lot of time explaining yourself to others or justifying your feelings and reactions. You may feel like you have to educate and inform others about what's going on, hoping a reasonable explanation will get them to see that things are unfair or hurting you.

Sadly, this approach will often fail since many of the people you've been caretaking haven't learned how to manage their own system without your help. The threat of losing your support will often shut down their cortex and make it impossible to really hear or see your point of view.

When this happens, it can be hard to accept that you're more alone and unsupported than you thought. After years of giving, it can be devastating when no one shows up for you in your time of need.

And even when you do have access to supportive people, it can be difficult to ask for or accept help. Since asking for help has rarely been safe for you, your amygdala may not even know that getting support is something that you could try. It might even think it's a *risky* option if you've been left hanging one too many times in the past.

If this is the case, then your system will probably skip over the option of looking for support and go directly to numbing out or clamping down when you feel drained, alone, or unprotected. And like the high-level functioning response, this can cause things to eventually fall apart one way or another.

Unfortunately, even though you are sacrificing a lot for others, you can also be adding to the relationship problems when you aren't taking care of yourself. You can end up secretly resenting others or breaking their trust when you can't deliver on all of your people-pleasing promises.

Now, if you're reading this section as a parent, you'll realize that one-way caretaking is going to happen when you're raising kids. So it can be easy to lose yourself and fall apart during these years, even when you're trying to be mindful of your needs and limits. Do your best to be patient with yourself. If you're interested, Chapter A in the Bonus Upgrades has some info and resources for parents.

Distracting

Distraction and avoidance can also be part of a combination response to stress.

Although this is similar to running away or shutdown, it's a bit different. When your body can't physically run away from danger and your system knows that shutdown isn't safe for you, then you need another way to **escape the stress**.

Avoiding and distracting are a key way that your system handles survival. This response is likely to happen during threats that you don't have the power to change or that don't have quick or easy solutions. You might use this response if you're being raised by parents who have addiction problems or if you have to work at a job you hate.

This response can also keep you from getting too stuck in a difficult moment or memory by redirecting your system to focus on other things.

In this response, slow-mode will keep some of your body numbed out while go-mode energy will help other parts of your body stay motivated. This will allow you to have the energy you need to keep facing a tough situation while also numbing out some of the discomfort. The go-mode energy can also give your cortex the ability to keep your mind distracted by other things.

Honestly, humans wouldn't stand a chance without this survival option. No matter who you are, your system would overload if it didn't have the chance to **dissociate and go offline** once in a while.

Life has a lot of moments that are hard to face, and it's normal to use distraction and avoidance to cope.

This might look like **building fantasies** in your mind about being famous or important, or daydreaming about living someone else's life. You might block out stressful experiences by reading books or getting lost in electronic devices.

Unfortunately, this response is needed a lot when you're raised in an abusive or neglectful home. Distraction and avoidance are often the only thing that can keep you going through so many years of helplessness and pain.

The challenge with this plan is that it can turn into a life of permanent avoidance even after you're safe. You may find yourself stuck here if you can't seem to focus on anything that needs to get done until the absolute last second. You can struggle with telling the truth when it might lead to uncomfortable situations. You might use humor to distract from important conversations. Or maybe you spend time thinking about plans that you never seem able to take action on.

It's tough if the only way you are able to cope with life is by living outside of it. It can get pretty lonely and frustrating.

Clearly, there are a lot of ways your system learns to deal with danger. No two people are going to have the exact same responses, but it can be helpful to see some of the ways your body handles go-mode and/or slow-mode.

The truth is that this list isn't going to cover every situation and person. Many people are a blend of all these responses. You might be a high-functioning people pleaser with episodes of shutdown. Or a passive-aggressive risk-taker who freezes up at work. You could be an overwhelmed parent who fights hard to protect your kids but blows up at them too. You could even be a teen who zones out during class and sometimes punches walls during panic attacks.

Hopefully you can see that **none of these responses are naturally bad**. Not everything in the world is safe and easy. It's really good to have survival options and to know how to deal with danger, even if it's not something you're proud of.

It does become a problem though when these responses are making your life harder. And it can get even more overwhelming when you can't figure out how to stop doing them. When survival starts to become your only operating mode, life can become pretty depressing.

Mostly, I'm glad our bodies protect us from such horrible experiences, but I'm so sorry if this is your story. No one should ever have to learn what it's like to *only* live in survival.

I'm glad you're here. And it *is* possible to heal and change these responses. But it's not an easy journey, and you can't just tell yourself to stop, which you are hopefully starting to believe by now.

In the next upgrade, we're going to discuss how these responses get stuck in your body and then give you more steps to manage your system in some healthier ways. But in the meantime, we're going to take a break again.

CHAPTER 14 – UNSAFE

If you haven't been through multiple traumas and/or difficult losses, you might wonder why we would take breaks during this book.

Bad experiences in your past are easy to stir up, especially when we're discussing specific reactions in your body. And your body is more easily triggered if we stay focused too long on the rough stuff.

Even though you now know that your amygdala is just trying to keep you safe, it doesn't change that you're still getting hijacked.

So, I'm going to keep offering more steps and information to help with that, but we're also going to take our time and be gentle with the process.

In fact, let me **take a moment to talk directly to any of you who are not safe right now**. You could be homeless, going through domestic violence, experiencing abuse, at risk for hate crimes, or feeling like you want to hurt yourself or others.

If this is you, you're going to need more support than the activities in this book can offer you.

(If this *doesn't* sound like you, feel free to jump to the next chapter and dive in. I'll wait here with everyone else, though.)

Using calming activities to imagine safety when you're really in a dangerous space isn't going to work very well. You can definitely still try them, but it's important to recognize that there are real dangers that won't allow your system to move out of survival.

For any of you who need some help getting safe, your best bet is to **start with a professional** who can help you.

Honestly, I recommend trying to find local support systems as they know your community and will be better able to work with you. **Mental health clinics or drop-in shelters** can be a good place to start. Their help will usually be private unless they have to report that there is immediate danger to yourself or someone else.

If that doesn't work for you, your local **civic center or library** will often have a list of places you can start with. Librarians have a ton of info and are really great researchers if you need something specific. You can also work with **police or fire departments** to be securely moved to a safe house and get help with filing protection orders or getting access to victim advocate programs.

If you're part of a **church community**, you can talk with the leaders to see if there are resources you might have access to. Local chaplains may also be able to help. Many hospitals and universities have chaplains on staff who are usually free to talk with and also keep things confidential. Chaplains are trained to be spiritual guides for every type of religion and belief and will usually know a lot about programs and supports in your community.

Some states and counties also have **support networks for folks experiencing discrimination or abuse** due to age, race, gender, sexual orientation, etc. You can find many of these through online searches.

Now, if these options still don't work for you, that's okay. Here is a list of **national hotlines** you can use to start getting help with your specific issues:

- Suicide and Crisis Lifeline: call 988 or visit 988lifeline.org

- The Childhelp National Child Abuse Hotline: call or text 800-442-4453 or visit childhelphotline.org.

- The National Center on Elder Abuse: call 855-500-3537 or visit ncea.acl.gov.

- The National Domestic Violence Hotline: call 800-799-7233 or text "Start" to 88788 or visit thehotline.org.

- The National Human Trafficking Hotline: call 888-373-7888 or text HELP to 233733 (BEFREE) or chat online at humantraffickinghotline.org.

- The National Sexual Assault Hotline: call 800-656-4673 or visit rainn.org.

- The LGBT National Helpline: call 888-843-4564 or visit lgbthotline.org.

- Racial Equity Support Line: call 503-575-3764 or visit linesforlife.org/get-help-now/services-and-crisis-lines/racial-equity-support-line/ (Available weekdays.)

- And if you need help with food, housing, or other basic needs, you can call 211 or visit 211.org to find help.

There are also plenty of other support networks that are easy to look for online if you need them, but these are the basic ones if you need help right now.

Getting help can take a lot of courage, so be patient with yourself. Chapter 56 has some tips about getting professional support, especially when you've been let down before.

CHAPTER 15 – SAFE

Okay, now that we have made sure not to leave anyone behind, let's move to our rest activities.

One of the cool things about your brain is that your body system can make **safe and comfortable matches** just as well as danger matches.

It's just tricky if you haven't had very many comforting experiences in your life. Your file on safe matches is going to be a lot smaller than your file on the dangerous ones.

Remember how a security team will spend time getting to know what a normal, safe day looks like so they can compare it to a dangerous day?

Well, that's one reason why repeating these calm activities can start to help your system. It will begin to show your body what safety feels like so it can add more safe matches to your files. That way, your amygdala can start to trust what it looks and feels like to be secure instead of always matching everything with danger.

This is why it will be helpful to go back to these activities a few more times as you work through this book. It will add some restful or comforting feelings into your system while we are bringing up all the tough stuff.

So let's go back to your **Calm, Safe Space.**

(If this exercise didn't work for you or you didn't like it, go on and skip ahead to the next activity in this chapter or take some time to do something else that feels calming.)

Do you remember what you named your Calm, Safe Space? If so, say that name to yourself or think of the name in your head. If you can't remember, just pause and be silent for a moment and see if it comes back.

Now, let's have you start to bring up the space that you made for yourself.

I want you to slowly pay attention to the things you're seeing in this space. It might have grown or changed a little since you last checked in. Some imaginations keep working in the background, so you might have to get to know your space again.

I want you to focus on the sights that make this place calm, safe, or secure.

When you're ready, start to notice the sounds around you. Try to pay attention to the softer sounds you may not have noticed before.

Then, slowly begin to check in with your feeling of touch and notice the textures against your skin and what you're experiencing around you.

Now, gently, check in with what's going on inside of your body. Does this place still feel calm and safe? If not, you can press the rain button to wash away anything uncomfortable (or you can use whatever clean up tool you came up with before.)

If things are feeling okay, let's keep noticing the sights, sounds, and textures, and then begin to notice what you're smelling and maybe even tasting.

Feel free to stay with this for a while. Some people settle in right away, and others need a few minutes.

We want to give your body a chance to get used to the feelings of safety and calm. It doesn't have to be perfect, but a few small moments of peace will continue to strengthen your safe matches and help your system get more comfortable with them.

If you need to, you can pause right now and start up again when you're ready. So go ahead and take a few minutes if that feels right.

Wonderful. You're doing great.

Notice how you're feeling. Was this easier or harder than the first time? Do you feel more safe or less safe than before? It's important to keep checking in so we get an idea of what is working and what isn't.

Hopefully the practice is making it a little easier and better, but it's not how it works for everyone.

We're going to introduce another rest activity.

That way, whether or not the first one worked, you have more options and ideas.

Okay. This one is called **Peaceful Flow**.

For the first step, I want you to think of something that has a safe or comforting vibe. Something that usually helps to boost your energy and/or helps you feel refreshed or relaxed. This could be a person you trust, the feeling of sunshine, a car, an animal, stars, nature, rain, or even the Calm, Safe Space you just created.

Once you've found or decided upon something, we're going to call it your *comfortable energy*.

Now try to focus on this energy and take your time to answer the following questions. Feel free to skip any questions that come up blank.

If this energy has a shape and size, what does the shape and size look like?

If this energy has color, what colors do you notice?

If this energy has texture, what does the texture feel like?

If this energy has a smell, what does it smell like?

If this energy makes a sound, what does it sound like?

If this energy has a temperature, what temperature is it?

If this energy moves, how does it move?

And, if this energy has weight to it, how heavy or light is it?

What did you notice about your comfortable energy?

If the energy feels healing and safe, go ahead and move to the next part of the exercise. But if the energy starts to feel uncomfortable or threatening, go ahead and find something else to focus on and go through the first part again. If you can't find anything that stays comfortable, then it's okay to skip this activity completely, or come back when you find something that works better.

It can be hard to find comforting energy in your life, especially when you haven't had a lot of safe experiences. I'm sorry if this is your situation. It's not fair that you have had to live this long with so little peace. It might be good to skip to Chapter 56 about finding some professional help. Sometimes the only way to take a break is to let someone else hold the safe spaces for you until you can hold them for yourself.

Okay, let's get back to our activity. If you were able to feel safe with your comfortable energy, then we'll move to the next step.

Now, I want you to carefully notice any part of your body that feels uncomfortable, painful, or tight.

If noticing this creates any sort of trigger or flood of stress that you don't feel ready for, then go ahead and switch back to your Calm, Safe Space until you feel less stressed. Then go ahead and try this again or skip it completely if you need to.

If you're still able to focus on your body (without feeling too overwhelmed) then go ahead and check in with the uncomfortable energy and ask the following questions, skipping any that come up blank.

If this energy has a shape and size, what does the shape and size look like?

If this energy has color, what colors do you notice?

If this energy has texture, what does the texture feel like?

If this energy has a smell, what does it smell like?

If this energy makes a sound, what does it sound like?

If this energy has a temperature, what temperature is it?

If this energy moves, how does it move?

And, if this energy has weight to it, how heavy or light is it?

Now that you have a sense of the uncomfortable energy in your body, I want you to bring your attention back to your comfortable energy.

Very slowly, I want you to invite the comfortable energy into the space around you.

Since it's a safe energy, it will be respectful and won't get pushy or forceful. It will only flow into the places where it's invited and welcome. As the energy moves around you, see how your body is feeling.

If your body still feels safe or relaxed as you do this, I want you to consider inviting the comfortable energy to slowly move into your body. You can imagine breathing it in, having it soak through your skin, or gently absorbing it through the top of your head like a ray of sunshine or drops of rain.

Again, this energy is not forceful or pushy and only fills any spaces where it is welcome. As this energy starts to take up some space in your body, I want you to keep checking in on how you're feeling. If it's making things feel worse than they were, you can pause or skip this activity. If it feels comfortable, continue to invite the energy in until it has filled every space that is open to receiving it.

Now, as the comfortable energy moves around or near the uncomfortable energy, I want you to notice what happens.

There are no right answers here. Every body has a different experience.

Take some time to notice the two energies inside of you and let them flow naturally. See if the uncomfortable energy will let the comfortable energy share or take some space. If it doesn't want to, the comfortable energy will respect that. And if more comfortable energy is needed, just invite more in.

It might take a few minutes for things to settle or come to rest, and that's okay. Take as long as you need and just allow yourself to notice what's happening. Go ahead and pause here until you're ready to come back to the book.

Hopefully, this activity was able to settle your body a little, even if it wasn't perfect.

Feeling a small amount of relief or safety means that this activity can be helpful and will likely get better with more practice. It's one you can use on your own, but I will also be reminding you to go back to it later on in the book.

If it didn't work at all, you can find another comforting item and try again. See if anything changes. You can even try adding a few comforting things together to make the energy stronger.

If you didn't like either of these activities, or if they don't seem to work for you, that's okay. Take a moment to do something that usually helps you to feel a bit more settled or grounded. I'll be introducing more activities as we go, so you can hopefully find something that feels right for you.

CHAPTER 16 – RECHARGING

Now that you may be feeling a little more settled, we're going to give you some more information to help you on your way to becoming a healthier system boss.

This information is about resting and recharging. Recharging is a really important step toward managing your system. Your body only has so much energy, and if you've been in survival for a long time, then your system is definitely running low.

Going back to our school comparison, let's talk about when there aren't enough resources, like staff or supplies, to keep everything running as it should. Sometimes this is a common, short-term issue like a teacher being on leave for a while or making do with old computers until the spring fundraiser.

But when the issue is long-term, like not having enough building space or money to run everything, then decisions have to be made about cutting salaries, reducing hours, or even closing whole departments.

The challenge is that these actions don't quite fix the problem since the school will still be expected to perform just like all the other schools. So school staff will usually have to take on extra work and get burned out from doing more than their share.

The same thing can happen in your body. **When there aren't enough materials or energy** to get you through the day, your system will have to find ways to balance the budget (so to speak).

Some of your **nerve centers will experience energy cuts** because your body knows how to prioritize where the energy goes when the resources are running low.

Generally, the parts that keep you alive, like the systems that control your heart and lungs, are going to be the top priority and get all the energy and supplies they need. Then come the systems that handle danger and survival (like your amygdala and emergency teams). And then the rest of the teams get sorted out depending on importance.

So, for example, when you get sick, your immune system gets more of the energy and supplies than other places so that it can keep you alive and fight off germs.

Or if you're going through something stressful or dangerous, your emergency systems will get priority. Go-mode will burn through tons of energy trying to make sure you survive. But then slow-mode will flip everything to shutdown to make sure that you don't die by using up the last of the energy.

And for anyone with a uterus, reproductive organs are prioritized for keeping the species alive, so they get special treatment as well. That's why you can struggle with low energy (and melting down) during periods and pregnancy and menopause, especially when you already have gyno issues. Lots of energy gets rerouted to the uterus and ovaries when things get active or are changing down there.

If your energy is getting used up like this, your system has to decide which **parts of your body get turned down or turned off**. This will help balance out the energy budget. That's why your digestion is almost always the first thing to shut down. It uses a lot of energy, but you can survive for a while without it running.

Another nerve center that is great to have, but isn't really necessary to stay alive, is your frontal cortex. It uses a ton of energy to coordinate and manage everything, so when your body is prioritizing things, **your cortex will almost always be on the list to get turned down or shut off**.

In our school analogy, this would be like cutting the principal and admin hours knowing that the rest of the school can keep things running for a while. And it's true that the school can survive this way, at least for a short time, but it's not a great long-term plan when you need to get back to the big-picture stuff and keep everyone on the same page.

In your body, this means that your cortex will get shut down or turned off when your energy is low day after day. And it will be hard to get a handle on the big-picture situations in your life.

And to make it even harder, **your amygdala will usually end up being in charge** since it ranks higher on the priority list and is the other nerve center that can run your body.

Unfortunately, your amygdala is not meant to handle the complicated situations that your cortex does, but there's no other choice when your cortex goes on standby. This is why you're more likely to end up emotionally reacting instead of on-purpose thinking when you're tired, stressed, sick, or pregnant.

Being stuck in survival takes a lot of energy and makes it hard to get your cortex back in charge and living in the big picture again.

That's why we're going to talk about ways you can rest and recharge your body systems. We've already introduced the activities for taking a break, so now let's discuss how to recharge and stay charged.

Again, these ideas may seem really basic, but it's important to remember that it will be hard to move on to more steps if you don't have enough energy to get your cortex and your body back online.

Further Study Recommendations:

Laziness Does Not Exist by Devon Price, PhD. This book can help you understand that your body needs rest more than you realize and that low energy is a sign of exhaustion, not laziness.

Rest Is Resistance: A Manifesto by Tricia Hersey. This book can help you understand the importance of making rest a priority for yourself and your community.

CHAPTER 17 — SLEEPING

Pretty much the best thing that you can do to get more energy back into your body and brain is to focus on sleep.

Now, I know this isn't as easy as it sounds because **survival often messes with sleep**. But sleep will still be the best place to start focusing your attention because it's the most direct way to recharge your body and get some of the energy you need.

When your system is stuck in survival, you might find that you **struggle to get enough sleep** and/or that you're **sleeping too much**.

Let's talk first about the idea of sleeping "too much." Many people believe that over-sleeping will cause mental health issues like depression. These people will usually limit their sleep time (or their children's sleep time) to protect them from depression or shutting down.

The truth is that sleeping a lot is almost never the *cause* of these problems. Sleeping a lot is a sign that your body is **low on energy and trying to recharge**.

If you had the flu and slept for half the day, you would be glad since you know it's helping you heal. So why are you concerned about sleeping too much when your body is drained and your energy levels have been overdrafted for weeks or maybe years?

Even if sleeping a lot is part of your shutdown survival response, we already explained how you can't just solve this issue by telling yourself to stop. And in the meantime, there's no scientific evidence that over-sleeping causes mental health problems. Most studies just show that they are related. Which makes sense when we know that survival drains your energy and impacts your mental health.

With any type of body recovery, sleep is actually going to be very useful. In fact, once people are able to get to sleep and use this as part of their healing process, they discover that they need more sleep than they expected because their energy supply has gotten really low.

I think this is why many people believe that giving in to sleep will make you want to sleep more. As your body gets permission to rest, it will use the opportunity to restore the energy supply and work to get your system back to a full charge. This will often look like getting *more* tired once you start allowing yourself to rest more.

Another challenge with survival is that you might be **sleeping plenty but not sleeping very deeply**. Stress is likely to keep some of your body in go-mode, even when you're sleeping. So your system uses up a lot of energy even while it's charging, which makes it hard to store up any extra.

A survival system won't just recharge overnight the same way phone batteries do, so it might take weeks (and sometimes months and years) for your sleep cycle to balance back out again, especially depending on how long you've been living in chaos and running on empty.

Keeping your system charged will be important throughout the healing process and for the rest of your life. Without this, it will be hard to get out of (and stay out of) survival.

Now, if you're worried that you're sleeping too much, try not to restrict your sleep. Obviously, this might be difficult to do if you have certain work hours or if you're raising children. But sleeping less isn't going to help much.

Part of the slow-mode signal is to tell your body to save energy and not let go. This means your body might be telling you to sleep all the time even though it never helps you to feel rested. Do your best to keep practicing the calming activities and the sleep improvement ideas we're about to go over. With time, they can help your system ease up on the survival responses so your body can finally get more *restful* sleep.

Okay. So, let's talk about sleeping for those who have a **hard time getting to and/or staying asleep**.

This is a tough cycle when you're in survival because, if your body isn't getting enough sleep to recharge, it often leaves you stuck in go-mode. And if your body is stuck in go-mode, it's hard to get to sleep and stay asleep.

It's a really frustrating cycle.

Try not to stress too much though. (I know that's easy to say and much harder to do, so just do your best.)

Even a little more sleep can help more than you'd think, and there are a lot of options for working through this. You probably won't get there right away, but you can start with the recommendations in the next few pages and see if you notice any improvement.

Now, some of you may actually feel like you're **stuck between the not-enough and too-much sleep** situation. For most people, this looks like a random schedule where you fall asleep at different times every day and sometimes can't sleep for days but then crash for a 16-hour stretch.

This pattern can be part of an up-and-down emergency system where you flip between go-mode and slow-mode, and your sleep is just trying to keep up. If this is you, these recommendations can also help you improve your sleep patterns.

But if you start to feel overwhelmed as you read through these recommendations, this might be a good time to consider getting some professional support. Asking yourself to make changes while you're stuck in this energy-sucking loop might be too much to do on your own, so it's really okay to find someone to guide you through the process. Chapter 56 can help you find someone if you want to head over there for a bit and come back.

In fact, even if you're not interested in other professional help, it can be really worthwhile to get a **medical check-up and a sleep study** done. You might have sleep apnea or dust allergies or pain that keeps you from decent sleep. Sometimes these issues can be easily treated so you can focus on recharging to deal with the other stuff.

Now, whether you talk to someone or not, we'll walk you through some basic ideas for getting better sleep that are based on the latest research.

Reset Expectations

First, let's go over average sleep times because you might think you're sleeping enough when, in reality, you're not. Some people believe they're sleeping too much when they're actually getting the right amount.

Adults need *at least* 7 ½ hours of sleep a night. As in, that's the minimum, and you may need much more than that. And, if you feel like you're in survival a lot, you may need closer to 9 or 10 hours a night since you're burning through energy all the time.

It's also important to remember that shutdown can be a sign that your body is clamping down on go-mode energy that won't turn off and is running constantly in the background. So your system might be fully drained even if you just hung out in bed all day.

Another important thing to know is that **teens need more sleep than adults**. They generally need between 8 and 10 hours a night because their neurons are still growing, and they are dealing with a lot of hormonal changes. And if they're also dealing with survival, they will need even more than that.

Reset Matches

One of the most important things you need to understand about your sleep process is that it uses matches like your amygdala security system. This means that **your sleep cycle is activated by the senses in your live feed**. When your body is ready to rest, your system likes to have clear signals that everything is safe and comfortable before it's willing to let your guard down for the night.

So your system keeps a file on sleep matches to help with this. Your body will start to know things are safe and you're ready for sleep when you're in bed, snuggling with your favorite blanket, listening to your fan, and smelling the laundry detergent on your sheets.

But, if you've been struggling to sleep, these matches can get muddy because you noticed all these same senses as you lay wide awake three nights in a row. Now your brain doesn't understand that these senses are the signal to sleep, not to stay awake.

So, let's go over how we use this info to improve this process.

1. **It's important to be ready to sleep at the same time every night.**

Your brain likes creating and using matches to stay consistent. Trying to keep the same pattern every night for two weeks can go a long way in resetting sleep patterns.

2. **If you aren't falling asleep, get up and do something else until you're sleepy again.**

If you try to read, scroll on your phone, or listen to music while lying in bed, then all your sleepy time matches may switch to wide-awake matches.

When you get up, go to a different room or area and do something boring (and do your best to avoid screens) until you feel sleepy again. Then go back to bed and try to sleep. If you aren't falling asleep after 30 minutes, then get up again and keep repeating the process until you do fall asleep.

3. **You have to keep doing this to strengthen the matches.**

This process might feel stressful at first when you think about how much sleep you are missing. We want a quick fix, especially when we're feeling crappy and tired. So it can be hard to have the patience to keep working at this. Do your best and get help if you need it. The more regular you can make this pattern (even if you don't fall asleep right away), the stronger your sleep process will get in time.

Reset Rhythms

Another pattern that can help you reset your sleep is to use mother nature.

Our body systems have run off of sun cycles for a long time, and it's amazing how much technology messes with that. Since we can keep lights on all night and usually watch a lot of bright screens, our brains get tricked into thinking that the sun is out when it's not, and we stay up really late while our bodies are waiting for a bunch of fake suns to set.

So **being mindful of your light exposure** is a simple way that you can support your sleep. For most people, the most straightforward way to do this is by changing your morning routine. Probably the most important step for resetting sleep is to **get bright light first thing in the morning**.

The very best option is to walk outside in the sunlight as soon as you get up, and then hang there for 10 minutes. If you aren't fancy enough to have a balcony or a yard to lounge in, you can find a window with some sunlight and hang around there.

And, just to be clear, I'm not asking you to look directly at the sun, just look around and soak up the rays. Also, if you wear glasses with a blue-light filter, it's best to take them off during this time because the blue light is what you want your eyes to take in.

Now, for those of you who are in a situation where the sun isn't around when you need her (like working weird shifts or living somewhere with dark winters), a bright LED light or ring light can be turned on first thing in the "morning" for a pretty decent amount of wake-up light.

After doing this at the same time every morning for a few days, it will usually start to help your brain and body get tired at the same time every night. This is also a good hint about when you might want to schedule your bedtime if you're trying to reset your sleep routine.

If you're struggling to get out of bed or fully wake up in the morning, find a bright LED light that you can keep next to your bed. (Be sure to avoid lights or lamps with UV rays as these are not safe without eye and skin protection.) Once you have this light, try to pay attention to how long it takes for your body to actually wake up in the morning once you get some light and set an extra alarm for that amount of time before your real alarm.

Then, the next morning, when the first alarm goes off, lean over and turn on the light. Then go back to sleep or close your eyes. Your eyes can actually get blue light through your eyelids, so it will help your system to wake up before your real alarm, even if you're sleeping.

Now, to improve this light process even more, you can also work on **dimming or filtering light in the evenings**. Some people do this by setting blue-light filters on their phone, turning off overhead lights, or even wearing blue-light filter glasses.

Giving your brain the signal of morning with the sun or a bright light and the signal of evening with dimmed lights and blue-light filters can really help your body get a better handle on a more natural sleep cycle.

Now, these changes might take a while to reset, so if they're not working right away, don't stress and keep doing your best.

The sleep suggestions in this chapter are based on patterns that work for everyone's brain and sleep cycles, so I would start with these before you jump into other ideas. Repeating them a lot may help improve things down the road, even if they aren't changing right away.

But if they don't end up working for you, check out the book recommendation below for more ideas and info.

Further Study Recommendations:

Why We Sleep: Unlocking the Power of Sleep and Dreams by Matthew Walker, PhD. This book can help you understand the scientific systems behind your sleep and how to work with your mind and body to improve your sleep.

CHAPTER 18 – EATING

A really important part of keeping your body recharged is eating.

Eating is something we all need to do to stay alive because it gives us energy. But **eating can be really difficult in survival**, especially now that you've learned how your digestion gets shut off when you're stressed.

Most people in survival really struggle with good eating habits. And I'm not talking about *healthy* eating, but just eating in general. It's hard to eat regularly when you don't feel hungry or you feel nauseous all the time. Eating enough is a very real issue when you're in survival.

I'm not going to talk about healthy eating in this book because that's a step you can work on when you're in a better place and have more energy.

I'm just going to talk about ways to help you eat when you're dealing with survival.

1. Try not to be hard on yourself about what you're eating. **Any food is better than nothing, especially when you're not getting enough to eat.**

Low energy will make it hard to stay motivated and make changes in your life. So eating enough will be an important focus as you heal. This is true no matter what size you are. Low appetite and digestion shutdown affect all body types.

2. If you're feeling nauseous all the time or struggling to feel hungry, you can try to keep snacks around and **eat a tiny bit every hour or so.**

This keeps your stomach from getting too full or upset but also helps to signal your body that it needs to switch digestion back on.

Just do your best. Having a little more energy will help your brain recharge and move out of survival a little bit at a time.

3. Another important thing to understand is that **eating is a really simple way to tell your amygdala that it's not in danger** and to cool down the emergency systems.

Stress eating might be one of the ways your body has figured out how to switch off survival mode. Trying to make major changes to this process right now might actually make things worse, not better.

4. **If you're worried about overeating or emotional eating, this is something you can deal with later** after your energy is more built up and your big-picture brain turns back on.

Eating more than you need is usually better than eating nothing since you can use the energy. You're working with survival here, so you're doing the best you can with where you're at. There's no shame in that.

Now, don't get me wrong, healthy eating can support better brain function, but it's probably going to take way too much energy for you to make major changes like that right now.

Plus, if you're a human in survival, you've probably failed to "get healthy" enough times that you really beat up on yourself about it, especially when other people are more than happy to tell you how they "cured" their stress with a good diet or finally got their energy back when they lost 20 pounds.

If that's true for them, that's amazing. But, like most things in life, nothing is a one-size-fits-all solution. Most people don't just kale or CrossFit their way out of survival.

It would be nice, but it's rarely that simple.

Okay. Let's pause for a moment. I'm really excited you've gotten this far.

We've gone through a lot of information, and you might be overloaded right now. Learning and changing is not an easy process, so it's impressive that you made it here.

If this is getting to be too much though, go ahead and take a break. You might want some time to sit with everything you've learned, and there's no rule that you have to finish every book you start. Or that you can't come back after a long pause.

Do what you need to, and the book will be here when you're ready for more.

Further Study Recommendations:

Health at Every Size: The Surprising Truth About Your Weight by Linda (now Lindo) Bacon, PhD. This book can help you better understand how impressive and complicated your body is and offer you simple and effective ways to make slow and steady changes that can help both your emotional and physical health.

UPGRADE 3.0
CREATING THE NETWORKS

CHAPTER 19 – DEVELOPING

Now that you have had a chance to see how these systems all work together, we're going to add a few more details. This upgrade will teach you a little more about how your body and brain develop the unique responses and reactions you have in your system.

To understand how this works, we're going to go back to neurons and nerves. We already discussed how neurons send messages back and forth in your body all the time and keep your system connected.

It's important to know that **neurons don't start out being all organized and clear** right when you're born. In the beginning, many of your neurons fire kind of randomly since you're just beginning to connect with the world and your own body. But then, **as you grow and explore** and learn, the **neurons start to fall into regular patterns**.

Let's go back to our school analogy and think about a brand new school starting out. It might take a while before the staff and students figure out their communication patterns and who is taking care of what. Staff will have to hold a lot of meetings and have a lot of conversations to figure out how to run the school.

And once things are up and running, there will always be more things to add or sort out based on the needs of the school and how it changes. Students might want a new after-school program or to start a student council. So the staff will have to figure out how to put together these new programs on top of their regular meetings and everyday duties.

This is similar to the pattern your neurons go through as they're growing and forming in your body and brain.

No matter how many things you learn and organize, there will always be more to sort out and put together.

You might have seen this in action if you've ever watched a baby starting to explore the world.

She will start to move her fingers and practice gripping and controlling the movements in her hands. Her neurons are learning the difference between a firm and soft grip, and how to adjust her fingers, wrists, and arms. This will build a group of nerves that work together to manage her hand movements.

At the same time, you might also see her building another group of nerves for her vision. You may notice her eyes crossing and readjusting as she learns to focus on and track objects. Her neurons are organizing visual patterns and trying to understand the images in the world around her.

Then, one random day, she'll catch sight of her own moving fingers and it will suddenly click that the hand she's seeing is hers and she's controlling it. She might even look surprised as she makes this discovery. After a bit of practice, she may figure out that she's seeing and connecting with a part of her own body.

Once this happens, these two nerve groups will figure out how to communicate with each other and work as a team. Together they will become her hand-eye coordination.

The connection of these two groups will continue to help her nerves grow. She will be able to use her eyes to develop her hand movements and her hand movements to practice focusing her eyes.

By exploring and practicing every day, her neurons start to build really strong patterns and connections with each other, and she learns how to handle and navigate the world one tiny piece at a time.

Your body system grows this same way. It uses these same patterns of practicing, connecting, and organizing to make you and your life truly unique.

Every new experience shapes and reshapes your neurons and nerve centers. So many years of your childhood are spent building and rebuilding these connections to figure out who you are and how to navigate your world. Your body and brain are still doing this every day, but it's not as obvious as it was when you were a baby and learning the basics.

As an adult, it's easy to forget how much your system is handling day to day because you've been doing it for so long.

CHAPTER 20 – EXPANDING

As these groups of nerves continue to grow, they build nerve centers like your frontal cortex and your amygdala.

In fact, your **frontal cortex** is so large and complex that it **can take about 25 years to be fully developed**. You need to build a lot of nerve groups and get a lot of practice to be able to coordinate such big-picture and on-purpose thinking. It takes a ton of training and experience to make decisions and take action that consider the past, present, and future.

Your amygdala, on the other hand, **starts handling security duties before you're even born.**

You can start saving danger and safety files at about 26 weeks in utero (which is about 3 months before a baby is usually born). Your body makes sure this part of your brain is developed early on so that your system knows how to keep you safe. From this point, and as you grow, your amygdala will save short clips of your senses as you go through different experiences.

While your brain is learning and practicing these matches, your system will use the *find a protector* emergency plan when threats come up. That way, your amygdala can learn from your caregivers how to survive each kind of situation. By watching them, your amygdala will become more prepared to handle threats, and it will build the emergency plans that will help you survive.

As you learned in Upgrade 1.0, your amygdala keeps a file of the memory snips that are connected with threats. Then, when anything comes through the live feed that matches one of these clips, your amygdala will sound the alarms and send messages to your body to follow up with one of the emergency reactions we reviewed in Upgrade 2.0.

Now let's talk about how these **emergency networks continue to develop.**

Although your senses and body reactions are important pieces of your emergency teams, they're not the only parts that get involved.

Emotions are another layer that can be added into the amygdala's emergency network.

Emotions are closely connected with your amygdala because they are a way that your body can quickly add up a lot of signals going off all at once. They are almost like a climate check or weather gauge for your system so you can get a quick understanding of what's happening and make sense of it.

Think about a time where an emotion gave you a good idea of what was going on, before you even realized there was something to notice.

Maybe you walked into a quiet room and felt somber and like you should keep your voice down but didn't know why. But then you realized that someone had just shared some bad news. Or maybe you were walking down an empty road and felt nervous only to realize someone had started walking behind you.

Emotions are often telling you something before all the incoming signals are sorted out and understood by your cortex. Because of this, emotions are a helpful part of your emergency team.

For example, if your emergency plan is to run, your body will interpret this as feeling scared. But if the plan is to fight, then you're more likely to feel angry. Emotions are your body's way of helping you get a quick idea of what's going on so that you know how to respond, even when a lot of complicated stuff is happening.

These emotion signals will start to take shape and become part of your emergency teams pretty soon after you're born.

Then, as you get older, **words and thoughts will begin to join into your emergency network too.**

Words are another way to sum up complicated stuff, so thoughts and words can also become part of your stress responses.

For example, if your go-mode helps you ace a test or gives you the guts to chat up a cute stranger, then you're more likely to think "I'm strong," "I'm successful," or "I'm confident." These words will then get matched with these situations and help you stay motivated the next time you face them again.

But if your emergency reactions are getting you stuck, or taking over at bad times, then you'll probably start thinking things like "I'm weak," or "I can't handle this," or "I'm helpless." And it's likely that your body will relive these messy reactions the next time these same thoughts pop up.

As you can see, there are a lot of layers that can get added into your emergency responses. Emotions, thoughts, body reactions, and senses all play a part in expanding these nerve connections.

CHAPTER 21 – NETWORK

Now, if these layers keep getting activated in the same way and with the same patterns, then the nerves in your body will begin to form really strong emergency teams made up of these expanded nerve groups.

Let's go back to the school analogy to understand this part.

Many schools will form emergency response teams to help the security guards when there are threats.

The idea is that you will need staff members in each part of the building to help carry out the emergency response and help everyone follow the plan. They will all be given two-way radios and separate instructions so they can take care of their zone and their specific part of the plan. Then, when they are called into action, all the members work together to handle the emergency as a team, even if they usually have jobs doing something else.

Similarly, **your emotions, thoughts, body reactions, and senses form emergency teams** in your system.

Each of these layers have their own part to play in your emergency response, even if they usually do other jobs in your system. But **the more they respond together, the more connected they become** until they form a nerve network that acts as one solid team.

This is why you can stop in your tracks when you think you hear your ex's voice at the grocery store.

As the voice comes through the live feed of your senses, your amygdala will match the sense with sound clips of fighting with your ex and trigger your system to go into emergency mode. Old snapshots of your relationship may flash before your eyes. Your body response may be to freeze and gasp for air, your emotion response might be to get flooded with grief, and the thought "No one will ever love me" might pop up.

Without meaning to, all these layers became bonded together in your system because your ex hurt you so many times. And now that those reactions have connected enough to form a nerve network, it's going to be difficult to separate them out again.

Let's go back to the school emergency teams to see how this works. Since the security guards and the other team members need to communicate quickly and directly with each other, they will switch to a special emergency channel on their two-way radios when the alarms sound. That way they can keep in touch with each other on a dedicated channel until the problem has been handled. Once it's over, they can go back to their regular jobs and switch their radios back to the main channel.

But if these issues keep happening all the time, then they're probably going to start keeping their radios on the dedicated channel and pay more attention to their emergency duties than their regular jobs.

And, since the whole team is now staying tuned into the emergency channel, any member of the group can pass along a message without having to wait for the switchover signal from the security guards.

So, if just one member of the team happens to notice something in their zone that matches the usual emergency pattern, they will immediately share this with the rest of the team and kick start everyone into action. Even if it's a false alarm.

Your neurons and nerves work in a similar way.

As these nerves connect together more, **they become a network**. And the more they respond as a network, the more they get **tuned in to the same frequency** and stay tuned in.

So, when a survival response gets activated over and over, each nerve group becomes so tuned into each other that **any part of the network can set off the rest of the network** with just one tiny match. And it doesn't actually matter which feeling, thought, sense, or body reaction signals first because the whole network gets triggered, no matter where the signal starts.

This means that you can start out only being triggered by your ex's voice but, eventually, the network can be activated just by feeling grief, or getting short of breath, or thinking "No one will ever love me." And this is true even if these feelings and thoughts are popping up due to completely unrelated situations.

This can be tough because **your system can keep adding more and more nerve layers to the network.** If more emotions, body reactions, senses, or thoughts start joining in regularly, they will also start tuning in to the same frequency and become part of this emergency network.

Because of this, people in survival often become a walking trigger factory where they start to get set off by nearly anything and everyone around them. This has nothing to do with being strong or weak. Your system is just doing the best it can, and it's trying to add as many early warning signs to the emergency network as possible.

It's really frustrating to deal with getting triggered all the time though. Especially when you probably have more than one emergency network that is taking over regularly.

Actually, it's pretty common to flip between different emergency networks with different reactions when you're in survival a lot. Your system might go through panic, anger, and shutdown all in the same hour. When one reaction doesn't "handle" the danger, then your system will look for another.

Remember how the shutdown response is often the backup plan that kicks in when your system realizes that go-mode isn't working, or if it's taking too much energy? This means that you might find your system going back and forth between go-mode and slow-mode, or even going through both at the same time.

This could look like getting a ton of energy and being anxiously productive for a few days and then struggling to get out of bed for the next week. It could also feel like you don't care about anything, but still find yourself freaking out over tiny issues.

It can become a really confusing and exhausting way to live.

CHAPTER 22 – MEMORY

To understand more about how these networks get so stuck, we need to go through some basics about how memory works in different parts of your system.

When you go through regular, day-to-day experiences and your cortex is mostly the one in charge, your memories save in a pretty straightforward way. This is because your cortex has help from a part of your brain called the **hippocampus.**

The hippocampus seems to have a few roles in your brain, but one of the really important things it helps with is **organizing your memories.**

In our school analogy, you can think of the hippocampus like the principal's assistant or school secretary. If you have been behind the scenes in a school, you will know that this is a *major* role. The principal's assistant keeps everything organized and running efficiently.

The hippocampus plays a very similar role in your body. It helps with storing and organizing the memories that you make while your cortex is in charge so that you can keep track of them later.

Throughout the day, **your brain records and saves memories to your short-term or working memory** where they can stay for a little while. But this part of your brain only has a small amount of storage space, so when it gets full, you have to file away or delete these memories to make room for new ones.

You might think of this like the assistant's desk. During the school day, many files and documents will pile up on her desk, and she'll have to decide what to do with them all. At the end of the day, an organized assistant will sort through everything so she can file away what's important and toss anything that's not.

Luckily, your brain has a similar process for backing up important memories so that they aren't lost.

Every night while you sleep, **your hippocampus** sorts through your short-term memories and **decides what to move over to your long-term memory.** This is called **memory consolidation.**

Usually your long-term memory is used for things that are important to you and help you with the big picture.

A lot of what your hippocampus decides to save depends on what you care about and focus on the most. You might memorize funny movie quotes, or sport stats, or ideas for remodeling your house.

You will feel more in control of these ideas and memories because they're things you're choosing to focus on, and they usually stay pretty organized. Your hippocampus can easily search and sort these memories by words, or pictures, or feelings, or pretty much any category you can think of.

If you want to see what I mean, try remembering something from 4th grade. Now think of memories where you felt excited. How about a few memories of buying shoes. Or your favorite memory with your best friend. You see how your brain can literally just search things up with an image, an idea, or a feeling?

I mean, how cool is your brain?

Now let's talk about survival memories and your emergency networks. Survival systems actually store memories in a much different way because they're saved when the amygdala is in charge.

Since your amygdala is more focused on your live feed and spotting danger matches than the big picture, it doesn't save your emergency networks in the same organized way that your hippocampus does. Instead, **survival networks get backed up into muscle memory**, which is a lot different than your long-term memory.

You see, your brain is always looking for ways to be more efficient and free up energy. So when you repeat a certain movement or task the same way again and again, your brain will actually store that memory in parts of your brain and body that run on autopilot.

Your body has a ton of these autopilot systems that you use every day. And they make it easy for your body to just feel and react to the common patterns in your life. That way, you don't have to waste your energy planning out or thinking too hard about a task that you always do exactly the same way every time you do it.

This can include things like riding a bike, counting, putting on pants, and always singing the wrong lyrics to your favorite songs.

Your amygdala works really well with muscle memory because they both work by matching, and they both directly link to the body for quick reactions.

But, just to be clear, not all muscle memory starts with your amygdala. Many of your muscle memories can actually start with your long-term memory. Your hippocampus can help save things in both long-term memory and muscle memory, but your amygdala can only use muscle memory.

An easy example to understand how your hippocampus helps to save things to both memories is when you think about tying your shoes. Most of you probably learned to tie your shoes when you were young. Your cortex spent a lot of time learning and practicing this skill so that your hippocampus could save the instructions in your long-term memory. But eventually, this task was also saved in muscle memory because it's something your body practiced the same way over and over again. And now you hardly have to think about it.

Down the road though, if you have to sit down and teach a kid how to tie *their* shoes, you can get thrown off. The autopilot will make it hard to slow down and adjust the movements for teaching someone else. But since this skill was also saved in your long-term memory, you can usually get your hippocampus to pull up the info so that you can pass the knowledge on to someone else.

With your amygdala, when your body repeats certain emergency responses the same way over and over again, they will also save as autopilot systems.

For example, when you learn to drive, your cortex does a lot of practicing and learning. But it's likely that your amygdala will take over during dangerous situations to help you hit the brakes a bit faster by using go-mode.

And it will only take a few brake-slamming situations before your body moves it to muscle memory. Then, once it's on autopilot, if the car in front of you slows down too quickly, your foot will automatically move to the brake pedal. If you doubt this, think about how many times you have tried to hit the brakes while you were sitting in the *passenger* seat of a car.

Having muscle memory for emergencies is really smart. It helps you recognize and respond to regular stress more quickly and automatically. But if your stress responses have been problematic or unhelpful, then having them move to autopilot can just make things more complicated.

If your body keeps responding to stress or emergencies in the same way and it isn't really helping (or stopped working after a while), then it's going to be more difficult when those reactions become muscle memory without your choice. Even your worst reactions can still end up in autopilot just from being repeated over and over.

This is why it can be harder than you think to stop throwing tantrums or walk away from fights, even as a grown up.

You should also know that **your memories can get a little complicated with two ways to record things**. Even though your cortex is not in charge during an emergency, it can still observe and save details of a stressful situation in your long-term memory.

So **your cortex and your amygdala can end up with two totally separate versions of the same event**. And depending on which file your system is pulling up, you might not realize that the details of your story keep switching, which makes other people confused or annoyed.

Plus, the more autopilot things get, the harder it is for your cortex to stay online and keep track of what's going on. So, your cortex will start disconnecting more when things are running off of muscle memory. And this can create **dead spots in your long-term memory.**

In a functional system, this isn't as much of an issue because the actions and responses that get moved over to muscle memory are usually helpful and appropriate for the situation. This is how you can drive home safely without remembering how you got there. Or how you can forget what you ate for dinner or what outfits you wore to work this week.

Unfortunately, in a disorganized and overwhelmed system, you can end up saving some pretty messy networks into muscle memory. And once this happens, it can be nearly impossible for your cortex to observe or record anything that's going on when these networks flip on.

This means that you can end up having full-on blackouts (with no memory of what you did or what happened) every time your system switches over to an autopilot emergency response. This is why some people will swear up and down that they didn't freak out or lose their temper even though you watched it happen with your own eyes.

This disconnection is a form of dissociation, which we'll talk more about in Chapter 50.

Another point that's really important to understand is that **your amygdala doesn't have a sense of time other than the present**. Remember how it's only meant to stay focused on the live feeds? This means that when emergency responses come from your amygdala, the network is only saved with a concept of *now*.

So when a really strong emergency network takes over, your system can end up in a timeless space where the experience becomes your whole reality. And with your cortex offline, you can't see the big picture enough to realize that the moment will eventually pass.

While these networks are switched on, two minutes can feel like an eternity. It will seem as if you've been stuck in that emergency forever and that you will always be stuck. Which is another reason why panic attacks or shutting down can feel so terrifying.

This also means that these networks save kind of like a **time portal where your mind and body get transported back** to all the moments when these networks were created *and* expanded. Every memory that has triggered this emergency network gets piled up together and flares all at once.

Your senses will replay the matching clips that your amygdala has saved. Your body will go through the same go-mode and slow-mode reactions. And your whole emergency network will get activated with all the emotions and thoughts that have been added in. The hardest part is that your system won't be able to understand that these experiences are memories and not happening live.

This is called a **flashback** in the mental health world.

These time portals or flashback moments can become even more challenging as your system moves these emergency networks into muscle memory. As they lose all communication with your cortex and your long-term memories, they stop getting updated. This means that these networks will literally get left in the past as the rest of your system grows and changes around them. And when they take over, it feels like all the old experiences are happening all over again *right now*.

So, when you get triggered, the network will make you feel like you're back to being 6 or 11 or 17 years old again. In fact, most people have a few emergency reactions that have been trapped in muscle memory since they were kids. And when these get set off, it's really easy to get stuck in immature reactions because the network hasn't been updated in a very long time.

This is why you can behave like a mature adult most of the year but lose your mind when you get together with your family for the holidays or celebrations. It's pretty impossible to grow up in a family without having some emergency responses that get matched with their voices, tones, words, actions, and faces. And you're almost guaranteed to trigger those old, immature reactions when you spend enough time together.

Having your *own* family can also be hard. Lots of moments in family life can match with parts of your childhood emergency networks that have been dormant for a while. And they can easily portal your system right back to those same immature responses you created years ago.

An important side note here is that you don't really have the ability to create long-term memories until you're about 2 years old because your cortex is still forming. So it's unlikely to have solid memories before this time.

But, if something happened that was highly emotional or stressful before you had long-term memory, it's possible to have some recall of these experiences. Since your amygdala, reward system, and emergency networks are developed before you are born and save sensory clips in your safe and danger matches and muscle memory, you may remember some details or feelings from very early on in your life.

CHAPTER 23 – EXAMPLE

At this point, I think it would be helpful to show you how this can work in real life by walking you through an example.

Since I want you to understand the idea, I'm going to use a pretty realistic situation that includes loud noises, yelling, and body responses of panic and shutdown. This might be difficult for some of you, especially if you have an emergency network with similar matches.

So, if you do want to go through the example but feel a little nervous, this could be another great time to use the tricks we reviewed in Chapter 10.

You can change the images into cartoons, or you can turn them black and white. You can also imagine turning down the volume on your senses or feelings. You can pull out something strong to smell, or you can put your difficult feelings or memories in a container if that worked before.

(And, you can also skip this if you're not ready. That's always allowed.)

Ready? Let's meet our example character. Her name is Hazel.

Hazel is a one-year-old girl with two loving parents and a safe home.

One night, as she is peacefully sleeping, a thunderstorm rolls in. As the wind starts to blow and the rain pours down, a sudden bolt of lightning shoots down nearby and makes a giant boom that wakes Hazel up.

In this case, because her amygdala was startled, it sounds the alarm to call for her parents. To do this, her body gets the signal to release go-mode energy, which makes her cry loud and her heart race.

But because of the noisy storm, her parents don't hear her crying from the other side of the apartment.

As she cries and no one comes, her amygdala switches up the plan and tells her to run and find her parents. But she can't get out of her crib by herself. And with nowhere to go, the adrenaline and energy that dump into her body start to make her legs shake.

As this is happening, Hazel's amygdala starts to record the images and sounds of what is making her feel unsafe. In this case, this will include the images of flashing lights and the sounds of loud booms since these were the senses that first startled her.

Then, because she tried to call for help and run away, her system has now linked the body responses of crying, a racing heart and shaky legs to the senses of flashing lights and loud booms. And since she couldn't get help or get out of her crib, the emotions of fear and helplessness have also been activated.

Luckily, Hazel's mom and dad decide to check on her a few minutes later and they rush to comfort her when they realize how upset she is. Because of the storm, they let her sleep with them for the next few nights.

At some point, Hazel is able to sleep in her own room again and forgets the storm ever happened.

Now, let's fast forward to a couple years later when Hazel is with her parents at her first firework show.

As the show starts, she's caught off guard by the flashing lights and loud booms. Because similar matches were saved during the thunderstorm, her amygdala immediately triggers the alarm and sets off the emergency plan in her body. This causes her heart to race and her legs to shake, and she cries out to her parents. All these reactions bring up the same emotions of fear and helplessness she felt when she was younger.

Luckily, her parents are able to help her feel protected again, but they have to leave the show in order for her to stop crying and to get her body to calm down.

Now that this has happened twice in mostly the same way, Hazel's reaction has become a little stronger in her body. All these reactions and feelings have teamed up into an emergency response that is more easily triggered by flashing lights and loud booms.

Okay. Let's move forward again.

Hazel is now 5 years old, and it's dinner time. Right now she is tired and refusing to eat. Her parents are also worn out and they start arguing about whether they should give her fruit snacks if she hasn't finished her dinner.

As she begins to realize that her parents are arguing about her, she starts to wonder if it's her fault that her parents are fighting. Then, suddenly, her mom stands up, pounds the table, says, "I've had enough," and leaves the room.

Well, without anyone realizing it, the loud boom from pounding the table will trigger the same emergency response all over again. Because it was loud and unexpected like the thunderclap and the firework boom, her amygdala matches the sound to danger and sounds the alarms inside of her.

Now, little flashes of the old memories will come up with the same senses, emotions, and body experiences that came with it before, and Hazel will probably have a meltdown as her heart races, her legs shake, and her eyes see spots as if there are flashing lights.

Her amygdala will also save the sounds of her parents arguing into this network, as this clearly came before the loud boom. Her amygdala will be trying to save any senses that might give her system more of a head start next time things get stressful.

On top of this, as her mom walks out of the room, her body is reminded of feeling lost from her parents on the night of the thunderstorm, and so a new emotion of feeling abandoned pops up and gets added to the mix. Since she's only 5, she'll have no idea what this feeling is called, but she will know it feels sad and scary when her mom leaves because she needs her mom around to help her survive.

And, finally, right before she was triggered by the pounding sound on the table, she had started thinking, "It's my fault." So now this thought has been linked with the survival network.

Unfortunately, at 8 years old, Hazel's parents start fighting a lot more, and it really begins to strengthen this survival network. Since her mind is triggered to think that their arguing is her fault, and she is too nervous to interrupt, Hazel's amygdala figures out another way to deal with the situation. Instead of crying and getting help from her parents, she runs away to her room and hides in her closet, using a combo of go-mode and slow-mode in her body.

The problem is that she's too young to understand that her parents are stressed out because her mom lost her job and not because of anything Hazel did. She doesn't have enough experience in her cortex yet to understand how unemployment could be stressful. And it wouldn't occur to her parents that Hazel is having life-or-death feelings inside her body when they fight or that she believes that their arguing is her fault.

So when Hazel's parents notice her hiding in her closet and crying after they fight, they say things like "Don't worry, you're fine" or tell her to stop crying and come out of her room.

Sometimes this triggers Hazel's amygdala even more for fear that she's doing something wrong or her parents might start arguing again. So she goes back to melting down since her amygdala knows that this response has worked before to get her parents to comfort her.

But now that her parents are more stressed out and tired from their own arguing, sometimes they have the patience to help her calm down, and sometimes they don't.

A few years later when Hazel is 11 years old, her dad finds her hiding in the closet after another fight. When Hazel starts crying, her exhausted dad yells at her to "grow up and stop acting like such a baby." In that moment, Hazel's usual emergency plans have now failed to protect her. Crying isn't working, and running away and hiding isn't working either. So her amygdala switches up the plan and decides to shut down.

Immediately Hazel's body goes limp and she numbs out. She's still awake and her eyes are open, but her gaze gets foggy, and she tunes out everything her dad is saying.

When her dad asks, "What's wrong with you?" and Hazel doesn't hear or respond, her dad believes she's giving him an attitude and gets more angry. When Hazel still doesn't respond, her dad says, "Fine, you're grounded" and walks out of the room.

As badly as this went, shutting down helped Hazel's system feel protected when it didn't have other options, so her amygdala adds shutting down as another option for her emergency plans.

Since Hazel isn't choosing to have these reactions, she feels that her body is betraying her, and she feels really guilty that she can't control her emotions. In fact, she is starting to believe that this is the reason everything really *is* her fault. So her cortex spends a lot of time overthinking how she can stop being such a big problem in her family.

Sadly, she doesn't realize that all the overthinking is causing her growing cortex to use up her energy and pushing her body to rely on the emergency systems more and more.

It's also hard because her parents can't understand why she's so sensitive to everything. From their point of view, an 11 year old shouldn't be having such terrible meltdowns, avoiding everything, and giving so much attitude.

They know that she is such a fun and creative kid, and they feel really helpless and frustrated that they don't know how to help her when things are bad.

After getting some advice from friends, they decide to spend more positive family time together and work with a therapist, which helps them communicate more and fight less. This seems to help, and everyone starts feeling a little better, but Hazel still feels too ashamed to share how she's really feeling deep down.

In fact, she doesn't really understand what she's feeling, so she doesn't have the words for it, even if she wanted to share. And none of the adults know to ask her about these things either.

Now, let's fast forward again to 8th grade. Even though things have improved at home, Hazel's emergency networks were saved to muscle memory years ago. She still has danger files and muscle memories that are triggered by yelling, loud booms, feeling guilty, shaky legs, numbness, feeling abandoned and helpless, a racing heart, believing something is her fault, or even stepping into her closet.

Since her parents have been fighting less and she's getting more support and attention from them, these triggers haven't happened much anymore, so everyone assumes these behaviors are fading away.

But one day after a school basketball game, one of Hazel's teammates comes up to her and yells that she missed too many shots, and it's all her fault that they lost the game.

Because the thought "It's all my fault" matches part of Hazel's muscle memory, her whole emergency network gets triggered and washes over her. This means that Hazel's heart starts to race, her legs shake, and she wants to cry. She starts to feel like a helpless and abandoned little kid. Her ears start to ring like she's heard a loud boom, and she starts telling herself that everything really is her fault.

Since Hazel's system doesn't know where to run for safety, and she doesn't see any adults to protect her, all her emergency responses get activated, and she gets signals to run, cry for help, and shut down all at once. The confusion turns into a panic attack. Hazel's heart is racing faster than ever, she can't breathe, she's dizzy and nauseous, and she starts seeing spots. She is genuinely afraid that she is dying.

Hazel tells her coach that she can't breathe and that she's going to pass out, so the coach calls an ambulance. When the paramedics arrive, they recognize the signs of a panic episode and recommend professional treatment to Hazel and her parents.

The tough part is that this same panic attack could have been set off by any feeling that matched with her muscle memory.

It could have been triggered while she was doing sprints for basketball practice and her heart started racing and her legs started shaking. Or it could have been set off because she was feeling extra helpless and lost in math class. Or it could have been set off by an unexpected loud boom from the band room.

As if middle school and hormone changes aren't hard enough, now Hazel has to deal with an emergency response that can get set off really easily *and* causes her to feel like she's dying.

Luckily, with the help of a skilled professional, Hazel and her family will get the support they need to reset and heal many of these patterns and networks. And this relief will allow Hazel to reduce her stress responses and feel like herself again.

Okay. Let's pause her story here.

Even though Hazel is not based on one real person, she is a general example of how people find themselves stuck in survival without understanding how they got there. And it's important to realize how overwhelming things can get when you don't understand what is happening to you.

This made-up example is actually pretty simple, though, and starts with one badly-timed storm.

In real life examples, it's definitely possible to end up in survival from one or two negative experiences like this, especially if the timing is just right. But most people in survival have been through so many negative events in their life that it can be hard to figure it all out and know how and why you got to where you are.

And it's also why it's so confusing to know how to get a handle on everything to change it.

CHAPTER 24 – LISTENING

Hopefully this example is making sense and helping you to understand how survival responses can become so difficult to live with.

Before we keep going, though, I want you to know that these networks *are* changeable. You might be feeling kind of hopeless right now as you're learning about these systems because they sound impossible to change. They are not.

It *is* hard to change these systems without understanding how they work, otherwise you'll keep trying things that are going to fail you.

Some of you are probably ready to get to the fixes, but remember, this isn't a quick-fix book. I will definitely keep giving you resources and guidance as we go, but we're helping you become more aware of your system so you can work with it instead of against it.

If I had magic shortcuts, I would definitely give them to you. But I don't.

I know it can be hard to trust the process when you've been let down a lot in the past.

You might also be feeling relief at getting some answers. Or frustration that there's so much to unpack. Or impatient because you just want to feel better right now, and this is taking too long. And maybe you're feeling all these things together.

There's no wrong way for you to deal with all of this. Do your best to be patient with the process and yourself. (Again, I know this is easy to say, and harder to do.)

Mostly, I am really proud of you for getting this far.

You have gone through a lot of information and upgraded a lot of difficult concepts. You've stuck with the book this far in spite of your doubts, and I'm hopeful you're learning to understand yourself a little more.

Now that you've gone through a few upgrades, I want to talk about why so many plans have failed you.

You probably remember that we touched on this when we were talking about your cortex and amygdala. It's hard to create plans when the cortex is not really in charge all the time.

That's definitely one reason you've been let down before.

Now that you understand more about muscle memory, you can see that **it's nearly impossible to tell your autopilot systems to just stop reacting**. It's like telling yourself not to shiver, or to stop feeling hungry.

Even though you can try to numb these feelings out, your body is going to do what it needs to do to survive. And your emergency networks are a big part of what keeps you alive.

Again, if these networks are working and only showing up when you're in danger, then there's no need to adjust them. But if you're stuck in survival feelings (when you are actually safe), it means **these networks have hijacked your life and need to be reset.**

So, let's talk about what it takes to reset these networks.

The first step of resetting these networks is something we've already been working on. As you've been going through the calming activities, we've been helping you create small networks that signal safety in your body. This is teaching your system how to take a break and feel more safe.

(If you haven't actually been doing them as you read, don't worry. You can always go back if you change your mind or wait for more ideas in the next few upgrades.)

The thing is, as you get stuck in survival, it's easy to feel betrayed by your body. Whether it's freaking out all the time, constantly going numb, or blowing up, it's really hard to trust yourself when you feel so out of control.

In fact, it's really difficult to make changes to your system when you're at war with your body because the only way to reset the system is to work *with* it. Avoiding it, hating it, judging it, or demanding things from it doesn't really get you anywhere.

Let's go back to the school comparison to understand this.

If the principal would like to change the emergency responses in the school, she's going to have to work with what she's got. Even if she's really bossy and demanding, the security team isn't going to just magically start listening.

Instead of lecturing everyone, the principal will have to start listening and paying attention to the patterns before any realistic changes can happen. She will have to start observing the school to see what's actually going on. Nothing much will change until she takes some time to slow down and try to understand how the system has broken down.

The same thing is true in your system.

If your cortex has been disconnected a lot or if you've been actively avoiding your body for a while, then **you will have to take some time to start listening to your system and figure out what it's been going through**. You're not going to get very far in the healing process until you can acknowledge that things aren't working.

This is another reason why we've been running through the calming activities and repeating them. It's hard to hear what's going on when there's chaos.

And it's also why we reviewed ways to recharge your body, because it's hard to practice new things without having some energy to do it.

When you've been in survival for a while, it can feel overwhelming to pay attention to your system. Numbing (or dissociating) will help you to tune out the pain and stress.

This means that your cortex ends up avoiding the present only to get fixated on the past or the future, or even get stuck living in a fantasy.

You can get obsessed with old memories to figure out where everything went wrong or who to blame. You can also get stuck stressing out about the next time you'll lose control. And sometimes you might get caught up fantasizing about the person you could have been or want to be.

When your system is regularly distracted like this, your emergency reactions will often feel like they go from 0 to 100 without any warning. And if your cortex is tuned out when these threats come along, your memory won't have enough details to figure out what was going on before your amygdala got triggered.

But, if your cortex can start to practice tuning into your body and staying present with the world around you, it can actually learn to notice the small changes that happen in your body before you get hijacked. It will also give you a better idea of the patterns around you that are keeping your system on edge.

This process is called mindfulness.

Mindfulness is any activity where your cortex practices **listening to and noticing your body without making judgments**.

This is a really key part of becoming a better manager of your system.

If you've ever had to work for a toxic boss, you know that a lot of the problems could have been sorted out if they just stopped to actually listen and pay attention once in a while.

A healthy boss will spend time observing and listening, even if they can't fix everything right away. This means that they will be open to understanding the strengths and weaknesses of their staff and acknowledge when things aren't working. That way they can figure out how to work with everyone instead of making unreasonable demands about what *should* be happening.

You can start to make the same changes in your system by practicing mindfulness.

CHAPTER 25 – MINDFUL

As usual, we're going to repeat our calming activities.

These activities can be stepping stones toward your mindfulness practice, and they can also help to create safe matches in your system.

There are many other ways to practice mindfulness if these activities aren't working for you.

Practicing mindfulness isn't always easy when you've been in survival. Activities that focus on silence or stillness may be really uncomfortable in the beginning. The openness might leave too much room for your inner critic or your anxious energy to flare up and take over.

If this feels familiar, you can look for *guided* meditations online or with an app. You can also join a mindfulness group or class to get more direction as you practice. And you can even add mindfulness into your favorite spiritual practices like prayer, music, worship, or rituals that enhance your peace.

Choose what works for you. Some activities focus more on calming your thoughts while others focus on relaxing your body. Some guide you through every step, and some set you up to practice on your own.

There is no wrong way to start. Later on I'll give you some ideas on more specific activities based on your experiences, but for now, you can just test some out and see if you like any of them.

It can be helpful to **set reminders or alarms on your phone** if you're planning to start this practice on your own.

Remembering is half the battle.

I have chosen these calming activities because they are gentle. You might need that if you're starting from survival. It can be tough to jump into connecting with your body when it's been numb or overwhelmed for a long time. There can be a lot of pain or fear underneath, so it's best to work up to it a little bit at a time.

Calm, Safe Space helps your body learn (or remember) what it's like to feel safe. Peaceful Flow gives you the chance to tune in to your body with the help of comforting energy so it's not too overwhelming.

Both of these can help you work toward more body awareness and mindfulness.

As promised, we're going to run through them again if you want to follow along, but you can also skip these and see if you find something that works better for you.

For those who are sticking around, let's go back to your **Calm, Safe Space**. Since you've done this a couple of times now, I'm only going to give you a few prompts as we go.

First, say the name of your place.

Try to remember the details you've created twice before and go back to the area where you felt the most calm and comfortable. Then take a moment to settle in and get cozy.

Check in with your body and see how it felt as you entered into that space. Was it easier to settle into this time? Or did it take a little while to get back into it?

Once you're feeling ready, go ahead and check in with your 5 senses and see what you notice in your safe space. Go ahead and pause here for a minute or two.

Now, see if you feel comfortable checking in with your body a little more.

See if you can show your body that you're working on becoming a healthier boss by tuning in, observing, and listening.

You might even apologize to your system for being so hard on it in the past. Or you might try to find some gratitude for your system now that you understand how it's been working to help you all these years.

Show your system that you're offering these mindful breaks now that you realize it's been working so hard.

It's possible that these steps might bring up some grief or guilt. If that happens, see if you can stay with the feelings as they rise and fall. It's okay to cry or yell or rock back and forth as they come up.

If staying with these feelings gets overwhelming at any point, go ahead and switch back to your Calm, Safe Space and focus your senses on what's going on around you.

You can even create containers to hold difficult emotions until you're more ready to face them later. Let your system know that you're not trying to avoid the feelings altogether but that you will return to them when you're more prepared to sit with them.

Take as much time as you need to stay here. Go ahead and come back to the book when you're **ready.**

Okay. If you're ready to come back now, let's check in again with your body and see how things are going inside of you. Were there any changes to the tightness or uncomfortable feelings? Did any part of you relax more? Did any part of you stress more? Do you feel any different than when you started?

If your safe space still isn't doing much for you, then it's okay to try something else. Three times is usually enough for an activity to start making a little difference. If you're not feeling it, then go ahead and skip this one from here on out.

Let's move on to the **Peaceful Flow** activity again and see how it goes for you this time.

Try to remember what you used as your comfortable energy. Was it spiritual, from nature, a person, an animal, a machine, or an idea?

Try to remember the details of your comfortable energy. What's the shape, size, and color? What's the texture? Does it smell like anything? What does it sound like? Notice the temperature. How does it move? Is it heavy or light or somewhere in between?

Does the energy still feel comforting for you? As always, you can pick another comfortable item and try again with something that works better. If it feels peaceful or settling, let's keep going.

Now, notice any parts of your body that feel uncomfortable or tight and pay attention to the energy that goes with it. If needed, you can skip this exercise go back to your Calm, Safe Space or another calm activity if this energy becomes overwhelming or too hard to handle.

If you're able to keep noticing your body even with the uncomfortable energy, go ahead and notice the details of the energy. What's the shape, size, and color? What's the texture? Does it smell like anything? What does it sound like? Notice the temperature. How does it move? Is it heavy or light or somewhere in between?

Now bring your attention back to your comfortable energy.

Very slowly, invite that energy into the space around you. Begin to notice the feelings from the outside of your body where the energy is flowing.

If it feels okay, go ahead and invite the comfortable energy to slowly move into your body in any way that feels safe. Remember that this energy is not forceful or pushy and only fills any spaces where it is welcome.

As this energy starts to take up some space, notice how your body is feeling. As the comfortable energy moves around or near the uncomfortable energy, notice what happens.

Spend some time letting these energies settle, and go ahead and pause until you're ready to come back again.

Wonderful. See if you can check in with your body and notice if there were any changes.

Did it help your body feel more peaceful or safe? Did it make things worse? Or did nothing change at all?

It's important to **be honest with how things are going**. Hiding your real feelings, especially from yourself, can make healing hard.

This can be pretty difficult if you've been numbed out or overwhelmed for a while. You probably don't have any idea how you feel sometimes. But even acknowledging that you don't know is helpful because you can start experimenting and paying attention to what's working or not working.

In fact, the most difficult part of this process might be admitting when things *aren't* working.

Survival can make you feel desperate and lose trust in yourself. So you might have pushed yourself into goals or programs that were guaranteed to fix everything.

And after nothing changed, you kept telling yourself that *you* were the problem. You probably told yourself that you hadn't been dedicated enough or committed enough. And kept blaming yourself every time it didn't work.

At some point, you might have started to feel that the only way to get anywhere was to discipline yourself until you finally got with the program and fell in line. Maybe it made you believe that you deserve to suffer because you're too weak and sensitive to control yourself. Or maybe you think that the only way to get better is to force and push and beat yourself into shape.

But, honestly, I've never seen this lead to true healing. No amount of self-punishment will get your system to stop surviving.

In fact, it will probably make things harder since you will just keep trying solutions that are working against your system or seeking advice from people who don't understand what's really going on.

If you've been doing this for a while, it's okay. Things can still change, and you were just doing the best you could with what you knew at the time.

Just take your time. This information and these tools are meant to meet you where you are. So use them in any order that feels right and skip anything that feels off. When you start listening, your system will help you to know where to go next.

CHAPTER 26 – INTERRUPTING

We're going to end this upgrade with one more tool that might be helpful if you're struggling with emergency responses that feel overwhelming or out of control.

As you start to listen to and reconnect with your body, you might discover some patterns that you may not have noticed before. This can help you **pay attention to the small changes that happen in your system** before the alarms take over.

You might notice that your fists ball up and your breathing gets heavy right before you blow up at your spouse. Or maybe your head gets dizzy and your vision blurs before your mind goes blank. Noticing these details, even if it's *after* the fact, shows that your cortex is getting better at noticing the changes in your body and picking up on the warning signs that show up right before your system gets triggered.

And once your cortex learns to **track when your system is about to flip**, it's possible to interrupt an emergency response before it hijacks your system. This will take a little time and practice, but these interruption skills can eventually help you to stay out of the time portals and avoid getting stuck in unhelpful emergency responses.

As you already know, these stuck networks don't just change by thinking at them. So we need to use what we have learned to approach them differently.

Since many emergency networks are saved in your muscle memory and mostly express themselves through your body, you can **hack the system by using your *body* to interrupt** instead of your thoughts.

Let's go back to our school analogy to understand this.

When the principal realizes that the school is getting ready to respond to a false alarm, she might try to talk to the security guards.

But they are probably going to ignore her or outrank her (like they are supposed to do) during a threat.

So when that doesn't work, she may be able to reach out to one or two members of the emergency team and get them to see that it's a false alarm and have them switch up their response. Since these team members have access to the emergency radio frequency, the change in their messages and actions will likely interrupt and confuse the security guards, who were expecting everyone to follow the usual procedure.

Once this happens, the security guards will likely have to pause and reassess the danger, even if it doesn't get them to immediately or fully back down from the emergency.

This is similar to how you can interrupt your own emergency responses.

When a stuck network starts to get triggered or activated, your cortex can communicate with parts of your body that are linked into the emergency network and have them interrupt the situation. Because these players are on the same emergency frequency as your amygdala, it will force your amygdala to pay attention and reassess what's going on.

Now, there are many ways to send interruptions from your body to your amygdala. But one of the clearest ways to send that message is through your lungs.

Breathing is one of the few places in your body that operates both on purpose and on autopilot. This means that it is a part of your body that you *can* communicate with during stressful events.

The other benefit here is that your lungs are linked into every emergency network in your system. Remember that breathing is one of the key parts of managing a crisis. Go-mode will cause your lungs to breathe heavily from your chest and get very full of oxygen. And slow-mode will cause your breathing to be very shallow and slow.

Since your lungs will stay linked to *any* emergency network that flares up, **changing your breathing can interrupt the danger signals** and encourage your amygdala to reanalyze the emergency.

In most situations, you can send this message by breathing more from your belly, with slow and focused breaths. Your amygdala will start to see that an important part of your body is not switching to survival mode, which will interrupt the threat signals.

Now, your amygdala is not going to immediately change the plan or switch up your mood when it notices the interruption, especially on the first try. You might already know this if someone has told you to breathe when you were mad or panicking and it made you freak out more or want to punch them.

One of the reasons that breathing can seem stressful during an emergency response is that everyone usually starts by taking air *in*. This is not actually helpful when you're in go-mode.

This is because your lungs are *already* full. Trying to pull more air into your chest will only feel terrible and might even make you feel more activated.

So during these moments, it's important to **focus on breathing out**.

And, it's actually really helpful if you focus on pushing the air out consistently and with a lot of pressure. You can do this by squeezing your lips together and focusing on slowly pushing the air out through the small opening. Then breathe in however you need to.

Breathing like this will start to bring your oxygen levels down and balance out the pressure in your lungs. (It might even cause you to make some farting noises, which isn't terrible since a little silliness can also help cool things down.)

All these small changes to your breathing will interrupt the threat signals. And this shift will cause your amygdala to rethink the danger and the emergency response, even if it doesn't turn everything off right away.

This technique can also help with slow-mode. Taking big breaths might pull you out of shutdown so quickly that you get dizzy and shut down again, so slow and focused breathing can help to bring you back slowly and gently. (As long as you're still conscious, of course.)

Now, I want to make sure you know that there are still challenges here.

One thing is that it is really hard to remember to do this *when* your emergency network is active since your cortex is likely to be offline. And asking someone to remind you to breathe during a freak out or blow up can be a recipe for disaster, especially since you might take it as a threat when you're already triggered.

So this step is more helpful in the moments *before* your system is hijacked. It's not that it can't work once you're mid-panic attack or in a fight. It's just that it's a bit easier to interrupt things when they haven't gotten too far.

This is why it's important to start with mindfulness. That way you can get better at noticing and catching the warning signs before your system hits 100. Sometimes this will give you time to interrupt a reaction, and sometimes you'll still just blow up, and that's okay. You'll keep getting better as you practice.

Now, if breathing isn't your thing, that's totally fine. There are still **other ways to interrupt your amygdala** and your emergency networks. Getting other parts of your body to do something out of the blue can sometimes interrupt the process and help shift your reactions.

Cold temperatures are another direct way to interrupt your amygdala. Splashing your face with cold water, jumping into a cold shower, or putting an ice pack on your chest are all things that will quickly interrupt threat signals. **Hot temperatures** can also work if you're not into the cold.

Also, **singing or dancing, exercising, whistling, laughing, coughing,** and **trying to poop** (yes, really) may also interrupt emergency networks just enough to get back a little control. If you're in public, some stealthier options can include **chewing gum, drinking hot or cold drinks,** and **sucking on hard candy**. And, of course, the calming activities we've been practicing can also be used as interruptions.

All these interruption skills can be hard to remember when you're getting triggered, and **it will take some time and practice** before things start shifting. But even doing them a few times can start to make it a little easier.

In fact, breathing and other body interruptions can be a good thing to start practicing when you're *not* stressed out.

Just like the calming activities, getting your body used to these actions can make it easier to switch over, even in a crisis. It can be even more helpful when these actions become part of your safe matches. That way, your amygdala will be more able to recognize a safety signal even if it has already flipped into emergency mode.

You can start by using these interruptions during moments that are just a *little* stressful and then work up to the more chaotic moments.

In the end, your body actually does want to feel better. So once you practice these activities for a while and they become more natural, your system will start to use them automatically when you get stressed.

And, just in case you might be worried, interrupting these networks won't damage your ability to respond to real danger. The only time your cortex can interrupt these responses is when it's clear that there is no obvious threat.

When there is a real danger or threat, you and your cortex will be freaking out along with the rest of the system and lose all interest in interrupting anything. Any of your emergency networks that handle real danger will be left alone and unchanged. So you don't have to worry about deciding which ones to interrupt.

And here you are. You've made it through 3 upgrades now, and it seems to me that you are pretty committed to healing. Congratulations on choosing to know yourself better and working on being a healthier leader for your system.

UPGRADE 4.0
STARTING TO SPIRAL

CHAPTER 27 – CYCLE

Now that you know the basic parts of survival, we're going to help you understand a little more about why your body gets stuck in emergency responses.

The truth is that most stressful experiences won't get stuck in your system if they're handled the way your body expects. **Your amygdala and emergency teams are meant to protect you and move on.** Once the threat is over, your cortex goes back to managing things, and your body and brain all work together to keep learning and improving. This means your system can go back to feeling safe.

In fact, if emergency plans work out as they are supposed to, your system can get pretty confident at handling high stress situations. For example, a functional survival response can help you sink free throws, hit the high notes at karaoke, make a tight deadline, or even stand up to a bully.

In these moments, the extra energy and focus from go-mode can enhance your performance and give you the guts to do hard things. And the more this happens, the more practice you get at managing difficult situations and the more your confidence will increase. You learn to trust that your energy and focus will turn up just as the pressure kicks in.

You see, **when an emergency plan is successful, you are more likely to walk away confident than stressed out.** Since you got through the threat and feel safe again, your body will feel in charge rather than overwhelmed.

We can understand a bit more about this if we go back to our school analogy.

The more prepared and well-trained a school security team is, the better they will handle threats. By learning and practicing many different plans and laying out step-by-step instructions, the security team will help the system feel more secure and ready for anything.

These emergency patterns are important because they help everyone feel confident that the danger will be handled and the school will be kept safe. This is how staff and students can get back to focusing on their essays and voting on the prom theme, even after a drill or minor threat. They have learned to trust the security team.

Your brain and body have similar patterns.

Your system has a natural cycle for responding to threats. And when this cycle helps your body to manage danger and stress, you are more likely to feel safe and secure.

So let's talk about the steps of this cycle and how they can help us get through emergencies.

Step 1 - Arrest/Startle

The purpose of the first step is to **notice that something is off**. It doesn't exactly mean that there *is* danger, but that there *could* be danger. This is the step when your amygdala perks up because it **notices a threat** in the live feed, or it **detects that something is different** than usual.

This might be the sound of a creaky door or the movement of an unexpected shadow.

Your amygdala is also wired to be on alert during new or unpredictable experiences. So when you're doing something you've never done before, your system will be more on edge to make sure you're paying attention.

This is why it's easy to trigger stress when you're trying something for the first time.

Now, if your amygdala does notice something is unusual or unfamiliar, or that there seems to be a danger match in the live feed, then your system will move to the second step.

Step 2 - Defensive Orienting

The second step is to **decide if the situation is dangerous or not**.

Not all creaky doors or dark shadows are dangerous, so your amygdala gets to scan your senses and decide if it all adds up to danger or if it's just a false alarm.

Either way, it will **signal your emergency network to be on alert and in defensive mode.** This means your body will prepare your system with go-mode or slow-mode. In this step, you're more likely to start with go-mode so you can scope out the danger. But slow-mode might also kick in to keep you quiet and stealthy.

As you'll remember from Upgrade 2.0, this means your body might get ready for a threat by tightening your muscles, changing your breathing, or shutting things down.

If it is a false alarm, your amygdala will signal the all-clear and your body will switch off the go-mode or slow-mode. It might take a couple of minutes for your body to cool down, but you should be able to go back to whatever you were doing pretty quickly.

You've probably been here if the creaks or shadows just turned out to be your cat. It's pretty easy for your body to readjust once you realize there's not a real threat.

If it was a false alarm, your system will skip the third step of this process and go straight to completion since you figured out there wasn't danger and you don't have any action to take.

But, if your amygdala decides something really *is* a threat, it will **decide upon an action plan** and send it out to your system so that you can protect yourself.

Step 3 - Self-Protective Response

The third step is all about **taking action on the emergency plan.**

If you remember in Upgrade 2.0, we talked about all the ways that your system might handle a threatening situation. Although we covered a lot of these reactions, there are only a few survival responses that can get you through each step of the stress cycle.

Finding a protector, protecting others, running away, and fighting are the responses that are most likely to get you through this cycle successfully. When the action you take **protects you and allows**

you to stay in sync with the situation, your system can move to the next step. (Even if it's with the help of someone else.)

Other emergency responses like caretaking, shutting down, distracting, or freezing can protect you from some types of danger, but they won't leave you with a lot of control in a threatening situation. It doesn't mean it's impossible to protect yourself with these responses, it just means your system is more likely to get stuck in this step if your body can't respond anymore and/or you're waiting for help that never comes.

Now, if your emergency response *does* get you out of danger and your system is still in control, then you will be able to move on to the next step.

Step 4 - Completion

The fourth step is all about **getting back to feeling safe**. If your emergency response worked and helped you to get away from the danger and back to safety, then your body will naturally begin to feel relieved.

When your amygdala has scanned and confirmed that the danger has passed, **it will signal the "all clear"** so your body will know that you've completed a successful emergency response and you are safe again.

Your brain and body will signal this by **releasing feel-good hormones** like dopamine and endorphins. These hormones can help you feel pleasure and excitement so that your body knows you're out of danger and can turn off survival mode. These hormones will also help to relieve pain in case you got hurt during the emergency response.

If you used go-mode to respond to the threat, your system might also have to work off some leftover energy. You might randomly get the shivers, feel like hitting the ground with a couple of push-ups, or find yourself taking deep breaths as the energy is trying to work itself out.

Crying is also a really common reaction here. It's a very natural way to work off energy and process complicated emotions. It can also help to release tension, which will signal to your system that you're out of danger.

Once your system is able to feel safe again, it will move on to the final step.

Step 5 - Integration

The fifth and final step is about **learning from the experience and bringing it all together**.

Once you successfully get out of danger and feel safe, you can return to regular life. This means your cortex will come back online, and all the parts of your emergency network can go back to their usual roles.

Your cortex, amygdala and emergency network will take the time to give each other **feedback and update the plans** for next time. That way they can keep working on improvements.

Getting through this last step is really important. It will allow your system to settle back into your regular safe mode. That way, your amygdala can go back to its normal security routine and make sure your system is ready and alert for the next threat, whenever that might come along.

This 5-step stress cycle is how your system can actually learn to feel confident about dealing with danger and threats.

Now that we've gone through these steps, you might have noticed that you've been through this pattern before without even realizing it. That's because **you automatically run through this cycle very quickly** and may not have noticed how many steps were involved.

It could be like the time you got out of the way of that car that ran a red light. Or when you chased off that #@%$ goose at the park.

Since the danger was simple and straightforward, it was easy for your system to get through all the steps and move on.

But, for those of you in survival, I'm guessing this isn't quite how your emergency systems have worked out. Somewhere in your history, you likely went through something (or many things) where you didn't make it through all these steps. And this can change everything.

CHAPTER 28 – TRAUMA

When your system doesn't make it through all the steps of a stress cycle, it can really throw things off. Your body and brain never figure out how to manage the threat, so your body gets lost somewhere in the cycle. This can eventually create an emergency network that gets stuck every time it's activated.

When something like this happens, it's commonly referred to as **trauma**.

Trauma might seem like an overused word these days, but it's important to understand that trauma can be totally different for everyone because it's so personal.

Some things may be traumatic for you but not for someone else. Two people can go through the exact same situation and end up with wildly different outcomes. So much of the experience depends on whether your system is able to finish out the steps of the stress cycle or not.

Sometimes this means that the moments you'd expect to be the most traumatic are easy to get over. And the ones you'd think would be easy to get over are pretty traumatic.

Getting called "fat" in the 5th grade might be harder to shake than getting mugged as an adult. Only you can know for yourself whether something really is traumatic or not.

The thing is, your system really wants to protect you *and* predict when you might be in danger. So when you go through **a stress response cycle that doesn't get resolved or settled**, then the emergency network is left hanging until things get sorted out again. In a sense, the experience **doesn't get filed away correctly**.

Let's think about the school analogy again. If a really awful thing happened one day, and the principal failed to have the right preventions in place, and the security team couldn't protect everyone, then there would be a lot of focus on trying to figure out what went wrong with the plan.

It's likely that the principal and the security team will bring up all the footage and recordings of that day and review everything that happened. They might spend a bunch of their time and energy trying to know what could have been done differently. They'll probably struggle to focus on anything else until they figure it out.

This is a lot like your brain and body.

Both your conscious and unconscious brain will keep running the cycle, over and over again, to find the glitch in the network so it can find something that resolves the threat or make the plan better for next time. This means that your on-purpose, big-picture cortex can get pretty wrapped up in these memories along with your emergency network teams. This includes your amygdala, your senses, your body, and your emotions.

In fact, dreaming and sleeping will often be impacted by these stuck experiences since this is when your system is backing up and organizing memories. Stressful experiences that haven't been filed away correctly will **keep trying to sort themselves out while you sleep.**

Sometimes dreaming can help your system to sort out a few of these stuck cycles. The creativity in your dreams can help your body to rerun the experience until it has reimagined and played out a way to resolve the stress. But this is pretty rare, especially when you're dealing with really overwhelming threats or a ton of disorganized files.

This is why you might have **nightmares** or **night terrors** where you feel just as helpless or angry as you did when the threat first happened.

Sometimes this can translate to extremely violent and gory nightmares. You might dream about ugly and brutal situations, even if you've never witnessed anything close to that. The stress stuck in your body can stir up some pretty horrific images.

Even when your dreams don't look like any of your trauma, if the *feelings* in the dream are similar, it's still likely working on sorting out those situations. Your system wants to go back to the network until it can find a way to make sense of it or organize it properly.

Unfortunately, for most people, the nightmares will just keep going, even though it's not resolving anything. As you can imagine, this usually makes things worse since it interrupts sleep and keeps you from feeling rested.

So, let's talk about some of the **reasons why it's so hard to get these emergency cycles unstuck** and back on track.

In some trauma situations, there was never going to be a way to handle the threat on your own. Which means that there was no way you were ever going to make it through all the steps of the emergency cycle when the danger happened.

When someone bigger or stronger is abusive, it can be impossible to get away. Or if a natural disaster comes without warning, there isn't much you can do. And you can even become traumatized when you learn about or witness bad things happening to other people that you couldn't do anything about.

Even though your brain wants to find some way that you could have stayed protected, it's just not going to happen. But it's hard to get your system to stop searching for those answers and stop blaming yourself for not figuring it out.

Another reason this is so difficult is that **it's nearly impossible to get an emergency response unstuck just by thinking about what could have been different**.

In order to unstick a stress cycle, the network has to be active and online so that all the parts of the system can get updated on the plan and adjust their responses.

But how is that emergency network supposed to participate in rerunning the emergency cycle when it doesn't understand the difference between the past, present, and future?

Since these emergency networks and muscle memories only understand the concept of *now*, it's going to be hard for them to work with your cortex to update the cycle without triggering a false alarm. Your emergency networks are likely to mistake these memories as live-feed threats and hijack the system.

This will make it hard to work with stuck emergency networks without getting sucked into the time portals and reliving the trauma over and over. This is especially true if your brain and body experience memories and feelings in really vivid and realistic ways.

Now the last challenge here is a big one. **Most modern-day threats can take a long time to play out.** The *sort of* life-or-death problems we discussed at the beginning of the book don't really fit into natural stress cycles. Without a sense of the big picture, it's pretty easy for your emergency networks to get confused by any threats with delayed outcomes.

Waiting on a cancer test or trying to get custody of your kids feels pretty life or death for a while, even if things work out okay later on.

These kinds of issues can take months and years to get resolved. Which means that **your system is left in an emergency cycle for *much* longer than it's meant to be**. And sometimes these situations never really get figured out because life doesn't always wrap things up nice and neatly.

Confusing or long-term threats can cause your emergency responses to get pretty jumbled. You might freak out for a week and then numb or freeze when nothing has been resolved and your energy gets low. And then go back to freaking out again when the energy comes back. You could also go back and forth between angry outbursts, struggling to get out of bed, and working on distracting projects between panic attacks.

These delayed outcomes also make it hard for your system to know when it's safe again since things like joint custody and chemo treatments won't feel very relieving to your mind and body. And it will still be hard for your system to let go and move forward, even if things get better.

So let's talk a little bit more about the different ways your system can get stuck and how it might affect the way that you have experienced survival.

CHAPTER 29 – STUCK

This chapter could be hard to sit with.

We're going to talk about what happens to your brain and body when your system gets lost in an emergency cycle during a threat. Although the information might be heavy, it may also help you to better pinpoint where your system is struggling and how to address it.

But this doesn't mean you have to jump in right now. Take a few breaths and see how you're feeling. You can always pause and come back when you're ready.

If you do want to keep reading and need some help getting through it, you can always use the tips and tricks we discussed before. You can picture cartoon characters, or turn down the "volume" on the experience, or use a container to hold the overwhelming stuff.

If you're feeling ready, let's get into it.

There are many ways an emergency plan can get stuck and create confusion for your system.

This can happen because you went through so much danger all at once that your system couldn't keep up. Or you might have had some bad luck and been caught off guard so you couldn't react properly. But sometimes you get stuck here because you were hurt or neglected by the people who should have protected you. We'll talk a little more about this in Upgrade 6.0 as this last one makes things a lot more complex.

For now, we're going to discuss how your system is likely to get stuck based on which step of the cycle goes off track.

Step 1 - Arrest/Startle

When a threat comes out of nowhere or your body wasn't ready to handle an emergency, your system might get stuck in the Arrest/Startle step.

This means that **your amygdala wasn't able to notice a threat before it showed up.**

An emergency network might get stuck here if you got into a freak accident or went through a sudden loss that you didn't see coming. This could also happen if too many threats happened too close together to stay ahead of them all. It's also really common to get off track here if you had stressful experiences before you could talk.

This could include medical issues, trauma, or abuse before you were born, during your birth, or in the following 2 to 3 years. You may also get stuck here if something traumatic happened to your family during your early years.

Since babies and young kids are still learning to connect with their bodies and their environment, it's easier for threat signals to get missed or poorly matched when you're little.

With all these kinds of situations, your amygdala can have a really hard time finding the right sensory clip for your danger file. It might create matches that are way too general or just completely missing.

This can lead your amygdala to be unprepared and mixed up a lot of the time. In fact, your go-mode and slow-mode response will be pretty out of sync because your amygdala is working with a bunch of incomplete files. And without clear danger signals, it will be hard to come up with an emergency plan, let alone complete all the steps.

When your amygdala struggles to predict danger, it will become really hard to trust yourself and your system. And it will be difficult to stay in sync with your own body and the space around you.

When your amygdala is not sure what it's looking for, it has to watch out for everything. It will probably get confused by or caught up in each and every sound, image, feeling, or movement.

Because of this, your body may often be in a state of **distraction and avoidance** or **false starts and missteps**. You can **miss obvious threat signals** or **get caught off guard** when you don't notice that your environment has changed. This could look like tripping over things, running into walls, or not noticing when someone is trying to get your attention. Your body may feel out of sync with the world around you and you may **feel kind of lost and empty** all the time.

Getting stuck in this step can also make it **difficult to let go** or grieve. It's hard to move forward when there are gaps in your experience. And when you always feel left behind, or like you're on the outside looking in, it's hard not to feel **isolated and depressed**.

To cope with these feelings, you might get stuck **building fantasies** about your ideal life or hoping you'll be rescued when your miracle comes. You can also spend a lot of time **blaming yourself or others** for the bad things that have happened. You may develop arrogant or judgmental attitudes to hide your shame and disappointment. And you might even feel like you have been cursed or that others have cheated you out of the life you deserve.

These attitudes can lead you to take on **rigid beliefs and expectations** that help you to maintain a feeling of certainty about your life and the world. And you might try to force these beliefs on others or attempt to control them when you feel especially insecure or helpless.

When you don't have the intuition to recognize danger, your system will encourage you to **hold back and shield yourself from new experiences and ideas** to keep you safe.

Step 2 - Defensive Orienting

When your amygdala does **recognize a threat but can't figure out what to do,** you might get stuck in the Defensive Orienting step. This means that your amygdala will get triggered without a clear idea of what the danger is or what to do next.

An emergency network might get stuck here if you were often threatened by a bully who never followed through or you got exposed to scary images or overwhelming sounds online. This response may also come up if you were a preemie or suffered neglect as a baby. You might also be here if you were abused, experienced discrimination, or got taken advantage of by others over long periods of time.

In all of these situations, **your amygdala gets confused about what's dangerous and what's safe**.

You can be exposed to threats that never show up, so your amygdala creates a lot of danger files with no follow up instructions. You may go through stress so early in life that your amygdala doesn't get a chance to make any safety matches. Or you might feel threatened so often that pretty much everything is flagged as dangerous.

In fact, this is a really common place to be stuck if you've been through emotional and/or sexual abuse in childhood. When bad situations start off with feelings of trust and safety, it's hard for your amygdala to figure out when things became threatening. So it's easy for your system to get confused and save the same matches in both your danger and safety files.

If your system gets stuck in this step, you can end up in a state where **you never really feel safe** and **your system is always expecting danger**.

This will cause your senses to be hyper focused as your amygdala keeps scanning for danger while it tries to come up with a plan. This means that your system is **constantly prepping for threats**, hoping that you'll eventually be able to do something.

Getting stuck here can overload your body with energy that has nowhere to go. **Staying busy** is a common response when this happens. When your body feels like you need to be taking action, you might feel better when you're cleaning the house, or playing sports, or working on your to-do list.

Unfortunately, getting stuck in this step might also leave you feeling **paranoid and panicky** all the time. It can look like keeping track of everyone who enters or leaves a room, or making sure you know where the exits are, or keeping your back to the wall so no one can sneak up behind you. You might even feel like you're always being watched.

For other people, the constant signals of danger can push your body to clamp down on the go-mode energy so it doesn't overwhelm your system.

This kind of **freezing** response can cause **long periods of exhaustion and depression**. And although this response may push you to **sleep more**, it might be **hard to feel rested** since your system is still getting threat signals all the time and can't fully relax. **High-risk activities** can become an easy outlet when this happens since it can help you break through the numbness and channel the blocked energy.

Over-functioning, **protecting others**, and **caretaking** can also show up when you're stuck in this step. A numbed-out body with energy to burn can support your cortex as it analyzes, prepares for, and manages everything and everyone around you.

This often means that you develop good insight and protective instincts for *others*. But it can also mean that you're distracted from just how lost and overwhelmed *you* might actually be. And with the up and down energy, you may end up **collapsing and isolating** when you hit your limits and crash into shutdown.

The never-ending threat signals can also wear down your body and create a lot of aches and pains since your organs, tissues, and muscles get overworked and stuck as your body is constantly preparing for danger

Sometimes the pain and confusion can feel so out of control that it pushes you to **find a protector** or **people please** to see if other people can handle things with you or for you.

Sadly, it's not unusual to get taken advantage of when this happens. People that get stuck in this step may be drawn to controlling personalities since their system is looking for protection or direction. In the beginning, the control can feel relieving since it gives your system clear expectations. But, in time, these same behaviors may also become unsafe.

This is especially true if that person is also someone you depend on for food, shelter, or basic needs. Fighting back or running away could risk your basic survival, so your amygdala isn't left with many options for taking action. This means that you will probably end up giving in or shutting down to survive. And this will make it harder and harder to stand up for yourself, even when you want to.

Having emergency networks that never figure out how to take action can be rough. Being **constantly flooded with fear** and/

or **numbed out** can make it really **hard to make decisions** and **protect yourself**. It might feel like you're **constantly adrift**, not knowing who you are and what you want or how to find the confidence to move in your own direction in life.

Step 3 - Self-Protective Response

If you go through a stressor and your amygdala is able to alert your system and send a clear plan, your body should be able to use go-mode to handle the threat. But if **your action doesn't work or gets overpowered**, then it's easy to get stuck in a Self-Protective Response.

This might happen if you tried to run from the cops but couldn't get over the fence. Or if your leg broke in an accident and you couldn't run for help. Or if you were humiliated by someone when you tried to stand up for yourself. This is also common if you've been through abuse, neglect, or discrimination and you tried to defend yourself without success.

Since your system wasn't able to manage the threat, your body will get **stuck holding on to or trying to repeat the same emergency responses**.

Your body will keep trying to execute the same plan you used when you first got stuck. This constant push to take action can make it **difficult for your system to be flexible** or take the time to see things from a different point of view. It might also falsely trigger your amygdala to **feel threatened or insulted by everyday interactions**. And this can often cause your system to be on the defensive, always ready to **attack or avoid**.

With a go-mode response, this will usually lead to **getting angry or running away**. You might yell at your toddler for skinning her knee or punch a wall when your feelings get hurt. It could also include running away every time your stepmom grills you about your missing school assignments.

Getting caught up in this step can also lead to a buildup of **aches and pains**. And you may even **struggle with injuries** when you don't realize that you're pushing your body too hard or going beyond your limits.

As for slow-mode, this is usually the alternative plan that will show up when your system runs out of energy. This can look like **feeling anxious or falling apart** when your actions aren't getting you what you want or your body is too tired or broken to keep going. For many people this can make it **feel like you're dried up or useless**.

A combined response can make you feel **indecisive and paralyzed by fear**. These feelings might signal to others that you need some help or protection, but your intensity and inflexibility might make it hard to let anyone in.

Another response might be that you look for opportunities to **protect and take care of others** so you can feel like your actions are accomplishing something. This response might help you feel a bit safer knowing that people need you and your efforts aren't wasted. Even with good intentions, though, helping others can still get tricky if you're too defensive to see their point of view or constantly trying to do things for them that they don't want.

Since your system is stuck repeating certain actions, you can get caught up in believing that your way is the *only* way things will work because you can't see other options. This can turn into **demanding** that people help you or **trying to control** their behavior because you need action *right now*.

Getting stuck in this step can make you closed off to change. When you get **stuck in your way of doing things** and you can't see the forest for the trees, it's **hard to notice when things aren't working**. And it's difficult for anyone else to get through your defensiveness when your system is constantly telling you to attack or run away.

Step 4 - Completion

In this step, you have become alerted to danger, come up with a plan, and successfully protected yourself by taking action. But going off track here means **you probably didn't know how to feel safe again**. So your body never really got the relief it needed to know that the threat was over. This can leave you stuck in the Completion step.

This might happen if you experience danger over and over, even if you are able to come out of it each time. Your system will never really believe the threat has passed since it keeps happening. This may also come up if you've been through stress or danger that lasted a long time and the signal of safety took too long to bring relief to your body.

Abuse, neglect, and discrimination can definitely be part of those long-term issues, especially when the people in your life are unwilling to resolve and repair problems with you or take responsibility for their mistakes. When you've been able to protect yourself from a threat, but you're not sure if you can go back to trusting other people or the world around you, it can be difficult to find relief.

If your emergency networks get stuck here, **your body has a hard time feeling like it's out of danger**. Your system won't be reassured that things are safe again, even when your amygdala isn't sensing any more threat. Without the all-clear, **your system isn't sure if there are still dangers or concerns** that haven't been resolved.

With a go-mode response that won't shut off, you can spend a lot of energy worrying that people are mad at you or that you've offended them. You might also try to find relief by **looking for reassurance and validation** from everyone around you.

The go-mode energy can also push you to **chase fun and/or risky activities** like extreme sports, street racing, shopping sprees, drugs, and romance since these moments can offer some temporary relief. Unfortunately, over time, relying on these quick fixes may lead to addictions or manic episodes where your body needs more and more intensity to find relief.

A slow-mode response that won't shut off might cause you to go through episodes where you **avoid people** or get flaky to keep from getting drained or hurt. Slow-mode can also cause you to **feel like giving up**. You might become pretty disconnected and struggle to feel like yourself.

And if you can't find relief from a combo of go-mode and slow-mode, your system will feel **unsettled and forgetful**, and your body may **freeze or feel restless**. The chaos in your system can make it hard for others to know how to support you. Your thoughts may get mixed up or your emotions might drown out your words. On the other hand, you might **lash out** at others when you get overstimulated or overwhelmed.

These disconnections from others can create a lot of fear about being left to survive on your own.

You might use **people pleasing and humor** to make up for your temper and/or to make sure you're likable enough for others to stick around. Even though this might help, it can also lead to **shallow relationships** where you're always expected to be chasing excitement and making everything fun.

It can even lead to relationships where other people become critical or controlling. You may tune out red flags and safety issues in your relationships so you can convince yourself you're safe even when you're not.

Life will get pretty tough when you're **constantly chasing relief and connection**. Being stuck here can easily burn you out and make it difficult for you to truly trust yourself and others.

Step 5 - Integration

For this final step of the cycle, your system has been able to notice danger, make a plan, take action, and return to feeling safe. **What's missing here is learning from what happened.**

Without Integration, your system will have a hard time wrapping things up. In fact, if you are stuck here, then it's highly possible that you are also stuck in some, or all, of the other steps too.

You can get stuck here if you were the victim of ongoing abuse, abandonment, rejection, discrimination, or bullying throughout your life.

Being hurt by other people is something that your brain has a hard time making sense of, especially when you're young, so it's common to handle this experience by blaming yourself.

Getting stuck in this step because of abuse makes it likely that you will believe that what happened to you is your own fault for not being good enough.

It might seem confusing, but **putting the blame on yourself** might be easier to handle than feeling unwanted or trying to make sense of disturbing experiences. If you're not good enough, you can hold out hope that things might be different when you finally change or get things right. In a way, you gaslight yourself to keep moving forward.

You might also be stuck in this step if you've served in a war, been a member of a gang, or served as a first responder. Being on the front lines is brutal.

Even if you were able to get out alive, it doesn't mean that you didn't lose yourself or a lot of people along the way. Plus, your heart never really understands why it all had to happen. You may even feel ashamed or guilty about the people you hurt. Or the ones you couldn't save or protect.

When your body goes through a massive amount of survival, it becomes **challenging for your system to make sense of what's going on**. Although you may have the intuition to manage danger and stay protected, there's often a limit on how many survival experiences your system can keep filing away until it's overloaded. And when your brain and body can't keep integrating these files into your system, **the networks get backed up, and things fall apart**.

In this step, it's common to handle this overload by **burying** and **disconnecting** from the memories. Unfortunately, this kind of **numbing can take over** everything. And you can't shut down these feelings without turning off a lot of other communication too. It will make it difficult for your body to feel and express emotions of any kind, even to yourself.

This can also make it **hard to open up and let other people in** so you can have meaningful relationships. Your system may **freeze** on you any time you try to be vulnerable. And your body can get pretty **anxious** if you start digging around and looking for some feelings and feedback.

This means that words or feelings might get caught in your throat or refuse to come up. You might also feel resistant to letting others help or get angry when they tell you what you should do. Friends and partners might have a hard time understanding this and feel frustrated when you always seem to **shut everyone out**.

Trying to bury all this chaos can lead to some messy places. When the **pressure gets too high**, you might end up **blowing up, burning bridges,** and **pushing people away**. And then feel too **ashamed** to repair and try again for **fear of being a burden**.

This kind of **disconnection** can make it **easy to turn to drugs, sex, or other thrills** to help you numb out and/or actually feel something anymore. This will often lead to a lot more shame and reinforce the belief that you will never be enough.

Sadly, many people in this situation are likely to have **thoughts and feelings of death** or wish they were never born since they feel so broken. Death often feels like the only way that anything can change long-term. Getting stuck here will make it difficult to feel grounded and remember who you really are.

If this is you, I would really consider getting some support through this process. The national 988 hotline can give you a place to start if you're feeling suicidal, or you can skip to Chapter 56 to get ideas on finding the right professional who can be patient with your disconnection.

Now, with a lifetime of survival, it might be that you have been stuck, or are stuck, in many of these steps, and it might feel really overwhelming to realize what trauma has done to your system.

Remember that we are talking about this so that you can get some clarity about what's going on and start moving in a better direction.

Many of these factors can improve as you learn more about how they work and how they've taken shape in your life. But if bringing up these ideas has been challenging for you, take another break before you move on.

You can always go back to the calming activities or anything else that helps you to feel a little better. We're going to review them again in a few more chapters, but you can stop anytime you need so that you're not pushing your system too hard or getting too overwhelmed.

CHAPTER 30 – CHRONIC

Now that you understand how your system can get stuck because of stressful experiences, let's talk about how this trauma can go on to create other long-term issues.

Many chronic problems can arise from survival, but one of the most common is pain.

In the first place, traumatic experiences can be literally painful. Some emergencies involve broken bones or dog bites. And now that you know how these survival networks operate, you might understand how easily aching or throbbing or stinging can get fused into muscle memory and keep flaring up long after the wounds have healed.

When **physical pain gets stuck in an unresolved trauma network** it can make it difficult to deal with the past or go back to survival memories. If it was just about remembering the images or sounds, it might not be so bad. But having to face the pain can be overwhelming.

And on top of physical pain, **many stressful or traumatic memories also have emotional pain.** Feeling helpless, or terrified, or abandoned all come with their own kind of hurt.

We don't often think of this kind of pain as being that bad, but it really is.

This makes sense with what you've learned about your trauma networks. Now you know that a lot of stressful moments will trigger your body to experience things like a tight chest, tense muscles, nausea, etc. These responses become linked with the overwhelming emotions in an emergency network. So it's very possible to experience discomfort or pain every time that network is triggered because of the body reactions that are matched with it.

In fact, the challenge with survival is that your body gets so used to activating emergency networks that your system is likely to get really exhausted after a while.

After years of being flooded with stress hormones, high energy, uncomfortable physical reactions, and/or buried feelings, **your body can get run pretty ragged**.

High blood pressure, breathing problems, digestion issues, fatigue, tinnitus, infertility, chronic nerve and muscle pain, fibromyalgia, sexual dysfunction, inflammation, and blood sugar issues are just a few of the ways this might show up.

This makes sense if you think about how out of sync your system can get if survival responses are running non-stop and always hijacking your organs, tissues, and energy.

Having your body constantly in overdrive and/or clamping-down stress can make it hard for your system to have enough energy to fight off diseases and clear out defective cells and tissues. Ongoing survival can really overwork and back up your system.

This all checks out when we look at long-term studies of health and trauma experiences.

Adverse Childhood Experience or ACE studies have found that **people who experienced trauma during their childhood are more likely to struggle with long-term health issues** like heart disease, diabetes, and cancer. It can even cause some signals to get mixed up enough that your body starts attacking itself, like in the case of auto-immune issues.

In many situations, **chronic pain and trauma can also impact weight and body size**.

For some people, it's possible that your body wasn't able to develop properly and ended up being pretty small. This makes sense if your system was constantly shut down and couldn't spare the energy or materials to focus on growing when you were younger.

And for those of you with bigger bodies, it's possible that a lot of danger and stress has encouraged your body to keep a higher than average fat storage. Since fat stores can be used for go-mode energy, it helps your system to feel protected and prepared.

This could easily be a reason that your weight loss attempts have failed so many times. Your body, especially when it's in survival, will use a surprising number of tricks to keep you from letting go of the energy storage. Even if you manage to lose weight for a while, your body will try to gain it back at the next possible chance in order to be prepared.

When your body is activated all the time and burning through energy, it might be hard to keep weight on, even when you're trying to eat enough. And when your body is in shutdown and storing all your energy for later, it can be hard to keep weight off, even when you're trying to eat less.

What's tough is that these weight issues are not usually the *cause* of your health challenges. It's often just another side effect of survival on your body. It can be frustrating to realize this, but remember that these systems are trying to help you survive.

Since trauma impacts both your health and your weight, it makes sense that those things almost always show up together in most wellness studies. Unfortunately, many scientists have missed the real connection between health and weight until more recently.

And many professionals still aren't aware of these factors and might blame you for being sick. If you have a bigger body, they might make you feel like you're not trying hard enough to lose weight. And if you have a smaller body, providers may not take your health concerns seriously when you don't "look" sick to them. Having the "ideal" body type can trick others into thinking you're fine when you're not.

These experiences with your body will often just add to the pain and trauma and can make you feel like giving up on taking care of yourself.

Sadly, the physical issues of trauma aren't the only way your body is impacted.

Scientists have also found that **physical and emotional pain share a lot of the same networks in your body and brain.** This means that your emotional pain can feel just as bad as your physical pain and sometimes be just as hard on your system.

No wonder we use phrases like "I was stabbed in the back," or "it broke my heart," or "what a pain in the neck" to explain emotional hurt. The nerves impacted by a betrayal might feel just as intense as getting stabbed. And the ache of losing someone may feel just as real as a heart attack.

Now, on top of all this, your body can also experience pain for other survival reasons.

After many years of shutting down and numbing out the stress and anger, **your body might not be able to drown out the pain signals anymore**. For many people, pain can come out of nowhere and be confusing and terrifying because it might be the very first time you realize your body is overwhelmed and dealing with anything.

Living with sudden or chronic pain or other health issues is an exhausting way to live. With these kinds of experiences, it's hard to believe that your body is actually on your side and that you could ever trust it again. And losing trust in yourself can lead to a lot of shame and self-hatred, which only makes it all worse.

Pain is meant to help you know when something is wrong so it can be addressed. Your system is trying to keep you from walking on a broken foot or bleeding too much from a cut.

But this can be really confusing when your lingering back pain or your dysfunctional digestion are related to traumas or negative life experiences that are long passed.

Another challenge with all this is that **you can develop a very high pain tolerance**. This means that you get so used to severe pain that you handle it way too well.

Not only is this an insane way to live, it also means that friends and family may get skeptical when you say your pain is a 10 out of 10 but you're not screaming and rolling around on the floor. It's also hard not to feel defensive about your pain when you know that your 10 would probably drop most people on the spot.

Even professionals can be hard to convince sometimes when you're struggling with chronic pain. When they can't find a scan or a blood test to diagnose something, they might tell you to eat better and exercise more, or blame the problem on your weight. They may shrug when they run out of treatment ideas and things still aren't better. And they might treat you like your issues aren't really that bad or you're being too sensitive.

When your doctor or provider doesn't know enough to connect it all together, their incorrect treatments or disbelieving attitude can often make the situation worse.

If you happen to have some of these chronic pain or health issues, you'll probably know how this feels. It's no wonder a lot of folks with chronic pain feel guilty for being sick and stop asking for help.

It's important to know about the toll that survival is taking on you. It's not about being too sensitive or too weak. You need actual support and treatment.

In fact, the right help and treatment will often change these outcomes. You're already beginning the process, just by reading this book and understanding your body systems.

Plus, you're beginning to have a clearer idea of what you need and what you're looking for, which will make it easier to find the right kind of professionals and treatments.

Now, before we finish the chapter, I want to discuss one more thing. The cycle between trauma and the body doesn't always start with trauma first.

Living with **disabilities or chronic illnesses can also be really hard on your system** and push your body into survival responses. Being born with a different body than most other people, or developing exhausting and painful diseases, can be its own kind of trauma. Especially in a society that's in love with perfect bodies.

Sickness and disabilities can cause your body to spend a lot of energy on your immune system and healing. Or when your body has to compensate for missing functions or physical damage, it will often be exhausted. This can make it hard to drum up the motivation to look for solutions and show up to treatments. And because your system gets pushed to its limit and overwhelmed, it will usually try to protect you by turning up your survival systems.

This kind of functioning will take energy away from your cortex and activate your amygdala more often. This means that being sick or struggling with a disability might actually be the reason your survival systems get stuck so easily. Which, in turn, won't make healing or existing in an ableist world any easier.

It can feel frustrating to learn that your survival systems are adding to the difficulty when your differences already make life challenging.

This is why it's important to realize that social and emotional support should always be considered when planning for any disability accommodations.

Now, whether you have any chronic problems going on or not, **it can be helpful to get a medical check up** and see if you have common issues like allergies, imbalanced hormones, blood sugar issues, low iron, thyroid problems, toxic levels of mold or heavy metals, etc. These kinds of things can cause your body to be more on edge or even mimic survival symptoms. So it can be a good idea to get these things checked out before jumping in with your stuck emergency networks.

With all these different areas to think about, finding the right treatment can feel really complicated. It can take some time to sort out whether you need a doctor, a therapist, a body worker, a functional medicine provider, or even a spiritual support. And handling the insurance and finances might take even more time and energy.

Survival systems can impact so many parts of your life that it can make it hard for treatment teams to know where to start or how to get to the core issues.

Getting help from more than one professional might be really useful in situations like this. Especially if you can find ones who are willing to coordinate with each other. Again, we'll talk more about getting help in Chapter 56.

Although this process can be complicated and take a while, the good news is that **proper treatment can actually help your body to reduce or let go of some of the pain** that you have been dealing with. It may surprise you how many of your chronic and difficult-to-diagnose body challenges have been related to (or made worse by) trauma and stuck emergency networks.

Further Study Recommendations:

The Body Is Not an Apology: The Power of Radical Self-Love by Sonya Renee Taylor. This book is not directly about trauma, but it can be a helpful book to work toward embracing the body you have and letting go of what you think it should be like.

When The Body Says No: The Cost of Hidden Stress by Gabor Maté, M.D. and Daniel Maté. This book discusses how long-term stress and survival can impact your body.

Why Zebras Don't Get Ulcers: The Acclaimed Guide to Stress, Stress-Related Diseases, and Coping by Robert Sapolsky, PhD. This book is a bit more scientific and may not read as easily, but it talks about how stress responses in the body can impact long-term health.

CHAPTER 31 – GRADUAL

Let's talk more about getting help and working on healing.

Now that you're getting some clarity, you might be feeling more motivated and ready to work on your stuck networks.

Sometimes, when we get answers, our brain wants to jump in and tackle these problems all over again, thinking that this will finally be the time where everything falls into place. On the one hand, it's nice when you get some energy back, but, on the other hand, **jumping in too quickly might get you stuck all over again.**

One of the toxic cycles your system can get into is rushing back into action every time you have a little energy. You do this because you hope it will finally get you unstuck.

There are lots of influential people who don't understand these systems and will tell you that the only way to succeed is to kick yourself in the butt and hustle your way out of the chaos. They might also tell you that we're all born with the same potential but only some people will work hard enough to unlock it.

Unfortunately, if you're stuck in survival, then this kind of attitude will almost always lead to crashing and burning.

Think about how this has happened in the past.

Have you ever made goals to eat better, exercise, quit smoking, use a planner, stop getting angry, or to stay caught up on chores?

Out of curiosity, how did it go?

Did you decide there was no room for error? Did you decide that the only way it would work is if you did it perfectly? And then did you use every last drop of energy battling your emergency responses until you collapsed or gave up again?

Because that's how this pattern usually works.

Forcing yourself to fight against a stuck cycle doesn't help your emergency networks to process through or file away the trauma.

Even if you could keep up with the goals and do them perfectly, it's not going to get you unstuck. You're just spending all your energy on side projects.

It's not very practical to take an over-stressed, exhausted body and brain and try to heal them by adding more things to remember and complete every day.

Remember how you have work, school, family, kids, relationships, a partner, a lawn to mow, dishes to wash, mouths to feed, menstrual cramps, etc.? There is no way adding perfection and huge projects to your list is going to help.

What's hard about your body is that you're going to have energy sometimes. And sometimes you won't. That's normal.

So, when you get a little motivation, it's easy to binge the energy on things you've been trying to get together. It's honestly hard not to. Because you don't know the next time you'll get another surge.

But, as you can imagine, this is a lot like keeping your system batteries at 5% every day. Even if you get to recharge here and there, you're going to be constantly running on empty. And on random days where you wake up with a decent charge, you'll probably drain it all trying to make up for all the days where you got behind.

So, **here's what we do instead**. I want you to think about being a little more gentle with your energy and paying more attention to it.

You can do this with a very simple technique called **One Thing at a Time**.

Here's how this works.

Obviously, there are things that you have to get done every day. Like eating food, or picking up your kids, or working.

Then there are things that you feel that you *should* do but don't really hurt anyone if they don't get done. Like shaving, folding laundry, or making your bed.

When you're checking in with your energy levels, it's helpful to **focus on the basic things that need to get done and plan your day around them.**

If you only have enough energy to get the basic things taken care of, then try to focus on rest and recharging as your task for the rest of the day.

If you *do* have some energy, or you get a chance to recharge, and want to get something done, then you can use the One Thing at a Time technique to jump in.

Let's go through how this works.

First, you'll want to **pick *one* task**. Then ask your system if you have enough energy to do that one thing.

Now, I'm not talking about cleaning the garage or catching up on all 500 of your unread messages.

I'm talking about *one* thing.

Ask yourself if you can put away *one* tool or respond to *one* message. And **if you have the energy, do it**. Then stop.

Then ask yourself if you have the energy for one more tool or one more message. And if you do, go for it. Then stop.

Keep doing this until your body says, "no." Then do yourself a favor and **take a rest until you have energy again.**

Focusing on tasks that make you feel better is a great place to begin. If clearing off the counter or changing a lightbulb will help your system feel more comfortable or less annoyed for the rest of the day, then start here.

It might seem overly simple, but this process is helpful in three ways.

1. It starts teaching you how to be mindful of your energy levels.

If you always seem to be shutting down, it can be a sign that your body is constantly running low on energy or overwhelmed by your to-do list. And if you keep bingeing energy and draining yourself every time you get a decent charge, your system is going to take over and start shutting down even more to protect your energy.

So, asking your body if it has energy for each tiny part of a task, until it says no, will keep you from going over the limit and forcing yourself into shutdown.

You might actually be able to clean the whole garage this way, but you will feel better afterward because it was broken into easier steps and you didn't have to force your body into a stress response halfway through.

Because this tool is also a type of mindfulness, it will help your system to be more aware of your low energy signals and the alerts that go off before you shut down. This will also help you to be more in tune with yourself and your body.

2. It helps your system become more energy efficient.

Since muscle memories are created from the things your system repeats, you can intentionally create healthier autopilot responses. As you practice doing things in small steps, it becomes more automatic and natural for you to do everything like this.

This can help your body to build up a ton of healthy habits by focusing on and practicing one skill at a time. And once these muscle memories are in place, these tasks will feel easier because they have moved to autopilot and don't feel as stressful or take as much planning.

This can eventually help with having more energy since your emergency responses and big-picture problem solving aren't constantly draining all the resources.

3. It's another step toward becoming a healthier system boss.

Healthy bosses notice when their employees aren't feeling good. They will send them home to recover or split up their workload. They realize that you'll be more functional overall when you don't burn yourself out in the short term.

By learning to do the same thing for yourself, you will build more cooperation between your body and brain.

Now, I know many of your survival systems might actually need a month off just to feel sane again and you probably can't just quit and lie in bed all day. But these small steps will help you to be more aware of your energy and how to use it wisely.

You can also include other techniques for managing your energy like setting timers or limiting the number of things you will do every day until you're caught up or feeling better.

For someone with a tight work schedule, this might look like picking up 5 things everyday after work. Or dedicating 10 minutes to clean the kitchen and stopping when time is up. Or sweeping and leaving the dirt pile to sit until tomorrow (or next week).

For someone who likes to stay busy and needs help resting more, it could be working on taking more breaks. It might be focusing on sleeping more. And then it might be adding 5 minutes of stretching to your day. It might be actually taking your lunch break at work instead of skipping it. Or it might be spending time with family without busy distractions.

For someone in a depressed place, it might be asking yourself if you can get out of bed. And if you can do that, then it's asking yourself if you can put on pants. And then if you can put on a shirt. And then if you can eat breakfast. And then going back to bed because you can't do any more than that.

Now, I want to acknowledge that some of you might be pretty non-functional.

Some levels of survival become so intense that it leads to situations where you literally can't get out of bed most days or keep up with the basics.

You might get so anxious you can't leave your house. Or you can't function without drugs. Or you can't stop cleaning. Or you can't do anything for yourself anymore.

In these situations, the small steps can also work for you, bit by bit, but you might consider starting with professional help.

Now that many professionals work online, it's possible that you can get help when you're stuck at home, or even stuck in bed. See Chapter 56 to get help with that process.

You might also think about applying for temporary or long-term disability or state assistance until you can get a better handle on things. These services are nothing to be ashamed of. They are there for situations exactly like this.

Although these programs can be difficult to apply for and won't take care of all your problems, they can free up some energy so that you can work on a few of the deeper issues.

If this is something you're thinking about, I would highly recommend looking for a local support group with social workers or case workers who can help you connect with these programs. They are trained to know what services might be available to you and can often help you apply to them.

You will usually find these services through your local civic center or library and non-profit mental or medical health centers.

Further Study Recommendations:

How to Keep House While Drowning: A Gentle Approach to Cleaning and Organizing by KC Davis, LPC. This book is amazing if you are feeling overwhelmed. There are tips and tricks for taking care of things when you just don't have the energy. There's even a shortcut through the book if you're really overloaded.

CHAPTER 32 – STRENGTHEN

So far we've discussed how taking breaks, recharging, listening to your body, and interrupting stuck emergency networks can begin to improve the connection between your cortex and your body. It's also important that you work on being mindful of your energy so that you don't end up biting off more than you can chew.

Practicing these healthy boss techniques slowly and intentionally like this can be really important because changing survival systems is a lot easier if you're being honest about your limits and learning to take it at your own pace. This approach will help to build trust between yourself and your body. That way, your system will be more confident and prepared to handle hard things as they come up.

As you get better at noticing your limits and prioritizing rest and mindfulness, it will become easier to work with the difficult truths, memories, and feelings in your emergency networks that are holding you hostage.

Since everyone gets stuck in different places, this chapter will go through specific ways that you can continue to work on mindfulness based on which step (or steps) of the stress cycle you're stuck in.

Step 1 - Arrest/Startle

One of the challenges of being stuck in the Arrest/Startle step is that it's hard to have **trust in your senses to notice threats and in your body to protect itself.**

You might feel like it's hard to let go of the past and that life is passing you by. You might find that you're getting taken off guard, over and over again. You might even feel cursed since you struggle to notice red flags or your own gut when you're getting into sticky situations.

Life can start to feel really heavy because it's hard to let go of the disappointment in yourself and others. It can also be hard to forgive yourself for missing the signs that might have kept you out of trouble or put you on a different path.

If you're stuck here, one of the things that can be helpful is learning to feel safe with your body. Considering that your system will likely feel disconnected and out of sync, this is not as easy as it sounds.

Practicing **mindful activities** that focus on connecting with your body and brain can help you to be more comfortable staying in tune with the present and move your focus away from the fixations of the past and future.

Mindfulness practices that focus on your body and staying in the present are called **interoception activities**. Practicing these activities can help you to reconnect with your mind and body and regain trust in your intuition.

Belly breathing is one way to work on this.

To practice this, you will want to sit or lay down and relax your shoulders. Place one hand on your chest and one on your stomach. Slowly start to notice your breath going in and out. As you get comfortable, see if you can inhale to move the hand on your belly a bit more and the one on your chest a bit less.

Spend as much time here as you need.

If breathing doesn't feel safe, you can look up other interception activities online and find something that works better for you.

If you're ready to look for professional support, a trauma-informed body worker like an occupational therapist or acupuncturist might be a good place to start. Or you can look into group activities like martial arts or yoga classes that can help your body learn to shift from protecting and holding on to letting go and opening up.

Step 2 - Defensive Orienting

When you're stuck in Defensive Orienting, **your body can feel like it's never safe.**

You might feel flooded a lot, get stuck in overthinking, and/or struggle with shutdown and freezing. Your system will feel like everything is dangerous, so you'll spend loads of energy and time being prepared for threats that almost never happen.

You might also find that you are easily affected by other people's energy and stress. Because you don't have a great handle on your own sense of safety and threat, it can be hard to separate your feelings and moods from others. If this is the case, you might end up taking a lot of responsibility for other people's emotions, and/or expect someone else to always take care of you and manage your feelings.

As we talked about in the first upgrade, a functional security system will take time to get to know safe situations as well as dangerous ones.

If you're stuck here, using mindful activities like **Calm, Safe Space** can help teach your body what safety looks like and feels like for you.

In these situations, it would be best to do these kinds of activities without distractions so that your system can start matching the senses in your environment with feeling safe and calm.

Obviously, it will be important that you choose a space that *is* safe to do this in. It will be hard to convince your body that you're safe when there's actually a threat or danger.

If possible, it can also be helpful to do this practice while you're alone so that your system can focus on your own feelings without being influenced by others around you. This will help your body stay more clear about which feelings belong to you. That way you can start to notice when your experience is getting blended with others.

But, it's okay if you can't do this alone right now. Don't force yourself to do anything you're not ready for.

As you get better at mindfulness and feeling safe, you can then work on using **interrupting activities** to cool down your body if it's flooding with anxiety or shutting down.

And if you're looking for professional help, it's probably best to start with one-on-one work. It's easy to get lost in a group or class when your feelings get mixed up with other people's feelings. A trauma-informed body worker, a mental health professional, or a spiritual or energy healer may be able to help you strengthen your feelings of safety and help you to unblend from other people's emotions.

It will be important that you look for someone who helps you feel safe but who is also good at holding boundaries. This may be difficult for you to recognize if that's something you already struggle with. So you might want to read through Chapter 56 to get some more tips on looking for support. And Chapter 53 may help with understanding more about boundaries.

Step 3 - Self-Protective Response

When you're stuck in a Self-Protective Response, it can be **hard to be flexible and see where other people are coming from.**

You might blow up at others or misunderstand their intentions. Instead of stepping back to regroup once in a while, you might just keep spinning your wheels with efforts that keep on failing, or on projects that keep you distracted.

You could also find yourself feeling frozen or uncooperative when you have to make unexpected decisions. Or you might be terrified of making a wrong decision.

One of the tools you can use for handling an angry outburst is the **Frozen Towel** technique.

For this activity, you soak a rag or towel in water and then ball it up and put it in the freezer. Then, when you're angry or overwhelmed, you can get the towel out and work at pulling it apart to redirect your energy until the feelings have passed. It can even be helpful to ask the people you live with to quietly set it nearby and walk away when they notice you are losing it.

Generally, the practices that you'll want to do when you're stuck in this step are called **proprioception** activities. These are activities where you guide your body to feel more in sync with others and the world around you.

When you learn how to get your body in sync with the outside world, it helps you to practice taking action based on the behaviors of other people and the signals around you. It allows you to be more flexible in your responses and be open to seeing more options before you decide what *should* happen.

This can be practiced by doing team sports, taking dance lessons, singing in a choir, or joining an improv group. The catch here is that you'll want to do something out of your comfort zone. If you join an activity where you feel like an expert or have expectations about how it should go or what it should look like, then it will be difficult to work on the flexibility piece that you're trying to strengthen.

If these activities feel too vulnerable, then you can start by tossing a stress ball or a stuffed animal back and forth with a friend or family member for ten minutes a day. After a while, you can increase the challenge by staying silent while the other person gives you random directions on how to catch and throw.

If you need it to be even more challenging, you can both be silent and try to direct each other's movements using body language. Ideally, you will want to do these activities while trying to let go of your expectations of how things *should* go and see if you can lean into going with the flow. It probably won't be that easy at first, but you'll get better at it with practice.

If you feel frustrated or annoyed during these activities, it will give you a chance to use some mindfulness and guide your system through new ways of responding.

As for professional support, you might do better in groups to work on proprioception. You can look for trauma-informed yoga or martial arts classes or find a mental health therapy group that fits your needs.

If you want one-on-one support, you'll want to look for a professional who feels confident about working with defensiveness and can keep a cool head if you get intense.

Step 4 - Completion

If you're stuck in the Completion step, it can feel like it's **hard to trust yourself or others**.

You might get flaky and stop following through to keep relationships at a distance. You might find it hard to focus and get randomly sad or drained a lot.

You can also find yourself hyper focused on pleasure as you're trying to find some relief for your system. This might include partying or having one night stands, but it can also motivate you to put all your energy into helping others feel good so that you can feel good too.

If you're feeling stuck here, **Peaceful Flow** is a great activity that you can practice to help your system feel safe again.

It can also be helpful to work on feeling safe by **spending time with people who recharge you**. Being playful and safely having fun with others can help to renew your energy and rediscover joy.

If you don't have anyone in your life who you can do that with right now, you can follow or subscribe to online channels of kindhearted and loving people. Kids shows like *Mr. Rogers* and *Bluey* can offer a lot of healing energy until you can build more trust in personal relationships.

You might even think about connecting or **reconnecting with a higher power** if starting with other people feels too overwhelming right now. This could look like traditional prayer, connecting with nature, tuning into universal energy, or reaching out to your higher self. Finding connection here can slowly strengthen your ability to trust again.

If you do have relationships that you want to improve, learning to use boundaries and repair can help your system rebuild trust in others. This can allow you to feel more protected and clear about your relationships and environments. Generally, this will bring more long-term relief that will allow you to feel like yourself again. Chapter 53 and 54 can help you learn more about this process.

If you're looking for professional help, one-on-one support might be the best option so you don't have to worry about people draining your energy. A good start would be a mental health therapist, an energy healer, a spiritual leader, or a trauma-informed body worker.

If a group option feels more doable right now, you can start with less social activities like restorative yoga classes or a meditation group.

These settings might be less likely to drain your energy while also helping you to safely reconnect with yourself and others.

Step 5 - Integration

For those who are stuck in the Integration step, **you might actually struggle with many of the areas we've already covered**, but you will also have your own challenges from being stuck here.

Since your system can't process everything you've been through, it's hard not to feel like you're broken. This makes it difficult to let others in and also makes you feel like you're always going to be a burden to anyone you get close to.

To deal with this, you probably bury a lot of feelings. For this reason, it can be hard to know what you're feeling, let alone know how to share anything with others. You might feel so passive that you let others walk all over you. Or get into substances, casual sex, or other activities that give you some energy or pleasure while also keeping you disconnected and numb.

You might really dislike being told what to do since you're protective of your energy and never sure who you can trust. In spite of your resistance, though, you might also spend time caring for others and feeling useful when they can depend on you.

Unfortunately, this can also lead to feeling like being used is the only way that anyone will choose you. Or it might feel like people will always end up leaving because you can't share or open up in the way that they want you to.

For this step, it can be helpful to **focus on your body**. Since your body will hold a lot of that disconnection and numbing, it will be important to **slowly work on regaining feeling** before you can do much else.

This is a tricky process and shouldn't be pushed too hard. Slow and steady is a really good pace when you've been numbed out or disconnected for a while.

Progressive Muscle Relaxation can be a helpful way to start working on this.

Progressive Muscle Relaxation is an activity where you go up or down your whole body to tighten and then release groups of muscles one at a time. This can help you to tune into your body while also finding and loosening up some resistant or guarded places.

There are many guided meditations for this online or in relaxation apps, and they shouldn't be too tricky to follow.

It can also be helpful to work on **strengthening your pelvic floor and stomach muscles** while you're doing this. Building strength in these muscle groups can help a lot with improving your deep breathing and reconnecting with your body's intuition.

Professional help can be a good way to get started on this too, and it might be helpful to look for trauma-informed body workers like massage or physical therapists, acupuncturists, stretchers, yoga instructors, or martial art instructors. It won't matter as much if the interventions are group or individual as long as you don't feel pressured to open up or move too fast in the process.

Although a mental health therapist can be useful here too, it will be important that they understand and engage body work as part of their practice. Unless you can learn to feel a little safer in your body, it will be hard to move forward with anything else.

Now that you have some idea of what strengthening activities might be helpful, I want to point out that you are welcome to use any of these options that feel like they are a good fit for you. Humans are not equations, and I'm only suggesting these steps and ideas so you have a place to begin.

You might not exactly fit in these categories, or you might be stuck in most or all of these steps. There's no cookie cutter way of dealing with your individual experience.

All of these activities can be helpful no matter where you're at. So it doesn't really matter which one you try, as long as it feels like a good place to start for you. Just remember to work on one thing at a time so you don't overload your system.

And if you don't like any of these ideas, you can keep reading and see if something else seems like a better fit.

Further Study Recommendations:

The Tao of Trauma: A Practitioner's Guide for Integrating Five Element Theory and Trauma Treatment by Alaine Duncan, MAc. This book explains how our bodies become traumatized and stuck in the 5 steps. The author uses her experience as a practitioner of Asian Medicine and her study of neurobiology to talk about simple ways to strengthen and work with stuck emergency networks in your body.

CHAPTER 33 – REFRESH

You made it again.

We're back to the calming exercises.

You're making great progress. This book is hard. I've tried to make the ideas as easy to understand as possible, but it can still be overwhelming to open yourself up to the process.

Especially for someone who is already worn out from surviving.

So take a moment to really appreciate how hard you've been working to stay focused and get here.

Even if it's slow. Even if you're not ready to take action. You're here. And that's legit all by itself.

We're going to repeat our calming activities again.

But if these activities aren't working for you, skip these chapters and try out anything from the previous chapter that feels like a good fit for you.

If you *are* still enjoying our calming activities, and want to go through them again, we're going to start back with **Calm, Safe Space**. But you can skip down to Peaceful Flow if you like that one better.

Okay. Think of the name of your Calm, Safe Space and say it to yourself.

Now go ahead and settle in and try to get cozy.

Use all five of your senses to focus on the space around you, and do that for a minute or so.

Now see if you can take a few slow breaths as you enjoy your safe space. Don't try to adjust your breathing or do anything differently, just notice the air coming in and out.

If this feels stressful, go back to using your senses to focus on your safe space.

(And feel free to use your protections or cleansers to get rid of outside stress or judgments if you need to.)

Take a moment to stay here.

Now, see if you can focus on breathing a little more from your belly.

Again, if this becomes stressful, go back to using your senses to focus on your safe space.

Take another moment to stay here.

Now, see if you can focus on breathing out a bit more slowly than you breathe in.

If not, just go back to your senses and your safe space.

And take one more moment to stay here.

Now check back in with your body and see if anything has changed. Does the tightness, discomfort or numbness feel the same or different? Is it better or worse?

Now, let's switch to **Peaceful Flow** and see how that feels.

Try to remember what you used as your comfortable energy.

Does the feeling of the energy come more easily than it did last time?

Is it easier to remember the shape, size, and color? What else do you remember about it?

Does the energy still feel comforting to you? Feel free to go back and change it if you need to.

Now check in with your body to find any uncomfortable energy. It could be tightness, discomfort, pain, or even numbness.

Can you identify the shape, size, and color of the uncomfortable energy? How about the texture, smell, sound, and/or temperature? Does it move or have weight?

Now bring your attention back to your comfortable energy.

As you have done before, invite the comfortable energy to fill the room and then slowly move into your body. Invite the energy into any area of your body that feels ready to accept it.

Notice how your body feels as this energy moves through you and around any uncomfortable spaces. Remember that the comfortable energy is always respectful and won't force itself to be anywhere it's not wanted.

Notice what happens as these energies settle in your body.

Take a moment to sit with this.

Okay. Let's pause.

How did that activity go this time? Was it easier or harder than the last time? Is the practice feeling helpful or frustrating?

You have now gone through this enough times that you probably have an idea of whether this is helping or not.

Again, these activities can get better with practice, but you don't have to keep using something that isn't working.

UPGRADE 5.0
SEARCHING FOR RELIEF

CHAPTER 34 – REWARDS

I'm excited that you've made it to the 5th Upgrade. I'm hoping that you're starting to see some small shifts in your daily life. Change is so much better when it starts to happen naturally and you don't have to overthink it all the time.

It's okay if that's not happening yet or you're still feeling impatient. It's hard to take it slow when things are miserable. Remember that pain is meant to get your attention so it can be handled. Your body has a hard time waiting when you're hurting.

In fact, this is part of what we will be discussing in this chapter. We're going to talk about your reward system and how it can help you to cope with pain and stress.

Your reward system is a really important player in your brain and body. It can be a great tool to support your mindful and strengthening practices, but it can also be a big distraction or even a drain on your system when it gets hijacked by survival.

To help you understand how it can be both, let's talk about how this player works.

Your reward system releases hormones that create positive feelings in your body. And, believe it or not, feeling pleasure is actually good for you. Pleasure keeps you motivated and helps you to learn and grow.

Sometimes the pleasure from your reward system will be super obvious and intense.

This will happen during enjoyable activities like having sex, eating chocolate cake, or waking up to 10,000 likes on social media. But you can also get this kind of pleasure from finishing a massive goal or solving a really difficult problem.

At other times the pleasure won't be as obvious because it's helping your system balance out negative feelings like pain or stress.

This often happens when your body has been overloaded and your reward system is trying to make things a little better. It might encourage you to do some online shopping or eat ice cream after a terrible day at work so your system can get a bit of relief.

Whether it's obvious or not, your reward system is constantly working to help you feel better. It's hard to feel excited, happy, relieved, or satisfied without it.

In fact, **your reward system is made to want and seek pleasure as often as it can.** It's always looking for ways to feel good and also balance out uncomfortable or difficult feelings.

Without this, you wouldn't have much interest in learning and growing at all. Life would also be boring and robotic. Not to mention that the human race would have died out a long time ago!

Wanting to feel good is not something to be ashamed of. **Pleasure gives us something to work for and keeps us motivated** to look for moments of happiness and connection.

Let's go back to the school system to see how this works.

In schools, there are usually a lot of awards and rewards. This might be with sticker charts, or pizza parties, or making the honor roll. But the main reward from school is being able to get an education, which is represented by completing each year and, eventually, getting a diploma.

School admins play a big role in handing out these yearly rewards, but many of the school staff will use small rewards like stickers or free time to help students stay on track for their bigger goals. And other staff, like counselors and social workers, will be there for students when they need support through difficult situations.

Through this process, students will learn that their hard work and effort will be rewarded, so they can keep working through each grade until they get their diploma.

Your body reward system is similar.

Just like the school admins, you have a couple spots in your brain that are more in charge of big rewards, but there are actually a lot of areas in your brain that help your body feel good and keep you feeling rewarded all the time.

And in the same way schools have a lot of different types of rewards to keep students going, your system also has a few **different types of hormones that make you feel good in different ways.**

You have some reward hormones that make you feel **satisfied**, some that make you feel more **balanced**, some that **take away pain**, and some that help you feel more loved and **connected** to others.

Now, your reward system is actually programmed to give you the most amount of pleasure the first time you are rewarded. And then, it's also programmed to give you a little less pleasure the more often you get that reward.

This may seem confusing at first, but it's important that your system is always looking for newer and better ways to feel good so that you're **motivated to chase after and work towards things**.

This doesn't actually mean you're only chasing cheap thrills and quick highs. In a healthy situation your reward system can actually be really good at looking for things that pay out for a long time, like improving relationships, exercising, and enjoying creativity.

Think about the school situation again. If students stopped getting new rewards after 5th grade, it would be pretty hard to stay motivated. Imagine being in 9th grade and still getting a 5th grade award each year. That would be kind of a bummer.

It's important that rewards lose their value over time and that new rewards replace them. This is how your system learns how to develop and stays motivated.

Let's go through an example so you can see exactly how this works.

When a baby is born, she has to eat to stay alive. So her body will send giant waves of pleasure as her belly gets full. You may have seen this level of happiness as a baby goes into a milk coma.

Every time she eats, her reward system will release positive chemicals to make her feel happy and satisfied. Her body will also start to notice that the pleasure of eating will take away the pain of her hunger and make the experience even better.

As her brain starts to realize that eating will get rid of hunger pain, she will start to have food cravings whenever she feels hunger. This means that she will become motivated to look for food or cry when her body needs to eat.

By repeating this cycle, her body and brain learn that it's important for her to eat to stay alive. But if her system just keeps rewarding her for drinking milk, then she won't want to eat anything else for the rest of her life. As she gets bigger, it will be hard to keep her fed and getting all the nutrients she needs unless she starts eating other foods too.

So her body slowly turns down the milk pleasure and, by the time she gets introduced to other foods, her system will find something new to feel great about. Through this simple process, her body eventually teaches her to look for food and eat any time she gets hungry.

Bodies are so legit that her system will learn what nutrients are in each food and give her cravings based on what her body needs, especially if she decides to get pregnant one day and needs loads of extra nutrients for the baby. Her reward system will be the key to this process since it gives her pleasure to seek out and eat the foods that she has been craving.

As you can see, the reward system can be an awesome tool for growth.

By turning down the pleasure on old habits, it pushes you to find all the different things that your brain and body need. It **teaches your system to look for goals that keep you satisfied for longer**. This is how your reward system can help you to be motivated to make routines that are good for you.

This process also means that your system learns **delayed gratification**. This is the ability to wait for a while before you get a reward.

Since your reward system reduces the level of pleasure as you repeat it, your brain has to look for more and more ways to feel good.

That means you'll have to look for bigger challenges that pay off in bigger ways and take longer to achieve.

What's cool though is that the waiting process can even feel good because of all the ways you can be rewarded in the meantime.

If your system has confidence that you will succeed, just imagining yourself making it to the finish line will release rewards and make you feel excited and energized to keep going towards your goals.

You can also have painkiller and mood-balancing rewards that can be released if roadblocks and setbacks get in your way. And you have connection rewards that will keep you close with people who support you while you work on your goals.

These different types of rewards can make it **easier to stay motivated and keep going**, even when things get tough.

If you grew up without too many challenges, your body can learn to feel positive and rewarded as you stretch yourself and work toward what you want. You'll also feel a lot of pleasure every time you reach a new goal because it will give you the highest reward.

It can keep you going through really long-term challenges like parenting and medical issues. And total failures won't be as devastating because you have confidence you can continue to find connection and rewards in other ways and try again.

When this system is working as it should, it's really helpful. You get rewarded for learning, growing, loving, and living creatively and curiously. You can stay motivated to make changes and feel confident in achieving them.

So let's talk about what happens to your reward system when you get stuck in survival.

But before we can do that, we have to talk about how survival changes the way that you see yourself and the world.

CHAPTER 35 – PERSPECTIVE

At the very least, **survival changes your perspective from long-term to short-term.** Since your system is only focusing on staying alive, it's hard to pay attention to anything else.

Your cortex gets turned down or turned off all the time *or* roped into doomsday prep and over-achieving. Either way, it can't hold on to the big picture. If you're putting out fires all the time or planning for the worst, it will get harder and harder to see beyond your fear and pain.

As your **big-picture view starts to fade**, your cortex has a harder time noticing or caring about anything unrelated to danger.

This kind of tunnel vision will make it hard to notice when you're hungry or hormonal or hitting your energy limits. And this will make you even more drained and extra sensitive to being triggered.

The more your cortex gets focused on danger, the more you start to feel like everything around you is closing in. And your point of view can get really narrow.

Sometimes this will make **it feel like you're not real or the world around you isn't real**. It might feel like you're watching yourself from the outside or like you're stuck in the Matrix. This is called **depersonalization** and **derealization** in the mental health world.

In other situations, you can become more **paranoid** since your cortex is spending a lot of time coming up with worst-case scenarios. This will often just add to the stress already coming from the overactive emergency networks. And since your body has no way of filing away all these imagined threats, the survival networks keep piling up and get stuck.

This pile up can easily make the tunnel vision worse as **your perspective gets more and more out of sync with reality**.

When your alarms are going off all the time, it's hard not to see threats in everything. It gets easy to believe that others are being critical or hostile, even when they're not.

This out-of-sync perspective can often lead to drama with others. You might get suspicious about other people's intentions as your system is looking for danger everywhere.

Your fight response might be activated by an image or sound that wasn't really as attacking as your senses made it feel. It can also lead to defensiveness where you shut down and put up lots of walls, which makes it hard for others to understand what's going on.

This can make it difficult to get along with bosses, or your kids, or your best friend when your life gets overtaken by survival. And it usually adds to the overall stress.

Another reason that you can get stuck in tunnel vision is because you end up with **dead spots in your long-term memory**.

Remember how the hippocampus can't save memories if your cortex is offline or not gathering info? This means that, if you're in survival all the time, your memory can end up with a lot of missing info, especially about what happened during your emergency responses.

Unfortunately, this can often get you pegged as being dishonest or a liar.

Other people will have a hard time believing that you really can't remember yelling at them. And they don't understand how you could agree to feed the dog but completely forget the conversation an hour later.

It can make it hard for others to trust you and for you to trust yourself.

Another challenge here is that your muscle memory doesn't really have a way of staying organized.

If you remember from Chapter 22, your muscle memories don't have a sense of time and aren't saved in the same way your long-term memories are.

The networks that are created while your amygdala is in charge will just pile up on each other instead of getting organized separately like they would in your long-term memory.

Survival memories don't come with any timelines, so it's really easy to get them all mixed up, even if they happened years apart. This is why trauma memories can get so blurred and jumbled up together. And why it makes them so difficult to sort out.

This means that when you're retelling something to your friends and you get the details of a lot of different situations mixed up together, they might think you're trying to brag or get attention by amping up the story. This might feel confusing when **your memory lumps different experiences all together**.

Now, as if all of this isn't enough, there's another way that survival can mess with your reality. This is by **reflecting and echoing the memories back through your live feed.**

Remember how muscle memory will get activated and all the parts of the network will get turned on? Well, it's possible to have your senses replay bits of the images, sounds, smells, tastes, and feelings that get piled up in the survival network.

Since they are just a bunch of short snips from your danger files, they can easily show up as random sensory interruptions or intrusive thoughts or feelings, and it may not be clear that they're jumbled up pieces of a trauma memory flaring up and replaying.

This can create something called **hallucinations**. This is where you **see, hear, smell, taste, or experience things that aren't actually there** but definitely seem to be coming from your live feeds.

This can also look like having **flashbacks** where the memory floods into your live feed and you get lost in a time portal. Remember that some muscle memories don't get updated and literally stay in the past. So when they get triggered, it 100% **feels like you're back in the original trauma.**

At times, these experiences can feel so real that they become **delusions**. That's when you **believe something is true or real that isn't.**

If your brain isn't having the same experience as other people, and your senses aren't fitting in with the world around you, it can feel really unsettling.

In situations like this, your cortex will work extra hard to make sense of it all, even if it has to come up with some pretty extreme theories to keep your system functioning.

It's not crazy to believe that you are being tracked by an ex or the government when your brain keeps showing you the same images of a man in a car every time you go out in public. This image may be a random clip from long ago that got saved in your danger matches and flares up when you're stressed. But that doesn't make it feel any less threatening right now, especially when you have no idea it's from the past.

If this is happening, it makes more sense to believe that someone is tracking you, or that your partner is cheating on you, than to disbelieve your own senses.

In some out-of-sync situations like this, **it's possible for people in survival to be abusive to others and still see themselves as the victim.**

You might scream at your sister for breathing too loudly and then walk away, genuinely feeling like you were attacked.

Since something about the experience triggered an emergency network with terrified feelings and images of danger, your system absolutely feels like your safety was threatened but may not realize it was only due to loud breathing.

Because of this, your amygdala gets triggered to intimidate her until she leaves the room. After your emergency network turns off again, you may have no memory of screaming at all. Or you might feel perfectly justified with your response since your survival network intruded into reality and told you that your sister was putting you in a life-or-death situation.

Wars have been fought throughout history where people on both sides truly believed that they were protecting themselves from the invaders on the other side.

If you struggle with these kinds of issues, you already know that it's not okay to hurt innocent people. Even if you don't show it, you probably feel ashamed of these behaviors when you *do* notice them. As you continue to learn about your system, the tools in this book can help you to heal these overloaded networks so they don't feel so overwhelming and out of control. And this can help you to take accountability for the things that you've done and find ways to heal.

It can be really hard to trust yourself when you start to lose faith in your senses, your body, or your reality. It can make you second guess yourself and downplay toxic behaviors like abuse, assault, or discrimination.

I mean, how do you speak up if you've always been accused of lying and you haven't been believed in the past? How would you trust that saying something will make a difference when you doubt your own experience? And how do you find the strength to protect yourself when you don't feel solid or real?

Not to mention that it probably feels easier to bury the memories when you realize that giving police statements and court testimonies will force you to relive the trauma again and again. And maybe in front of your abuser!

Speaking out and standing up to abuse is much, much harder than it would seem from the outside. It's amazing that there are so many people who still find the courage to do this, especially when it opens them up to judgment or harassment.

It's no wonder it can take some victims so long to be ready to come forward. Every statement and testimony has the potential to trigger trauma and pain all over again. And experiencing doubt from your family, officers, and/or juries can easily eat at your confidence and further skew your sense of reality.

If your networks have any of these challenges, it can be hard to feel like you'll ever get out of the tunnel vision or that there's any point to making goals for a future that you can't even see anymore.

And if you are trying to help someone with these experiences, it can get really complicated if you try to force someone to see the "truth" or "reality." It *is* their reality since the feelings and experiences in their system are 100% true and real for them. If needed, Chapters B and F in the Bonus Upgrade can give you more insight into helping others in these situations.

Okay, now that you understand how survival impacts your perspective, we're going back to your reward system to explain how this tunnel vision can eventually lead to unwanted habits and addictions.

Further Study Recommendations:

Hearing Voices Network USA. www.hearingvoicesusa.org. This online community is non-judgmental place to get support for those who experience hallucinations.

NeuroLogic: The Brain's Hidden Rationale Behind Our Irrational Behavior by Eliezer Sternberg, MD. This book isn't directly about survival systems, but it can help you understand how the brain is always trying to make sense of the world even if your perspective is out of sync.

CHAPTER 36 – FIX

When your body gets stuck in pain and stress, your system will dedicate a lot of time trying to feel better and calm down the uncomfortable feelings.

Your system does this by recruiting your reward system to search for **quick fixes** that can distract you from the chaos and pain.

In this setup, the motivation and curiosity parts of **your reward system will help you look for and find easy pleasures to cool down** emergency responses. This could be drugs and alcohol or sex and gambling, but it could look like a lot of milder things too. Cat videos or Reddit threads can also be pleasurable when you're stressed.

Other common fixes might include shopping, dating, parties, reading, perfectionism, high adventure, TV, movies, listening to music, social media, sports, collecting things, food, tattoos, exercise, and cleaning.

They can also include keeping up with current events, doomsday prepping, getting validation from others, fantasizing about the future, dieting and exercise, or sexual fantasies. Some research even suggests that stimming and tics can also be ways that your body resets and manages stressful networks.

And, actually, avoidance can also become a quick fix since it takes you away from having to deal with the stressors and situations that get you worked up to begin with. So putting off stressful conversations, distracting from your chores, and tuning out your spouse can all be quick fixes too.

Honestly, **quick fixes can be nearly anything**. Just like your amygdala, your reward system keeps files on reward matches. And, when you need it, your system will encourage you to do the things that have brought you pleasure and relief in the past.

By the time you're an adult, the list of things that can deliver fast pleasure or relief is going to be very long. And none of these things are naturally bad.

But, as usual, survival and tunnel vision can easily turn these quick rewards into something more challenging.

When your brain can only focus on right now, and you're overloaded with pain, numbness, bad memories, or stress, then it's hard to do anything except look for right-now fixes. And it can be hard for your system to give up these fixes when the survival never stops.

What's frustrating is that your reward system is usually just trying to help you manage your stress. But sometimes it makes everything worse.

Remember how the 4th step of the stress response cycle is to feel relief when you're out of danger? Well, when you keep getting stuck in trauma responses and your body doesn't know how to finish out the steps, **your reward system will try to find ways to provide relief and force the network to complete the cycle** when it's not moving forward naturally.

Although the fix can help your body feel relieved and cool down the emergency for a while, **this doesn't actually unstick or sort out the trauma** cycle you're stuck in.

Also, when you're living in low energy and tunnel vision all the time, your system doesn't have the focus to go after big picture goals, and it's easy to fall back into the fixes you already know. But it can become really tough to feel satisfied since the pleasure fades out over time and you'll have to keep chasing after more relief.

Once this starts to happen, you'd think your system would just switch gears and find another harmless fix to start the process over. But survival is not that simple.

When your body gets used to a quick fix, it knows it's going to feel good. So your reward system will actually **start to release pleasure hormones before you get the fix.**

This means that any time you head toward getting a reward, your brain is going to be thinking about how much better you're going to feel when you do it. And it's already going to be releasing these hormones in anticipation.

But if the pleasure is going down each time, then getting the fix isn't going to live up to the hype your brain is creating.

With your reward system out of sync like this and only looking at the short term, it's convinced that the old fixes still have the potential to pay out big. It won't have big-picture feedback from your cortex to see that it's not working anymore. So it will just keep pushing you to do more of what you've already been doing.

This leads to a cycle where you get really strong urges to go to a specific fix and expect it to feel great or take away the pain, but then nothing much happens. So then your body feels like you just have to do more of it or throw in some modifications to make it new and interesting again.

Because of this, your reward system starts to get really out of balance as the fix stops living up to the anticipation and the chase. Your system can get sucked into **hyper-focused looping** and **rabbit holes** where you lose all sense of time and spend hours and hours **chasing after a satisfaction that never really comes**.

This is how substance use may lead to harder and harder drugs, or why trying to get skinny might spiral into starving yourself, or how a porn habit can escalate into illegal activity, or gambling can lead to bankruptcy.

To see how this works, let's use an example.

After a long and stressful day at work, your friend sends you a link to a funny video. Your reward system realizes that this video makes you feel relief and logs it away for the next time you have a stressful day.

Fast forward to a few months later, and you find yourself in the middle of a messy break up. As you come home from work and find yourself feeling lonely, your reward system will probably encourage you to look up funny videos. Although this doesn't fix your broken heart, it distracts you and helps your body take a break from the pain.

Now, this setup doesn't mean you will automatically get sucked into a scrolling addiction. There are many different directions this habit might go from here. But if you are dealing with a lot of stuck emergency networks, and you're exhausted from your job all the time, then it's possible that your reward system will encourage you to scroll more and more.

Then, after months of scrolling, you realize you've seen almost every type of video imaginable, so your reward system has reduced the pleasure you get when you actually find something that you like. But now as you open your laptop or phone, your body starts feeling pleasure since your brain is *anticipating* that you're going to see something good. This is how you can find yourself endlessly scrolling, even when you just meant to check the weather.

Your brain gets stuck looking for anything that will give you the same level of pleasure that you got when you watched your first video. But now that you've seen so many clips, you're less and less likely to find a video that's as good as your brain expects it to be. So you just keep scrolling, feeling drawn in by the anticipation but ending up with a lot of mind-numbing blah. And since you're only seeing the short term, your cortex will struggle to notice that you're getting lost in these never ending quests.

Not to mention that you probably do find new and exciting videos every so often. And when the satisfaction comes rolling in, the quest for new content gets reinforced because your reward system sees that there are still treasures waiting to be found.

Hopefully this example can help you to see how your reward system is another player that can get hijacked by survival.

Now, if you feel like your survival systems spend more time with **obsessive or intrusive thoughts paired with compulsive behaviors**, then it's important to realize that your emergency networks and quick fixes are more likely to get stuck on future fears rather than past traumas. (Although it can definitely come from both.)

Obsessive feelings and intrusive thoughts are more related to the high-level functioning and people pleasing survival responses that are trying to predict the dangers lurking around every corner. And this future fear can definitely amplify your survival networks even if you haven't been through very many traumas in the past.

If your body spends more time in future fear, then your reward system is going to be dealing with **worst case scenarios that won't stop running through your mind.**

These obsessive and intrusive fears of the future can lean toward almost anything. You might be worried about germs, plane crashes, losing control of yourself or your body, being corrupted by evil, losing family or friends, gaining weight, being in places that are chaotic or disorganized, being caught off guard, etc.

And, generally, the quick fixes that cool down these intrusive feelings will be **behaviors or thoughts that help your system to feel protected from these future worries**. These quick fixes can include washing your hands, praying, wearing your lucky hat, or making lists.

Just like other quick fixes, none of these behaviors are naturally bad. But it can get really out of hand when these behaviors **become compulsive and take over your life**. You may have to **spend hours every day getting things "just right"** so your body can feel safe or settled again.

You might get obsessed with cleaning, exercising, performing rituals, purging, overanalyzing and over-preparing, repeating things to yourself, constantly reorganizing, debating other people's beliefs or opinions, counting calories, checking and rechecking everything, or just generally trying to keep a handle on as many things as possible.

It can feel easier to face the uncertainties of life when your system has a **false sense of control** about the future. And since these compulsive behaviors offer relief from your fears, it can trick your brain into thinking that they're necessary to avoid the doom.

Since most doomsday scenarios don't actually happen 99% of the time, though, your brain starts to believe that your behaviors are what's actually keeping these things from happening. And it only makes your system more convinced that these behaviors are protecting you.

Many eating disorders fall into this pattern, too, as your eating and dieting fixes are often trying to avoid or control the worst case fears about your image, body, and acceptance.

As you can see, getting stuck in quick fixes can be challenging in many ways.

Now, one of the hardest things about quick fixes is that, underneath everything, your emergency systems are still on alert and continuing to sound the alarms. **And the more you try to quiet things down with temporary relief, the more your system will turn up the alarms so they don't get missed.** Which means that your reward system will just keep working harder and harder to drown out the chaos and the pain.

And as if this cycle isn't difficult enough, getting stuck in quick fixes can make people feel pretty weak or foolish, especially when they don't know how to quit.

If this is you, it might feel embarrassing when you need quick fixes just to get through each day. This can be especially true when it's something that you don't actually want to be doing all the time, like drinking alcohol, avoiding everything, throwing up your food, spending money you don't have, or reorganizing the garage for the third time this week.

The more you have to rely on quick fixes, the more you probably judge yourself and feel ashamed. And then this shame usually leads back to negative feelings or intrusive thoughts that are likely to trigger your survival systems all over again, which means you'll need another fix.

I'm so sorry if you're stuck in this cycle. You're not weak and you're not dumb. You got here because your system didn't want to keep suffering, and it didn't have another solution for the pain. I hope with some help and support that you can find a way back out of the fixes and the pain to find the valuable person you've been all along.

CHAPTER 37 – HARM

Now, all this leads us to a very serious topic that I want to talk about: self-harm and suicide.

I want to cover these in their own separate chapter because they are difficult and heavy topics.

You can always skip this if you don't have the space or energy right now. You can also use the tips from before. Turning down the "volume" on feelings, smelling something strong, or using a container to hold things might help this feel less overwhelming.

These topics can be really triggering, and it's okay to take care of yourself or just take your time before you get into it.

So, first, let's talk about self-harm.

Self-harm is any kind of **action you take to hurt yourself.**

It can be cutting yourself, hitting yourself, starving yourself, or burning yourself. It can also be doing risky things like shooting heroin or carelessly racing on the freeway.

As you might have already guessed, **self-harm can become a quick fix** for bodies and brains in survival.

You see, the stress response cycle that we reviewed in Upgrade 4.0 has five steps that help your system deal with crises and threats. And during that cycle, your body totally expects to get beat up, bruised, and bloody. Even if you don't get attacked or mauled, running at top speed or being clenched and frozen for a while is still going to be hard on your body.

This means that when you get to Step 4 and you've escaped the danger, your system will be able to notice the damage and pain. And being able to focus on the damage and pain will be one of the signals to your emergency networks that the danger is over. (I mean, you're not going to pay attention to a blister or a cut while a bear is still chasing you.)

So noticing your injuries is one of the signals to turn off the alarms and cool things down. And your reward system is going to provide pain relief in the form of endorphins and dopamine since your body has been through something intense.

Now, if you think about how this process works, it makes sense that some folks would figure out that self-harm can move things forward when an emergency cycle gets stuck.

When you can't get yourself to stop panicking or shutting down, then harming yourself might be **a way to pull yourself through a stuck cycle**. It will draw attention to pain and/or blood, which will signal that the danger is gone and it's time to send relief.

In fact, most people who self-harm report feeling a lot of pleasure or relief when they do this. This makes sense because it's actually hacking the stress cycle to complete an emergency plan when your system gets stuck.

And, since your reward system gets good at sending relief just by anticipating something, it makes sense that self-harm doesn't even end up being painful after a while since the relief gets delivered *before* any of the harm starts.

For some people, self-harm can also provide some temporary relief in other ways.

If your body is stuck in shutdown and dissociated a lot of the time, then self-harm might also be a way to get yourself to feel something instead of nothing. This might even be a way to check that you're still real and not stuck in an alternate reality.

For other people, harming yourself can also be a quick way to do something high risk and help your body feel energized again. Activating adrenaline can help your body feel excited and motivated.

In other situations, self-harm might be used as a punishment.

If you go through your life constantly feeling like you need to be perfect and that you're messing everything up, then hurting yourself can be a way to prove you're sorry, or that you're getting what you deserve, or to show that you're trying to make up for not being good enough. In this way, it's also a quick fix to appease or calm down critical thoughts.

Another reason for self-harm might be that it can show other people how bad you are feeling.

When you struggle to express how miserable you are, or people dismiss your experience, self-harm can be a pretty clear statement. When this happens, it's not always a clear decision. Some people find that their emergency systems will often take over and do this. We'll talk more about how this can happen in Chapter 51 when we talk about protections.

It's really sad when you have to hurt yourself just to get other people to believe that you're in pain. Unfortunately, this doesn't always work, and the people who were already ignoring your inner pain might just continue to ignore your outer pain too.

Now, obviously the trouble with self-harm is that, deep down, most people really don't like hurting themselves. Just like many other quick fixes, **self-harm doesn't solve the issue**, and it usually makes everything a lot worse.

In fact, if you do this, you probably feel shame around it and hide it from others. It's hard to explain to other people how this helps you to feel better, and it can make you feel like a freak.

If this is something you're struggling with, I want you to know that your body has been doing its best to give you relief. You're not a monster or stupid. And there are ways to overcome this habit.

As you are able to work on strengthening your system and getting more in sync with your body and brain, you'll find that **it does become easier to sit with the urges and let them pass by** without doing anything. It takes time, but you can get there.

Now that we've covered a bit about self-harm, let's talk about suicide.

Suicide is what we call it **when you take action to cause your own death.**

Many people in survival will think about suicide, even if they never take any action.

Your survival systems are built to handle life-or-death situations, so it's actually really normal for your brain to bring up thoughts and feelings of death when you're stuck and overwhelmed.

This is why you can have those gruesome nightmares, even when your trauma hasn't been that gory. And it's why many people with a trauma history never expect to live into adulthood or old age.

Also, when your system has been shut down and out of control for a while, suicide may start to feel like the only way to end the pain or be free from the heaviness.

This might seem confusing since the whole goal of survival is to keep you alive. But endless suffering is its own kind of hell. So your system might start to feel like death is a better option. Or, if you believe that you'll go to hell for dying this way, you figure that you might as well trade one hell for another.

In this way, suicide becomes the ultimate escape plan.

Thinking about and imagining death can also become a quick fix for your system. Reminding yourself that you have the option to die can actually give your system a bit of hope that you can end the suffering if you need to. And this thought will often come with a bit of relief.

Sadly, this is why many people finally seem happy or relieved right before they attempt suicide. And it's also why suicidal thoughts can get so common and even addictive for someone in survival. Focusing on death might become the only way to feel some relief and hope.

Suicidal thoughts and feelings may be another way to survive and hold on. Knowing that you can end it when you've finally had enough may actually help you to feel a little more in control again and stay motivated to stick around a little longer.

If you're dealing with suicidal feelings and thoughts, I'm so sorry that your life has come to this point. It's such a heavy burden to live like this, and it's hard not to feel like you'd be better off dead.

I want you to know that your pain is real. Feeling suicidal and engaging in self-harm does not make you weak, pathetic, or lazy. You are suffering more deeply than most people realize. And it's not crazy that you hurt yourself or that you think about ending the pain.

This also goes for those of you who are still here after attempting suicide.

I wish I could personally sit with each one of you and help you hold some of this heaviness. I want you to know that I believe that you are still worth caring about. No matter where you have been. No matter what you have done. And no matter what anyone else thinks. I know that you have walked a road that many people could never imagine.

Part of the reason you're feeling so stuck is because your brain can't see past today. The tunnel vision is going to make it nearly impossible to trust that you'll feel better one day.

Even if you feel a bit of hope right now as you're reading this, it probably won't last very long. One spark in the darkness is going to be hard to hold on to. You're worn out. And your system has been overloaded for way too long.

This is why I would really encourage you to look for professional help. When someone can be there while you're dealing with all this, it can take a bit of the load off. Since you can't see a future for yourself right now, try to let someone else hold that hope for you.

I also know that it can be extremely difficult to get help when you feel like this. Your fears of hospitalization or being treated like you're crazy can make this process difficult. And they are valid feelings when you don't know what to expect.

It can also be hard to find a professional who is comfortable sitting with you in the hopeless spaces and who won't let their own fears get in the way. Self-harm and suicidal conversations can make many providers uncomfortable, and you might feel like you have to protect them from your pain and heaviness, which won't be of any help to you.

See if you can reach out to someone who has experience working with self-harm and suicide. Before you sign up or share any information, you can always ask them how they approach these issues in their professional practice. This will give you an idea of whether or not they may be a good fit.

Chapter 56 can also give you some more guidance on finding someone to help you. But it's okay if you still need time before you're ready. In the meantime, remember that you can always use the national 988 line to talk things through with someone for free.

There are also apps that can help to support you through suicidal and self-harm feelings. This can be nice when you don't have the energy to interrupt your own feelings or have the brain space to do these activities yourself. If you can just remember to open the app, it will walk you through the rest.

Clearly, survival can make things feel incredibly dark and overwhelming. You're not weak. You're just exhausted from carrying so much heaviness. The fact that you're still here in spite of all these feelings proves just how intense and relentless your survival systems have been.

I'm sorry you've been carrying so much for so long. And I hope that you get a chance to unload some of these burdens and find more peace.

CHAPTER 38 – HOOKED

We're going to talk about another heavy topic in this chapter, so check in with yourself and see if you need a break before you go on.

Now that we've talked about rewards and survival, I want to talk more about when quick fixes become a serious problem.

If you are struggling with compulsive behaviors, eating disorders, or addictions of any kind, then there are some important things you'll want to know as you're trying to heal.

First, when your reward system gets really focused on a quick fix, your cortex can actually get recruited into the process.

Remember how your cortex will lose track of the big picture during survival because it has to focus on safety and threats? Well, your cortex can also be recruited by your reward system when you're hooked to quick fixes.

Since rewards are a big part of surviving, your reward system has a lot of power when things get bad. I mean, if you're dehydrated and looking for water, the reward of finding a drink is going to be a big priority for your system. So both your emergency teams and your reward system will join forces to keep you from dying of thirst.

This means that, during survival, your reward system actually has the power to get your cortex and all of its big-picture energy to help search for fixes. Your cortex will shift its energy and focus on finding relief. This is how you can get pretty clever and creative when you're hooked and a fix is on the line.

This is also how rewards will become so urgent that you can't stop, even when you're spending more money than you can afford, or missing work, or neglecting your children, or breaking the law, or wrecking your body. Your cortex brings a powerful force to your reward system.

Second, rewards are matched in your muscle memory much like your amygdala and emergency networks.

After repeating rewarding behaviors over and over, your reward system saves the sounds, smells, images, tastes, and feelings that match and keeps track of the settings and places where you get your fixes.

This means that any time these sensory matches show up in your live feed, they can easily activate your reward system, especially when you are dealing with stress or you need a boost. And eventually these matches and actions all get saved together in muscle memory.

This makes it extremely difficult to just quit. Since your survival networks and your reward system are in charge and they've recruited your cortex into this process, your brain won't be able to notice when the quick-fix moments are getting triggered, let alone how to stop them.

It gets really difficult to figure out how to interrupt these behaviors since your cortex goes offline the moment the compulsion begins and doesn't come back until the task is finished. Every promise and vow you have ever made to quit will fade away the second these systems get activated.

In fact, if your urges are triggered by stressful feelings or trauma memories (which they usually are), then your cortex will be checked out long before your reward system is called up. This means that your brain will already be so fuzzy and dissociated that you will hardly remember when you switched gears to get a fix.

You will suddenly find yourself ordering another drink, or purging your dinner, or scrolling porn, or snorting coke, or refolding the towels for the 26th time. This disconnection between your intentions and your actions can feel so frustrating and embarrassing, even though it's not happening on purpose

The third thing you should know is that getting hooked upsets the balance of your reward system.

When a quick fix stops being a choice, it's because the satisfaction of the fix starts to be less rewarding than what you expect it to be. This means that your brain develops a huge gap between the anticipation and the reality of how good it feels.

After a lot of fixes, your body needs a large amount of reward hormones to feel anything since the expectation has gotten *so* big. But if you've become hooked, then you've used the high payoff rewards so many times that they're tapped out and will only give you a trickle of relief.

This gap can make it really hard to walk away from these behaviors because your body struggles to find anything that feels happy or satisfying to do instead. The activities that used to be satisfying won't do much since your body is now looking for such a high dose of rewards.

This means that if you are trying to quit these behaviors and looking for things that will fill the void, most healthy activities are going to feel pretty blah for a while. In this case, your reward system can take a long time to kick back in and work properly since the blah feeling doesn't really motivate your system to keep moving toward better goals.

In fact, most people end up getting hooked because they're fighting trauma memories, loneliness, and pain. So this gap can be extra difficult when quitting leaves you dealing with all the stress you've been numbing out and hardly any reward feelings to help you stay motivated.

Lastly, shame is a huge factor in this process. It's often what fuels the quick fix cycle.

When your cortex switches back on after you've found relief, you're very likely going to feel incredibly ashamed.

You will probably feel like you're not worthy to live or love or exist.

And at that point, your brain often thinks something like "Who cares now? Clearly I am the screwup everyone thinks I am. What's the point of stopping?" Which will activate your stress responses and trigger the need for a quick fix all over again.

This is why overcoming shame will be a large part of this healing process. Shame generally goes along with being alone and feeling like you don't belong. You will see in the next upgrade how much this impacts survival and how addressing shame can help to cool down the need for fixes.

The good news is that all these systems can heal, just like everything else. Although it can't happen overnight, your cortex can come out of recruitment and help your system close the reward gap and find satisfaction again.

To do this, you will have to start working your way back toward big-picture rewards to slowly reset the gaps in your system.

This can be a frustrating process when you have to train your body to go against the cravings it's feeling right now and look for other rewards.

This can feel extra tricky when you're also working on becoming a healthy system boss. Saying "no" to yourself while also trying to listen to your body and acknowledge your feelings can get confusing.

But being a healthy system boss doesn't mean that you always give in to anything that your body wants. It means that you are acknowledging the feeling and taking it into account.

If we go back to our school analogy, it's important to realize that the principal can listen and validate things while still being in charge. For example, the science department could ask for 90% of the school's budget for really cool chemistry equipment, but it doesn't mean the principal has to just accept this.

A healthy principal will do her best to be understanding, but she will also be able to say no. She will explain that the budget can't work like that and will do her best to find more sustainable ways to support these teachers in their roles.

As simple as it sounds, you can try to work with your system in the same way.

Mindful activities can help you to notice some of the patterns and triggers that signal your reward system. And by using interrupting and strengthening skills, you can learn to acknowledge and validate the cravings from your reward system without giving in.

You can let your system know that you're trying to practice using healthier rewards until your brain is able to close the gap and get back to feeling satisfied with big-picture rewards.

Obviously, this will be a lot harder if your system ended up here because of survival.

If you have been surviving for many years and your body hasn't really known what it's like to feel safe, then it's possible that your system only understands the quick fix version of feeling good. Which is honestly pretty devastating and explains why your reward system didn't know how else to cope all these years.

When you haven't had many experiences of safety and support in your life, then it's hard for your system to know what that looks like and to go after it. Your cortex probably won't know either and may have filled in a lot of blanks from stories or movies or watching other people's lives.

Having very few healthy rewards to fall back on can make it really hard to give up a quick fix on your own. It's probably in your best interest to look for treatments or groups that can help you as you start working with these hooks.

Since quick fixes are often helping you to deal with stress and trying to fill the emptiness, it's pretty unlikely that you will be able to change many of these patterns without other people being with you and supporting you as you go. Plus, it's nearly impossible to try and deal with shame all by yourself.

Many **professionals and recovery groups** understand these pieces and will try to make sure you're not alone in the process. They can help you find activities to fill your time and will work with you on healing shame through honest and open meetings or interactions. And they can help you to eventually face the trauma or experiences that are at the root of your pain.

Now, for many people, it's going to be nearly impossible to get your cortex on board with the healing process when it's still recruited by your reward system all the time. It will also be hard to face the pain in your survival networks when your quick fixes keep your brain and body constantly disconnected.

So finding support that focuses on quitting the behaviors *first* will often help your system to be more open to the rest of the healing process.

You can still get help without being ready to quit. It will just be difficult to get your cortex fully back online and your gap closed up without a break from the behaviors.

If you're not ready for that right now, that's okay. Try to be gentle with yourself and keep doing what you can.

For anyone who is feeling hooked by screens, it's possible to download timers and blocks to stop or reduce your use of certain apps and websites. These can be pretty helpful tools since you can't just get rid of your computer or phone and go back to the 1800s.

If you are working on quitting something else, it might be helpful to rearrange your space or routines regularly. As odd as this sounds, changing your environment and patterns can disrupt the muscle memory of your fixes. Since these networks have matches with your senses and actions, you can create space interruptions in the places where you're most likely to be triggered.

You can change the scent of the room, swap around decorations, rearrange the furniture, jumble up the apps on your phone, drive different roads than usual, or reorganize the cupboards. These kinds of changes can help to disable the autopilot systems that hijack your body. These adjustments will also force your cortex to stay online instead of checking out because you'll have to pay more attention when you're doing the everyday stuff differently.

Now, changing and reorganizing your environment is probably not a great tip for someone dealing with any type of obsessive and compulsive behaviors. The rearranging might just become another obsession.

So, if this is you, you will want to work on acknowledging and sitting with the obsessive thoughts and feelings without giving in to the compulsive behaviors. The next chapter can help you understand how to get used to sitting with these feelings of uncertainty. This can be really difficult on your own, so consider getting help through this process.

Hopefully you can see that quitting is not easy, and it has very little to do with willpower or being strong enough.

But even though being hooked can feel overwhelming, the practices we've been going through in this book can still help your system to feel more calm and mindful. Just like with emergency systems, these interventions will strengthen your cortex and help your system to notice the patterns that start to come up before you're hijacked by your reward system.

Further Study Recommendations:

Freedom from Obsessive Compulsive Disorder (Updated Edition): A Personalized Recovery Program for Living with Uncertainty by Jonathan Grayson, PhD. This book can help you work through obsessive thoughts and compulsive behaviors. Many eating disorder behaviors can also be addressed by working with the approach in this book.

Tourette Syndrome: Stop Your Tics By Learning What Triggers Them by Sheila Rogers DeMare. This book can help you work to reduce tic behaviors by working through the thoughts and feelings that trigger them.

Trauma and The 12 Steps, Revised and Expanded: An Inclusive Guide to Enhancing Recovery by Jamie Marich, PhD. This book can help you understand how to work on healing trauma while you attend and use 12-step programs.

Unbroken Brain: A Revolutionary New Way of Understanding Addiction by Maia Szalavitz. This book talks about different parts of addiction and discusses other ways to get help outside of 12-step programs.

CHAPTER 39 – FACING

Now that you're seeing more of the full picture in your system, you might feel overwhelmed with how much you're facing. There are a lot of players and processes that can make it feel impossible to change and heal.

This is why we keep repeating mindful activities. These will strengthen and support healing even if you're just following along as you read.

Take your time in this process.

Healing can be a big job.

It won't all be solved tomorrow. It will keep taking time and intention. Remember that you're still learning about how these systems operate, and you don't have to change it all right now.

That's why we've been taking this information one section at a time. In order to take your system out of survival mode, **you will have to learn how to face the memories and/or feelings that have been keeping you stuck.** This can feel pretty stressful and overwhelming since these networks are scary and painful time portals that you want to avoid at all costs.

This is why it can feel frustrating and confusing to keep going with the healing process. No one wants to relive their trauma. So here's what we have to do to reset your survival networks.

1. You have to activate the networks that you want to change. Because you can't reorganize them while they're offline.

2. You have to do this in a way that doesn't go into a full-blown emergency and shut down your cortex. Otherwise, we lose the big-picture support and all the info you've been learning.

3. You have to figure out where the network is getting stuck and guide your body through the cycle in a different way.

Now, if this sounds really straightforward, it definitely is not. It will take time and some trial and error to reset survival systems.

The really good news here is that your body can actually help you a lot in this process. Once you spend some time listening and learning, you'll see that your system has a natural intuition and wisdom that will help guide you through these experiences. And the other great part is that you have already been learning about and practicing the tools you will need to do this.

One important thing that you need to be aware of as you do this is that **being critical and angry does work temporarily** to interrupt stuck networks. **But it's not a long-term solution.**

Anger and criticism can work in the moment because your amygdala can prioritize fear and switch to whichever emergency seems worse.

So, even if you're terrified of spiders and you notice one in your car as you're driving on the freeway, it's unlikely that you will crash because your amygdala knows that an accident is the more deadly threat.

This means that being critical or scary can be an easy way to get yourself or others in line for a moment, but it's only going to be a quick fix and not a solution. You might tell yourself that you'll get fired if you don't stop panicking during your project presentation. Or you might yell and intimidate your kid so they stop throwing a fit at the store.

Interrupting survival responses like panic attacks, avoidance, or angry outbursts with intimidation or force can sometimes be an important way to protect yourself or others. But this way of interrupting doesn't help to build any big-picture understanding since it just activates and strengthens more emergency networks.

So it's important to learn how to interrupt and handle stress responses in other ways. Otherwise, you just train yourself and others to function by shutting down and living in more fear.

In order to learn how to interrupt survival networks safely, there is a technique called **titration** that can gently teach your system how to maintain control when something triggers your survival network.

In trauma work, the word titration means that you **work on facing your survival networks in small doses over time**. This practice makes the process a bit easier and helps your system build up a tolerance for the pain and stress that is activated by your trauma memories. That way you can slowly and carefully work up to facing and resetting them.

Hopefully you can see that you have already been practicing different pieces of this process as you have been strengthening your calming activities and getting better at interrupting false alarms. You have been increasing your ability to stay present and resist getting sucked into time portals and worst-case scenarios. You've also been giving your system more rest and confidence to slowly get in touch with the survival networks that are holding you hostage.

Once these skills are in place, you can use titration techniques to teach your system how to **stay in control while you move in and out of emergency networks**.

There are many ways to work on this, and you can check out the Appendix to learn more about different healing methods that can help you in this process.

In the meantime, you can follow along as we practice a simple version of titration and see how your body deals with it.

Feel free to take a break before you jump in, though, or skip the next 3 steps if you don't feel ready yet.

Make sure you read through each step before you try anything. Then decide what stressful experience you want to start with. If it feels easier, you can practice titration with memories of slow traffic or waiting in long lines to see how it goes before you get into anything traumatic.

Once you are feeling ready, here are the steps to **practice titration**.

1. Spend two to three minutes in your favorite calming activity. You can set a timer if that helps.

2. Once your body feels settled, bring up *one* tiny piece of a stressful emergency network. This could be a thought, emotion, body response, or sensory memory. Then notice that tiny piece of stress for 10 seconds. Feel free to count out loud or set a timer if you're nervous about getting lost in a time portal.

3. When 10 seconds are up, bring back the calming activity you started with and take as much time as you need for your body to cool back down and feel safe or settled again.

If 10 seconds feels too long, you can go as low as you need to get started. You can also adjust this process by asking your body to only share a small percentage of the experience from your survival network. 2% or even .001% of an emotion or sound might be more than enough to start with, depending on how sensitive your system is feeling.

As your body learns to tolerate the difficult feelings or thoughts, you can slowly increase the number of seconds that you stay with the experience, or you can increase the percentage of the network that you connect with. If you're not feeling enough of the distress by only noticing one part of the network, you might want to pull up two or three parts together. For example, you could pull up the sound of a horn, the feeling of your heart racing, and the thought of "I can't handle this."

By practicing going in and out of trauma memories, **your system builds confidence that it can come back to the present** and won't get stuck in the past or the future. This can make it easier and easier to face stuck networks and have your cortex recover control of your system.

It won't be easy to keep an exact balance between safe and dangerous networks as you learn to titrate. So this process might be difficult some days. And you may even find that your tolerance changes from day to day depending on your energy levels and your other stress.

If this titration activity is feeling difficult, **another thing that you can add is movement**.

Now, movement doesn't mean the same thing as exercise. Movement is literally just **a way to keep your body a bit distracted** while you face stuck networks.

Moving your body is one of the ways to interrupt your emergency response and create random signals that keep your system distracted from autopilot. This means that you can work on titration while you move your body so that your emergency networks stay interrupted and are less likely to take over.

For this process, you really only have to be walking or doing small movements to keep your body distracted. If you're not very mobile, you can tap your hands or feet, nod your head, or double blink your eyes every few seconds. What's important about this movement is that it's not too painful for you. If it is, try to find something more comfortable.

Once you feel okay with the movement, see if you can add one round of titration while you're moving and see how it goes. Again, you're allowed to **adjust this process until it works for you**. Try to be gentle with yourself as you do it. Check in with your body before and after every titration round and see how you're doing.

Now, this process might be a bit more confusing for you if your main emergency response is to be numb.

When your body has been numb for a long time and you've spent too much time in your head, then you may not even know or feel the stress that your system has been covering up.

This can make things complicated as you don't know how to get back in touch with your body, let alone how to pull up difficult feelings or memories. It's possible to have trauma networks that your cortex is not even aware of. Your emergency responses can protect you so well that they may be hidden from you.

In this case, it can be really difficult to know where to start. And the truth is that you will have to work on unnumbing your body in order to heal and move forward.

And honestly, this isn't easy.

Since shutdown is usually the way your body turns off go-mode, you're going to find that you have a lot of intense feelings that have been stuffed down, bottled up, and ignored for a long time.

Although titration can be really helpful for unnumbing, it can also take a long time. This is especially true if you're working through many years of trauma and stuck memories on your own.

Even though **titration will help you to uncover networks that have been numbed out**, your system can get overloaded as this brings more and more feelings to the surface.

As you reconnect with your body, these **networks are going to flare up and reawaken the pain and emotions** that have been buried or frozen over. After years of numbing, this can feel brutal. It's kind of like the pins and needles you have to go through after your arm or leg has gone numb. This means that **the healing process is going to feel worse before it gets better**.

This is also true if you're trying to get yourself unhooked from behaviors or substances that bring relief. Not being able to use a quick fix when your feelings are surfacing will be difficult. And you can't face these feelings if you keep shoving them back down with temporary fixes. So this process can feel super overwhelming from both sides.

If this is your situation, I am so sorry. I wish it didn't have to be this hard.

In this case, I would highly recommend finding a body worker or another professional who can start to guide you through reconnecting with your feelings in a safe, slow, and gentle way.

In fact, wherever you start in this process, it's not going to be easy to do this by yourself. Facing traumatic experiences over and over is exhausting and overwhelming.

Now that you have a better sense of where you're at and the kind of interventions you need, it can be helpful to look for a professional or support person who can join you in your healing journey.

There are treatment methods that use titration to heal and process stuck networks. And there are also many intuitive professionals who understand how to gently help you face your difficult feelings so that it goes at the pace you need.

This is important because you won't get very far if you're drowning in the process. The Appendix has a list of approaches that might help you to get started.

If you're still not there, that's okay. You'll know if and when you're ready to get help. In the meantime, we're going to return to our calming activities.

Further Study Recommendations:

Healing Trauma: Restoring the Wisdom of Your Body by Peter Levine, PhD. This book can help you practice working through stuck networks and using titration in your body. I would recommend listening to this as an audiobook as it takes you through many guided activities.

CHAPTER 40 – REPEAT

We're back to our calming activities again.

Since you now have a better sense of where you are at in your healing journey, feel free to **choose a healthy boss activity that works for you.**

You can focus on relaxation or yoga movements. You can also practice one of the strengthening activities like Belly Breathing, Calm, Safe Space, Peaceful Flow, or Progressive Muscle Relaxation. You can also experiment with some titration and movement if you feel ready.

You can also do a totally different mindful activity that feels good for your system.

If you want to do something but need more direction, go back to Chapter 33 for our guided activities.

Once you know what you're doing, go ahead and pause here. Take as much time as you want, and come back whenever you're ready.

UPGRADE 6.0
DISCOVERING THE ROOTS

CHAPTER 41 – CONNECTION

Now that you have a pretty good overview of how the connections in your brain and body work, we're going to switch gears and talk about the connections we make with other people and how those relationships also impact survival.

This can be a really hard topic when you're not quite ready to go there. You might learn things about your current relationships that might help you to improve them, but it might also make you see things you don't want to face yet and that you're not ready to deal with.

Check in with yourself and see how you feel about it. Remember that you can wait until you're ready. Trust your intuition. If you need to, put a bookmark here and come back when the timing feels right.

If you do want to keep going, try to take it slowly and keep checking in with yourself.

Connection is maybe *the* most critical tool of survival. Attachments to other people play a large part in our everyday lives and quality of life.

When you feel safe with others and trust them, your system will have an easier time feeling relief and staying calm. Safe connections keep your body in sync and well balanced.

In the mental health world, we often use the word **regulated** to describe when someone's body is feeling settled and stable like this.

It usually means that you have a good balance of *interoception* (which is the awareness of the feelings and senses in your own body) and *proprioception* (which is the awareness of how your body fits in the space and world around you).

When your body is regulated, your heartbeat, breathing, muscles, tissues, and organs will easily communicate with your brain and adjust their energy and speeds when you go through different experiences.

Your system will **easily switch between different emotions and adapt as things change**. Your body can move from calm to playful and from excited to relaxed without much effort. Even stressful or sad moments don't feel as overwhelming in a regulated body.

And if your system does go into survival mode, a regulated body is much more likely to get through all the steps of an emergency response and find relief again. So it's easier to handle threats when your system is in the habit of being in sync with yourself and your surroundings.

Many people also call this the **rest and digest** state of the body. When your system is regulated, it is easier to feel relaxed and rested. And your food gets digested more easily since your body isn't getting shut down by stress.

For most people, it's much easier to regulate your body when you're with people you trust and who feel safe to you. Knowing that you will have someone to support you when you fall apart or to comfort you when you're stressed helps your body to feel more confident in your everyday life.

Humans can actually help each other to regulate their bodies and reduce stress just by being around each other. This is known as **coregulation.**

When someone you trust can be with you or hold you through difficult experiences, it will help your body to find relief and allow the stress to cycle and process through your system. In fact, for most people, coregulation is one of the fastest ways to tell your amygdala to switch off the alarms and that the emergency is over.

This isn't just a nice thing that your body does. As you might remember from Upgrade 2.0, it's the very first way your system learns to survive. Before you can even understand the importance of food, water, and shelter, you survive by being connected to and protected by others.

In fact, being attached to others is so hardwired into your system that many of your nerves and networks won't be able to develop without connections to others.

This is due to something called **mirror neurons.**

Mirror neurons are a special kind of neuron. They are similar to other neurons because they send and receive signals about your system. But they are different because they also **send and receive signals that copy and match the actions and behaviors of the people around you.**

These neurons help you to sync up with and mirror people when they are close by. This helps you to feel connection and empathy, which is the ability to feel what other people are feeling and put yourself in their shoes.

This is important when you're first born because you don't know how to move or talk or take care of yourself, so your mirror neurons get messages from the bodies around you that **teach your body and brain how to develop**, just by tuning in and copying them.

You'll learn how to move your body and focus your eyes as people talk to you, and look at you, and grab your hands, and give you attention. Your brain will start to mirror and reflect the movements, expressions, and sounds of the people around you until you can get a handle on these tasks yourself.

You'll also learn how to understand and organize your own feelings based on the care you get from caregivers.

Remember how babies' neurons fire kind of randomly at first and don't get organized for a while? Well this is how that process gets organized.

When the caregivers in your life spend time holding you, feeding you, making sure you're safe, and trying to understand what you need, then your system starts to learn how to take care of itself. And it learns what it's like to feel safe and regulated. This is where those safety matches start to save up.

For example, when a baby cries, she can't take care of her own needs, and she doesn't actually know what's wrong. She just feels really uncomfortable, and her stress response gets her to cry. So her dad will have to help her get comfortable again.

If her dad tries feeding her and she still feels uncomfortable, she'll continue to fuss. Then if he changes her diaper and her discomfort goes away, her system gets the message that the stress is over and she's safe. This relief will then cue her body to stop crying. With these interactions, her dad helps her system to organize and make sense of all the different signals that are firing inside of her.

As her needs get met every day, her neurons will begin to learn the difference between the discomfort of a squishy diaper and a hungry stomach. And, with the help of her dad and other caregivers, her body will learn to move in and out of stress cycles safely.

Over time, these connections will help her neurons to grow and organize until she can laugh, roll over, walk, talk, play, etc.

In fact, this process is important throughout childhood. Although kids take on more tasks as they grow, receiving this support through childhood and adolescence helps them to regulate and organize their networks until they learn how to more fully take care of themselves.

If a child doesn't get this kind of attention and connection, she will have a hard time figuring out what's going on in her own body and struggle to know what she needs.

She will sit in a diaper or go without being fed so long that the signals will get muddled together and overwhelm her system, even when she finally gets some help.

If this happens a lot, she will have a hard time noticing and connecting to what's going on inside of her or around her. The confusion and lack of regulation in her system will get in the way of her ability to focus on anything but the stress and discomfort.

This learning and developing process is so dependent on bonding that babies can literally stop growing and even die if caregivers are doing the bare minimum to keep them alive. Neurons need way more interaction to grow than just feeding and diaper changes.

Children need connection, touch, and warmth with their caregivers and community. Without this regulation and safety, it will be hard to keep their survival networks from taking over all the time. And if a child's brain and body get stuck in survival, it can keep them from developing the rest of their system.

CHAPTER 42 – FOUNDATION

Thankfully, **babies can actually begin to form connection and safety before they're even born**. That way they're able to feel comforted and safe with their families right from birth.

From the inside of the womb, you can learn the rhythms of your mother's heartbeat and movements, the flavors and smells of household foods, the sounds of your siblings playing, and the laughter of your grandparents.

By the time you're born, you will already have some recognition of these patterns and experiences. Usually these senses will already be safe matches in your system and help your body learn how to stay regulated.

Unfortunately, though, if your time in the womb was stressful or traumatic, **you can also be born with many of your senses matched with stress responses**.

This means that you can be born with emergency networks that have already been activated and strengthened in the womb. Generally it takes a lot for this to happen, and these kinds of networks will usually be created **when your mother goes through serious traumatic events** like abuse, accidents, or injuries.

In other cases, some babies are **born premature or with medical issues**. When a baby needs medical help to survive, they are usually taken from their parents and given life-saving treatment. Of course, this needs to happen, but it can easily create stuck survival networks as well.

Even when doctors and nurses are gentle and caring, the only safety matches that a baby may have experienced so far are connected to the patterns of their parents and family. It's unlikely that someone else is going to match those patterns well enough to fully soothe and coregulate with a baby who's confused, distressed, or in pain.

These experiences of stress with NICUs and medical treatments will start to organize the baby's emergency networks and make them stronger than many of their other nerves. Obviously, this can become more difficult if parents can't safely touch and connect with the baby to coregulate and help them feel safe.

This is especially complicated because infant pain levels are difficult to measure when they can't talk. Not to mention that many treatments and medications can be risky and difficult for babies to process, which means pain management can be extra challenging.

In fact, up until the late 1980s, many babies and children would receive invasive medical treatments and surgeries without pain medication or anesthesia. Sadly, many people in the medical field believed that babies and children couldn't feel pain or that they were young enough they wouldn't remember the experience. And in many cases, there wasn't enough research to know if these medicines were too dangerous for babies.

If you were born before this time and had any difficult medical treatment as an infant or child, it's possible you didn't receive enough pain management. Your body may still be stuck sorting out pain and distress that got piled up in your system before you can even remember.

Unfortunately, after these kinds of experiences, it can be very difficult for a baby's system to be coregulated, even with the help of really skilled parents. The baby's emergency responses can get strong enough that their body defends against or avoids coregulation with their caregivers.

These early stress situations can also cause your system to have some **really broad and fuzzy matches in your danger files** since your baby senses weren't very clear yet. This often leads to stuck emergency responses that get **triggered by pretty much everything**, such as all loud noises or any sudden movements.

When a baby goes through these kinds of experiences, they are also very likely to grow up with shutdown responses.

Since **a baby has no ability to feel safe by themselves**, and they cannot run or fight, **their only option is to numb.**

Since crying and coregulation didn't get their needs met, their system learns that only shutdown and freeze will clamp down and manage the stress. After a while, it becomes hard for their system to even attempt other survival methods because the shutdown moves into muscle memory and becomes their autopilot response.

This is why children who grow up in institutions and orphanages can end up with so many medical, emotional, and mental health issues later on in life. Their system can struggle to recognize basic body signals after years of numbing and a lack of connection with caregivers.

Shutting down is also really common for toddlers who go through traumas or medical problems before they can talk and form long-term memories. Things like infant asthma, or surgeries, or severe sicknesses can do this, especially if they had to be held down to get treatments. This will reinforce that they can't escape, move their body, or find protection, which will switch their system to shutdown.

Now, it's important to note that some things can still go sideways even with good-enough caregiving and safe experiences. There might be neurological differences like autism, sensory overload, or developmental delays that can interrupt the safety matches in a child's brain and make it difficult to help them manage their stress responses. (If this applies to you, Chapter F in the Bonus Upgrade section might be useful for your situation).

This is also why many adopted or surrogate babies may struggle to bond to their parents. When all the sensations are different from their biological family, it makes it hard for a baby to feel safe. And, for an infant, these small differences can feel threatening and may get in the way of coregulating with their caregivers.

If it's possible, it might be helpful for adoptive parents or medical professionals to keep babies in contact with their birth parents as much as possible to get through adoptive family transitions or medical treatments. This won't be a perfect solution, of course, but it might keep things more manageable.

It also makes sense that a recording of the mother's calm heartbeat, a clip of the birth family's voices, or a piece of clothing with the mother's smell might help a baby's system transition a little better in situations where the birth parents won't be part of the caregiving.

Now, if you or someone you love has been through **trauma or connection issues before the age of 3**, then your best bet is to find a professional who feels comfortable working with **preverbal trauma**. This is hard to address on your own since you may have no memory of these stressful experiences, and they can be more difficult to get a handle on. Chapter 56 and the Appendix can give you tips on finding the right support for these experiences.

Another thing to note is that **life changes can often be hard on older children too** because they lose connection with the people, places, and things that have helped them to regulate and feel safe.

This is why kids can fall apart when a caregiver leaves, or they move to a new house, or there's a divorce, or they change schools, or a parent goes to prison or dies.

Since children don't have control of their own life and environment, it can be really difficult for them to process the loss of something that is a safety match in their system and helps their life feel predictable. They also don't have a lot of big picture thinking yet to figure out how things will be okay again.

In fact, just general life transitions like going into middle school or getting their first job can feel really overwhelming since it's something they haven't done before. Without much life experience, it can take a while before their system gets used to the new situation and builds new connections and safety.

CHAPTER 43 – CAREGIVERS

As you can see, connection is a really major part of human survival and that means that caregivers have a big role to fill.

In our school analogy, it might be helpful to think about caregivers as training schools.

When a newly formed school has access to training and preparation support, they will more easily learn how to function as a system. The new principal can get direction and support from the trainers as they learn about running their unique setup.

And with enough time together, the principal also gets to watch how the training schools manage their own systems and understand what healthy functioning can look like.

In this analogy, mirror neurons would be like setting up communication feeds between the training schools and the new school. This allows each department to get regular support and feedback from the trainers as the staff and students are learning.

Your brain and body work in a similar way with the people around you.

Because of mirror neurons, **you and your caregivers share feelings and signals and your networks learn from each other's patterns.**

In fact, babies are born without a frontal cortex. This part of your brain needs to make a lot of connections and learn a lot of things before it can even start to have a big-picture view and coordinate your system. It's hard to navigate the past, present, and future when you're new to the world and don't have life experience yet.

So, in our school analogy, the training schools have to be in charge of running and supporting the high school while also spending hours every day training the new principal how to *be* a principal. The training schools will have to do this constantly while also giving the new principal chances to try running small things on her own sometimes.

Similarly, **parents and caregivers have to share their big-picture cortex with their kids** every day so that their kid's cortex can slowly develop and build a larger view of themselves and the world.

This is a challenging process because kids need help for a long time. And their system will change a bit every week as their cortex learns and masters different things. It can become hard for caregivers to know what to teach, when to teach it, and the best way to go about it. It can also be difficult to know when to take over and run things yourself and when to let children do things themselves since it might be 20 to 30 years before their cortex is ready to handle most situations.

What's more challenging, too, is that babies are born with their amygdala and emergency teams ready to go since their bodies need to handle danger. They also have their reward system ready to go since they need to feel pleasure to learn what's good for them, like eating and learning to talk.

So caregivers have a huge responsibility as they manage and take care of other bodies in addition to their own body.

Also, as you grow up, **your system learns how to respond and survive by using mirror neurons and following what your caregivers do and say.** And because you learn so many basic things this way, you will usually have a lot of the same behaviors and characteristics that they do. And this will influence your danger and reward matches and which emergency responses you build over the years.

Now, this isn't a straight across match, because we all come with our own unique personalities and preferences. But, this means that many of the basic things you learn will be copied from your caregivers.

And caregivers don't just mean your parents or guardians. You can pick up a lot of things from siblings, grandparents, cousins, neighbors, teachers, and daycare staff. All the people who mentor and take care of you can influence how your brain grows and wires, especially the more time you spend together.

If any of your caregivers know how to regulate their own body and system, especially when they're overwhelmed or in survival, then you have a better chance of learning this too. Since they can provide a good model to you and show you how to use these skills, you are more likely to develop these same patterns.

If any of your caregivers hold you and wipe your tears when you are in pain, your system will learn that it's okay to feel hurt and that you will be cared for even on your bad days. This will also give you a great model for how to be a supportive caregiver when you're older.

If any of your caregivers take accountability and apologize when they make mistakes, then your system will know how it feels when someone cares enough to be vulnerable and accountable. And you will also learn how to repair issues with others when you make mistakes.

In fact, research shows that **children are much less traumatized by difficult events when they have at least one safe mentor or caregiver** in their life who is regularly there for them during stressful times.

Generally, these caregivers are good at regulating their own bodies, which helps them to patiently coregulate with kids while they're learning to sort out their emotions. They can also help you feel safe by protecting you and standing up for you when you are in danger or threatened.

Connecting with these types of people in your childhood will usually teach your body how to cycle through and handle stressful situations instead of getting stuck in trauma.

But, **if your caregivers struggled with their own survival history, then they probably didn't learn how to be a healthy boss** of their own system, let alone yours. And they probably had a hard time connecting with you and modeling safety when they couldn't regulate their own body.

This is really tricky when a caregiver becomes neglectful because they're overwhelmed by their own issues. And it's outright damaging when their dysregulation leads to abuse.

Clearly, **abuse can activate survival in children, but so can emotional neglect**.

Even if a child has food, clothes and shelter, but they don't have safe-enough adults to help coregulate their body and train their cortex, then their amygdala and reward system will likely become the most active players in charge of their brain and body.

And when your caregivers aren't connecting to you, protecting you, or modeling healthy behaviors, then your system will end up using survival responses to deal with most situations. Without a developed cortex or a safe adult, a child has very little control over their own protection.

Not having a safe connection with caregivers can feel just as threatening to a child's body as being held at gunpoint or being stuck in a burning building. **It really is life or death to a kid when they can't trust that their guardians will protect them.**

To survive these moments of disconnection, **kids will often find a way to stay connected** to caregivers even when it seems dysfunctional.

For some people, this means that you learned to take any attention, even if it was **negative attention**. Maybe you got angry, needy, demanding, mouthy, or manipulative, or you turned into a show-off.

Caregivers usually do pay attention during these times since these behaviors tend to annoy them. They don't understand that you are feeling unsafe and seeking connection. And even though you don't want to be in trouble, it might make your system feel a tiny bit better knowing that you can still get through to them if you need to. Sadly, this will often get you branded as a problem child.

In fact, this type of child can often be labeled as "spoiled." Many disconnected caregivers use quick fixes to try and shut kids up rather than take the time to teach them how to handle and communicate their feelings. But a child who just gets their way every time they feel bad will never learn how to identify and manage their experiences. And they will only continue to act demanding or aggressive when their deeper need for connection and guidance continues to be ignored.

When a child only learns how to get attention or cared for in this way, they are set up to fail a lot of opportunities and relationships since they were never given boundaries or shown deeper ways to connect.

At other times, you might have tried to **get attention by being compliant**. This approach may seem positive from an outside view, but it can be just as damaging. These survival techniques can include avoiding, overthinking, blind obedience, people pleasing, and/or taking care of caregivers.

When your needs aren't being met as a child, you might learn to get connection and attention by comforting others or being perfectly behaved so that your caregivers will want you around.

You might figure out how to make everything about them and help them feel happy or proud or less stressed. You can learn to do this so well and so regularly that everybody gets tricked into believing that it's *your* job to manage their emotions and not the other way around. They may even justify this by saying that they keep you fed and sheltered, so you owe them your gratitude and respect.

Unfortunately, to survive like this and stay connected, your system will actually learn to bury and numb out your own feelings in favor of everyone else's. You'll start to feel that your everyday needs and emotions are a burden since they are always ignored, criticized, or minimized. You'll figure out how to take care of yourself and be as independent as possible.

You might grow to believe that your normal human emotions are too much or too heavy or too sensitive since your caregivers probably got annoyed or overwhelmed during the rare times that you did express your feelings or tried to get support or tell the truth.

Although helping others can seem positive because you learn to be independent and empathetic, it can also lead you to lose your own identity and/or feel like you're never enough. This can make it hard to feel connected since you've always gotten the message that you're only loveable if you're sacrificing your life for someone else.

Now, when you *do* grow up in a family where your caregivers are taking care of their needs as well as yours, then you are more likely to learn that you are as important as everyone else. And this is not just because *your* needs get met. Since your caregivers valued and listened to their own needs too, they regularly modeled what it looks like to prioritize self-care and to not give more than they had to offer.

This kind of **healthy caregiving teaches you that you are worth other people's time and attention** and you don't have to hide your emotions or challenges in order to feel safe.

You also learn how to be considerate of others because you have been shown by your caregivers how to balance your needs and the needs of others. You understand that it's okay to admit when you're struggling or own up to your mistakes. That you don't have to be perfect to be accepted by others.

And when you feel like you belong and that you are as important as everyone else, it's pretty hard to get stuck in survival. If something bad does happen or you make a mistake, then you trust that **you will be able to get the help and support that you need** until you can get back on track.

This is called **secure attachment**.

Parents and caregivers don't even have to be perfect for this to happen. Research shows that to feel safe with your caregivers, they only have to get it right about one third of the time, as long as they own up to their mistakes and face and repair the problem when things go off track.

But, if you grow up in a family that is stuck in survival, this is going to be much harder. How can caregivers teach you how to grow and learn and feel important when they didn't get the attention and connection that they also needed?

In fact, **survival living is usually passed down through caregivers**. It's really hard to model a healthy relationship with *your* children when you've been abandoned, abused, or neglected by your own parents or guardians. It will be difficult to pass on secure connection to your kids without a lot of dedication and effort.

And, when you're a child, it's hard to understand that your caregivers were just surviving. You couldn't understand why they would selfishly choose quick fixes and emergency responses like anger, substances, avoidance, and abusive relationships instead of connecting with you.

Unfortunately, many people in survival will have children, hoping that this will finally give their life meaning, or unconditional love, or motivation to improve. Without realizing it, they expect their children to help them feel better and make their life worth living.

Sadly, this can put an unspoken burden on children who are raised to believe it's their job to help their caregivers get out of survival. Instead of helping their child to learn how to run their own system, the caregiver will turn the roles around and expect the child to help them function.

When this happens, a child can struggle for many years to get their needs met and end up being robbed of their innocence and childhood as they have to handle adult feelings and responsibilities.

If this was you, maybe you were expected to reassure your caregiver's insecurities or boost them up when they were down. Maybe you had to help protect your siblings when your caregivers were abusive, depressed, or really disorganized. And maybe you had to bury your own feelings and needs so your caregiver didn't explode or give you the silent treatment all the time.

This setup can be even harder if you tried to speak up or share that something was wrong and your caregiver just didn't hear you or got upset.

Your caregiver might have also made you feel ashamed or guilty by saying things like "You have nothing to be upset about," or "You're so ungrateful after everything I've done," or "You're right, I'm a terrible parent," or "You're just making a big deal out of nothing because you're so sensitive."

These kinds of interactions will push you to be **more concerned with your caregiver's feelings and beliefs than the truth of your own pain and experience** so you don't end up abandoned and alone. This probably taught you that the pride of your caregivers is always more important than being honest about your needs.

In situations like this, children are forced to numb, or avoid, or pretend away their own needs and pain so that they can stay connected with their family and survive.

Further Study Recommendations:

Adult Children of Emotionally Immature Parents: How to Deal with Distant, Rejecting or Self-Involved Parents by Lindsay Gibson, PsyD. This book can help you understand some of the challenging patterns of your family and identify ways to start making improvements.

Silently Seduced, Revised and Updated: When Parents Make Their Children Partners by Kenneth M Adams, PhD. This book can help you learn more about the traumas and stressors that come from being expected to take care of your caregivers' needs.

Understanding the Borderline Mother: Helping Her Children Transcend the Intense, Unpredictable, and Volatile Relationship by Christine Ann Lawson. This book can help you find some validation and support if you were raised by a parent with a personality disorder and/or extreme disorganization and trauma responses.

CHAPTER 44 – GENERATIONS

The sad truth is that most parents or caregivers who modeled insecure patterns were probably children who also didn't get the attention and connection they needed to feel secure.

Families often pass down survival systems because of how they were raised and their genetics.

This doesn't make abuse or neglect okay. But it can be important to understand where it comes from.

If you come from a family that is stuck in survival, it's probably because that pattern was established many generations ago and continues to repeat.

When survival overtakes someone, it can live on over and over through their kids and future generations. Raising children is incredibly difficult. And it's even more so when your system is stuck in survival.

It's possible that many of the emergency responses that you're stuck in are ones that didn't start with you. They may have come from your parents and grandparents.

Throughout human history, many people have experienced enslavement, genocide, sexual trafficking, wars, domestic violence, holocausts, family abuse, and other horrors. As you can imagine, survivors of these nightmares can't help but walk away with bodies that are overflowing with unresolved trauma networks.

And because children develop their body and brain by using mirror neurons and copying the patterns of their caregivers, stuck survival networks can literally be transferred on through the generations. Even if your family has hidden or forgotten the stories, you can still find yourself stuck in the exact same trauma cycles they were.

Genetics also contribute to getting stuck in these cycles since biological parents and grandparents can pass on a lot of survival patterns through DNA.

Although DNA doesn't change much from generation to generation, there are things called epigenetic markers that do change.

Epigenetic markers turn DNA programming on and off to help your system adapt to unique situations. These markers have learned how to manipulate genetic codes based on what your ancestors went through and what kept them alive. So these markers are kind of like a file of instructions that your system gets from the people who survived before you.

Many times epigenetic markers will be turned on or off during your parents' or grandparents' experiences and passed on to you with these adjustments still in place, even though you didn't go through these things yourself.

This also means that when these markers detect changes in your system, they can make switches to your DNA programming based on what the instructions tell them to do. And these adjustments can be passed on to your children too.

This is important to know because **you and your family can be born with an epigenetic system that makes your bodies more defensive and prone to certain survival responses.**

Now, these epigenetic markers *can* actually be switched back again when your system starts healing. As you get better at healthy boss skills, you can help your body to switch off epigenetic markers that increase survival mode. Which means that you can influence your children's healing as you work on your own healing.

This is true whether or not you had your kids before these markers changed in yourself. As you change your survival responses and you learn how to repair and connect with your children and model healthier relationships, they are more likely to mirror your changes and shift their epigenetics too.

And even though it might seem too late, you can sometimes help to change these patterns with your adult children and grandchildren. As you work on your own healing, you'll become more capable of facing things you didn't know how to address before, and it may become a bit easier to repair things that used to feel too confusing or heavy.

In some cases, you might even motivate your caregivers and/or siblings to work on their own repairs as they see you repairing and healing these cycles in yourself and/or your children.

Unfortunately, though, it's pretty common for some caregivers to feel like these changes are threatening. **Not only are traumas passed down through your family, but so are the fears of their discovery and the shame that goes with them.**

Honestly, most generations have someone in the family who tried to change these patterns or tell the truth about what was going on. And they often got criticized, bad-mouthed, or abandoned, which taught the rest of the family to stay silent at all costs for fear of also being rejected.

So your family might have emergency responses, shaped by your parents and grandparents, to lash out or put down anyone who questions or tries to change these patterns. They may even accuse you of betraying the family pride or rejecting them after all they've done for you. This is how pain, grief, and secrets become ingrained in each generation. Your body learns to be terrified of facing the truth without knowing why.

If you're raised in a family where hiding the pain is more important than facing the truth, then it's going to be pretty hard to live as your real self while also staying safely connected.

When you are constantly **criticized for being your authentic self**, then you get direct proof that you aren't accepted as you are. And if you're always hiding your true feelings to fit in, then you will often doubt that you truly belong because you're **always holding parts of yourself back**.

This pattern is often called **insecure attachment**, and it goes hand in hand with shame.

Shame is the feeling you have when you don't feel like you actually matter or belong as you are.

It is the belief that your needs are a burden. And that something is so wrong with you that you will never be good enough to be accepted. That you are only worthy of connection if you're perfect, or achieving, or taking care of others. That no one will ever want you or choose you when they finally learn who you really are.

Sadly, many people develop this kind of shame to survive difficult family patterns.

By believing and trusting that your caregivers are doing a good enough job and that *you* are the problem, you can often stay motivated to keep going when things are bad.

It's usually easier to believe you're defective than it is to admit that you are alone and won't ever get the support you need. If you're the problem, then you can try to weed out the bad and ugly parts of yourself and get rid of them, or fix them, or bury them, or avoid them.

This gives you a pretty powerful hope that you can eventually be good enough one day to get the love and attention that your system has been aching for.

Shame like this is created by having insecure relationships in your life, especially with your caregivers.

It convinces you that you always have to fit in by being perfect and hiding the weakest parts of yourself. It makes you feel like your true expressions will always keep you from being accepted. It encourages you to keep silent about the things you're going through in case you're rejected because of them. It drives you to criticize and judge yourself and others for imperfections because you've been convinced that these make people unlovable and a burden.

Unfortunately, you can become so convinced that you are unworthy of love that you always expect rejection and become skeptical of anyone who tries to connect or show you love.

In the mental health world, experiencing this kind of **insecure attachment and internalized shame** is also known as **complex trauma**.

This can be confusing because we often think about trauma as something that has happened to you or that you have witnessed. But complex trauma can also be about what *didn't* happen in your life. Even if your caregivers weren't abusive, inappropriate family roles and/or a lack of emotional connection can also be traumatic.

Many childhood experiences will be overwhelming without the support and guidance of a safe adult. Children will be left to survive alone or to fill adult roles that they aren't prepared for. During difficult times, they will be forced to rely on themselves and their survival instincts instead of receiving support to develop long-term goals and connection.

This lack of connection will also **make them believe that they were not good enough or didn't do enough** to get their caregiver's protection and support. This will generally encourage children to distrust themselves and keep things buried for fear of rejection.

As a result, they will become more and more isolated as they lose confidence in themselves and don't learn how to rely on others. This will force them to deal with situations in a very all-or-nothing way that often leads to high functioning and/or total shutdown and avoidance.

Unfortunately, this can lead to added trauma as they become **easy targets for bullies and perpetrators** who recognize the signs of **isolation, shutdown, and internalized shame**.

Going through this kind of complex trauma **can also lead to extremely controlling or manipulative behaviors** that help these children survive and get their needs met. If their system never got a chance to develop past the finding a protector stage, then throwing a fit, acting helpless, and demanding attention may be the only survival responses they know.

Most people with personality disorders like narcissism or borderline will struggle with these patterns due to severe neglect, abuse, abandonment, and/or rejection in their childhood. They learned how to survive by using childish bonding behaviors to stay connected to *and* protected against emotionally immature caregivers.

When you feel so insecurely attached that you believe you have to hide who you really are to stay connected, it can force you to **navigate relationships in dangerous and harmful ways**.

Unfortunately, when you feel like you don't belong and your survival responses and quick fixes feel out of control, it's easy to convince yourself that you're right to be ashamed of who you are, which will almost always spiral back into survival, quick fixes, and feeling insecure. It's a vicious cycle, which is why it can be so complex to treat and heal.

This is especially true when you find yourself **repeating the toxic patterns of your family** that you swore you never would.

Maybe you've taken on the same negative behaviors as your controlling father, your absent mother, or your violent grandmother.

When your system becomes so out of control that you can't seem to get it together, no matter how hard you try, it may confirm your worst fears: that you are doomed to become the kind of person you've always hated. It makes you feel that you really are broken and unworthy of love.

These beliefs will encourage you to keep hiding who you really are and the real needs and pain that are being buried and neglected. You might become like the rest of your family and lash out at anyone who tries to connect with, expose, or uncover the shame.

But when you live like this, it's almost impossible to keep all the pain and loneliness and grief from bursting out now and again. It will usually show up as stuck emergency networks and quick fixes when you feel overwhelmed or lonely.

This will make it **hard to trust yourself and others** and to open up or be vulnerable. And without this openness, it can be hard for others to understand what's going on and to prove that they can be gentle with your pain.

In fact, you might find it hard to be vulnerable with anyone, including therapists or other professionals. Everything you've ever been through tells your system that opening up is a severe threat, and it will make it hard to overcome the hiding and the shame.

Further Study Recommendations:

Break the Cycle: A Guide to Healing Intergenerational Trauma by Dr. Mariel Buqué. This book can help you learn more about how trauma passes through families. It can also guide you through different healing activities and resources.

Permission to Come Home: Reclaiming Mental Health as Asian Americans by Jenny T. Wang, PhD. This book offers support to Asian Americans as they're trying to understand more about intergenerational trauma. Although it is directed toward Asian folks, it may also be helpful for children and grandchildren of immigrants from any country, especially if your family left a collectivistic society to live in a more individualistic one.

CHAPTER 45 – RELATIONSHIPS

Now, if you are someone who has been through insecure attachments and a difficult childhood, you probably still long for safe relationships and belonging, even though you struggle to trust.

Of course you still want connection. You're a human. **The desire for love and acceptance are wired into your system**, no matter how much you feel like you don't deserve it or doubt that you'll ever get it. Belonging helps you to feel safe. It helps you feel like you can survive.

You can't really run away from that, no matter how hard you try.

For most people, **you'll do your best to connect with others, even if it gets messy or doesn't work very well.**

If you learned that people usually pay attention to you when you're angry or pushy, then you might get really **demanding and aggressive** when you're not feeling connected.

You might threaten to harm yourself or others. You might get critical and controlling. You might push people away, expecting that they're going to leave anyway. You might even get abusive and dangerous as you try to force or manipulate others into staying with you.

If you learned that others would show up when you were anxious or vulnerable, you might **show a lot of helplessness and desperation** when you feel like you might be abandoned.

You might beg people for their time and attention. You might suddenly get sick or stop taking care of yourself to show that you're struggling and need help. You might let anyone be in your life, no matter how toxic they are. You might become obsessed with getting people to like you. You may feel like you have to constantly explain yourself or convince others that your needs matter. You might push people to get close before they are ready.

If you learned that numbing out helped you survive, then you might **shut down to keep yourself safe** in relationships.

You might ignore your feelings or numb out so you don't become a bother. You might struggle to ask for help since you don't want to burden anyone or expect too much. You might avoid conflicts to protect yourself from rejection. You might hook up a lot or fantasize about the perfect romance and avoid long-term relationships where you might have to dig up buried feelings. You might go along with what others want just to make peace.

If you learned that you could get attention through manipulation or charm, you might use **dishonesty or deception** to get what you need.

You might make up stories that give you the emotional attention or connection that you crave. You might make promises that you can't or won't follow through on, hoping it will delay the abandonment. You might have a hard time being straightforward or honest since you only feel safe telling other people what they want to hear. You might spend a lot of time trying to convince people that they can't live without you. You might even figure out how to live a double life so you always have someone to fall back on.

If you learned that helping others or being self-reliant was the only way to fit in, then you might **sacrifice your needs to focus on others** so that you stay connected.

You might work hard to become independent and take care of others so you don't have to feel like a burden to anyone. You might feel like you have to be the life of the party to get people to stick around. You might spend your life doing service for others that they never asked for or may not need. You might give up your own goals or future to support someone else. You might work in a helping profession like first responding, nursing, or therapy to give your life purpose. You might feel like you have no value if you're not productive.

You might find yourself always looking for a guru to guide you through your life. You might feel like you have to hide or sneak your needs and walk on eggshells around everyone else. And you might only feel like you fit in if someone needs you.

For most of you, you'll probably have a few favorites that you use all the time. But it's likely you use different strategies at different times when the situation calls for it. Even if it makes you feel all over the place.

Emergency systems will take some pretty bold steps to survive. And love and connection can feel really life-or-death sometimes.

Now you know why.

It's the very first way to survive.

This is why you can find yourself in messy relationships over and over again as an adult.

When you grow up with certain survival strategies, **you will end up matching with other people who fit in with those patterns.**

In fact, you probably won't feel that great when people with healthy or secure attachment try to be in your life. Even though you logically want someone safe and consistent and supportive, your survival system just won't feel very comfortable with safe patterns. Their behaviors and actions will probably confuse you or make you feel suspicious. And you'll probably feel like a burden or guilty when they help you or take care of you.

Unfortunately, **your system learns to feel comfortable with people who are predictable to you and who you know how to fit in with.** But that doesn't automatically mean that they're safe or supportive.

Your safety matches are probably going to be glitchy since you had to connect with unsafe or unpredictable caregivers to survive. So you might feel comforted by tones, behaviors, and senses that remind you of who you grew up with. That's why you can feel a connection with people who are toxic for you and how you fail to notice all the red flags until things are super messy again.

Trauma bonds can be really hard this way.

When someone else understands what it's like to grow up the way you did, it can actually feel really great at first. It's not always easy to explain what it's like to be abandoned, or abused, or full of grief when the other person hasn't experienced this. And it might feel safer to open up about these things with someone who gets it.

So when you find someone who has been through similar situations, it can feel like your relationship is meant to be. Like you can talk about anything and that you'll finally be accepted for who you are. And you might even feel hopeful that your old wounds might finally start to heal.

Whether it's a friendship or romantic interest, it can feel really amazing to finally connect with someone in an authentic way.

The problem is that when **you both struggle with insecure relationships and/or trauma responses,** then it's going to be hard to keep all that from getting in the way of communicating and bonding in healthier ways to keep the relationship together.

It doesn't take long to **get stuck in old cycles** of anger, blaming, defensiveness, shutting down, feeling threatened, hiding your true feelings, overthinking, controlling, saying things you don't mean, and all the other ways your system gets stuck.

Usually this ends up with all your old wounds being ripped back open, feeling even more pain, and believing you're more unlovable and unworthy than ever before.

Now, in some situations, insecure relationships can actually be something that you experience for the first time in adulthood. In fact, it can be really confusing to understand the messy behaviors of your traumatized friends and/or partner when you grew up feeling pretty secure.

Hurtful words or false accusations from a once-trusted friend or lover can be pretty damaging and create a lot of shame. Or a divorce or break up out of nowhere can feel really confusing and painful. So you don't always have to grow up with these situations to get some experience with how they feel.

Further Study Recommendations:

The Power of Attachment: How to Create Deep and Lasting Intimate Relationships by Diane Poole Heller, PhD. This book can help you understand more about your attachment wounds and teaches you how to find more security in all your relationships.

Secure Love: Create A Relationship That Lasts a Lifetime by Julie Mennano, LMFT. This book can help you understand how insecure attachment relates to your romantic relationships and offers activities that can support connection and healing between you and your partner.

CHAPTER 46 – TRUST

Now that you understand how important connection is to feeling safe and how survival relationships can damage your trust, you might be feeling overwhelmed again.

As hard as it is, being honest about your childhood and relationships is an important step toward healing. Until you can clearly see the patterns that have harmed you, it will be difficult to know what needs to shift.

In fact, many of you probably know that you come from harmful patterns and keep spinning your wheels trying to get away from it. But if you haven't felt or experienced trust, how are you supposed to know what it looks like and where to find it?

Truthfully, this isn't an easy answer.

Reading about it in this book won't magically make trust easy or immediately bring healthy people into your life.

But it will start to give you a sense of what you might be looking for.

In order to trust, your relationships have to be safe and predictable. And something can only become predictable if you experience it over and over. That means that **trust takes time**.

It's also important to realize that being predictable doesn't always make something safe.

For example, you can predict that your boss will come in every day and make fun of your outfit. Or you can predict that your spouse will get defensive when you bring up money.

So safety and predictability have to go hand in hand.

Now, this might be a simple process if it was easy to always have respect, concern, love, and attention in long-term relationships. But that's not real life, even in the best of circumstances and the healthiest connections.

For most people, when you build relationships, you want to be seen and understood. You want to feel connected. Your system is looking for someone who you can coregulate with so that both of you can feel comfortable being yourselves with each other.

Again, this is true whether you're seeking friends or romantic interests. As relationships deepen, it can feel so nice to be your true self with someone else.

But we all go through terrible days, or weeks, or years. And survival moments can bring out our worst behaviors, especially with the people we trust the most. Shameful secrets can also surface.

And these are moments that can easily trigger old feelings of abandonment or rage. They can make you feel ashamed. They can push you to hurt before you are hurt or leave before you are left.

The truth is that **every relationship will have negative moments**. So the real test of building trust comes from learning how to resolve and repair issues in a way that creates safety and predictability for both people.

This might not make sense at first, but **vulnerability is the way that relationships can stay safe and predictable** like this.

Vulnerability is being able to expose your fears and hurts to another person and accept help and support to move forward.

When you've been through messy relationships, vulnerability will feel like the last possible thing that you want to do. In past relationships, these behaviors probably made things worse. Maybe people took the opportunity to shame or hurt you when you opened up to them. Maybe they took advantage of your fears to control or manipulate you.

Or maybe *you* did all these things to *them*.

And this is not okay.

You do not have to be vulnerable with anyone who uses your openness to hurt you or shame you or control you. And no one is required to do this when *you're* not a safe space for them either.

These behaviors show that there isn't a readiness or willingness to be able to repair issues together.

Being vulnerable with someone only works when both people are willing to be open with each other.

When two people work to be honest and vulnerable, they can build a relationship that's pretty safe and predictable. Even when things go wrong, they can genuinely apologize and repair instead of becoming resentful and holding things over each others' heads. They both take responsibility for making things work and sharing their needs or accepting help.

Here's the challenge though. **Vulnerability is risky.**

Vulnerability wouldn't feel vulnerable if you could always guess how the other person is going to respond. So **opening up can feel threatening and stressful** even in the best of situations.

Another challenge is that you will also have to learn how to be safe when others are vulnerable with you. When you can't offer being a safe place in return, **you can dead-end other people's attempts to deepen a relationship** without even realizing it.

Many times your own experiences with rejection will make it difficult to know how to accept vulnerability from someone else, especially when you've rarely seen it modeled in a healthy way.

Unfortunately, **vulnerability can feel impossible when you struggle with shame.**

Shame is the fear that you are bad. That no matter what happens, you will never be worthy of love.

If you have shame, your system will be terrified that vulnerability will expose your badness and the "truth" that you are unlovable. Your system will be way more sensitive to abandonment. You might think that others are threatening to leave, even when they aren't. So being vulnerable is going to be an extremely difficult step if you've been through a lot of survival.

Now, ironically, one of the best ways to work through shame is also with vulnerability.

This is a vicious cycle, though. If shame is going to make it hard to be vulnerable, but vulnerability is the way to heal shame, then it's difficult to know how to start.

But **being vulnerable doesn't have to be big and intense.** And you don't have to just dump all your secrets out at once to be vulnerable.

In fact, most vulnerability in relationships actually comes from practicing small bids for other people's attention and connection.

Bids for attention and connection are **moments where people reach out and try to connect with each other**. It's a small way to communicate that you want time and attention from someone.

You can learn a lot about safety and predictability when you see how others respond and engage with your small bids for attention.

This can be a daughter asking her dad to play Lego together. This can be a friend calling to share that she got her promotion. This can be a sister trying to race her brother home from school. This can be a spouse initiating sex. This can be a teenager wanting to talk about their crush.

Children usually learn how to use bids very early on. As they spend time playing, they learn the subtle give and take that is required to get their needs met in a way that keeps them connected.

If you learn that others will respond and engage with many of your bids for connection, you will feel more confident that someone will be available when you need them. It makes those relationships safe and predictable. That way it's easier to share the hard and deep stuff when you need to.

These small moments will also have a great impact on your system. Feeling secure and protected will calm your survival systems, and your reward system will release more connection and pleasure hormones.

But if you had to grow up too fast or didn't feel safe playing due to **complex trauma**, you probably **lost a lot of opportunities to**

practice bids and now you feel awkward not knowing how to easily interact with others.

It's also possible that your bids for attention went ignored or got mocked by your family, so your survival system ended up making vulnerability a danger match. Now you'll avoid reaching out at all costs and protect your inner world any way you can.

When you struggle with feeling safe in a relationship, you probably find yourself avoiding, running away, arguing, or criticizing a lot more than you would like. You might also try to control how others respond to you and bully or intimidate them, or you might even hide or punish yourself.

If this is your situation, there is hope.

With practice, your system can reset by learning how to give and receive bids for connection. This is usually easier when you can start somewhere that isn't too personal.

There is a lot on the line with personal relationships, and your system will be way more stressed about changing or trying new things with a close friend or family member than it will be about acquaintances or strangers.

Volunteering or joining an activity group or class can be a simple way to practice giving and receiving bids without putting as much personal risk on the line. Since playfulness is one of the natural ways to do this, the more enjoyable the activity is, the better.

Your local library or civic center will often have information about volunteer programs, or you can search online for opportunities using sites like UnitedWay.org or JustServe.org. As for community activities, there are yoga classes, church choirs, improv groups, gaming communities, music clubs, martial art studios, book clubs, theaters, exercise groups, drum circles, and many other activities.

Remember that coregulation is the first way that you learn to be safe. So when you can do activities with others that bring your bodies, voices, or energies into sync, it can help your system improve your safety networks and help you practice the skill of give and take.

You can even start with online groups if that feels easier right now. Online situations usually allow you to be anonymous, which can help you practice bids in a way that's not too overwhelming.

Gaming groups can be a nice way to start if that interests you. Role playing games like Dungeons and Dragons can be a great opportunity to learn relationship bids. Being able to play a character and express imaginary feelings can be a much safer way to feel out what it's like to be vulnerable.

Board game websites allow you to chat with others while you're playing. Online fan groups or support groups can help you find people with your same interests or challenges.

Of course, it's important to be safe online and be aware of any private information you're sharing or sending. Unfortunately, some people online can be good at faking trust and safety, so try to be mindful and take it slow.

Sometimes it's hard to care about being safe when you're overwhelmed with loneliness and survival. So, if you're not sure, go with your gut and get advice from a trusted friend, family member, or professional. You can always search up tips for staying safe online based on your age and the activities you're doing.

Now, if you do decide that you want to practice being vulnerable with your survival history, then you can always look for therapy groups, recovery groups, trauma-informed poetry slams, storytelling groups, drama therapy, healing ceremonies, or mindfulness workshops where it will be more appropriate to be open about your experiences and progress.

As you gain more practice in being open and vulnerable, it will be easier to bring these skills into the relationships that matter the most to you. It can also help you to form more meaningful relationships if you have struggled to create these in the past.

Again, if you're not ready to work on bids and vulnerability, that's okay. We're going to keep talking about things you can do to keep working with yourself in the meantime.

Further Study Recommendations:

Daring Greatly: How the Courage to Be Vulnerable Transforms the Way We Live, Love, Parent, and Lead by Brené Brown, PhD, MSW. This book can help you understand more about how vulnerability can help you to reduce shame.

The Relationship Cure: A Five-Step Guide to Strengthening Your Marriage, Family, and Friendships by John Gottman, PhD, and Joan DeClaire. This book can help you to understand more about using bids for connection and improving your relationship skills.

CHAPTER 47 – SEX

As we talk about trust, it's important to identify that sex will likely play a part in your connections and attachments in your romantic relationships.

Sexual intimacy can be another way to help your system regulate and feel connected.

You might think about sexual intimacy as an **advanced version of coregulation**.

During sex, your body actually takes advantage of your go-mode and slow-mode systems in the ebb and flow of the arousal experience. Adrenaline and go-mode can make your heart race and help your blood flow, and slow-mode can help your body to maintain control and timing.

Sex can be a pretty vulnerable setup, so it might be hard for some people to reach climax without a general sense of safety. Things like safe words, foreplay, asking for what you do and don't want, and respecting your partner's boundaries are all ways to help sex feel safe.

By keeping in sync with subtle energy changes and staying in touch with each other through the process, it allows your system to eventually reach orgasm and release one of the most potent mixes of reward hormones that your body can produce.

For most people, fulfilling climaxes come when you and your partner are tuned into yourselves and each other. That way everyone gets enjoyment and satisfaction.

When this ecstasy is achieved with a connected sexual partner, it allows your systems to coregulate in a very powerful way. The hormones that are released help your body feel blissful, connected, and satisfied. And the intimacy can reconfirm the safety and predictability of the relationship.

Interestingly, your reward system can actually continue to activate high levels of rewards even after many years of sex with the same partner.

If you and your partner spend time and energy investing in each other and working through challenges together outside of the bedroom, then you get to know and care for each other in deeper ways. This means that the relationship continues to evolve, and so does sexual intimacy. This ongoing growth keeps your reward hormones from tapping out over time.

Now, obviously, there will be ups and downs in this process for most people. Having kids, shifting hormone levels, going through health issues, break ups, and other changes will adjust what this looks like over the years. The importance of sex may shift throughout your lifetime.

Since trust and connection constantly change and grow, there's always potential to find new ways to have intimacy and rewards in your romantic relationships, with and without sex.

Unfortunately, **when you're stuck in survival, sexual satisfaction and intimacy can become difficult.**

When sex becomes the only way that your system is comfortable being vulnerable and intimate with a partner, then it's going to be **hard to stay fulfilled long term.**

When sex isn't paired with learning and growing, the satisfaction from your reward system will drop over time. When this happens, you might make up for this by adding new bedroom material or looking for a new partner to make things fresh again.

If you and your sexual partners are not looking for a deeper connection, then this may not be a problem. Unfortunately, many people find themselves in this pattern when they *are* looking for a deeper attachment and don't realize that they are missing other connection skills that can help the intimacy to continue to develop and stay fresh.

Another challenge with sexual intimacy is that the go-mode and slow-mode energy that comes up during arousal and orgasm can **trigger survival responses** that hijack your body.

This is especially true if you have a history of sexual abuse or assault. Since the go-mode and slow-mode responses can match stuck networks in your body, it can make it difficult not to activate survival responses during sex, even with a really safe partner.

This can also be complicated when your **insecure attachment patterns can make it hard to feel safe and trusting**.

Since your system can have a hard time staying in tune with other people and yourself, you might misread cues from the other person, or not even realize what you're feeling.

You might not be as interested in having sex as you thought. You might just be going along with it because you feel like you should or you don't want to disappoint the other person or be rejected.

In other cases, you might feel ashamed to show your arousal feelings or express your passion. You may feel guilty for your desires or worry that your preferences or needs might be mocked or rejected.

For other people, it's possible to **get hooked on quick fixes like porn or one-night stands** when you struggle to feel connected in your day-to-day relationships.

Your system intuitively knows that sex is a way to increase connection. So when you don't know how to actually feel close with someone, sexual quick fixes might seem to fill the void for a bit. But, long term, this could also leave you feeling even more lonely when you can't make any intimate connections over long periods of time.

In fact, if you haven't had a lot of good experiences with coregulation and giving and receiving bids, then porn and casual sex might trick your brain into thinking that this is *all* that there is to intimacy and attachment.

Unfortunately, this means that when you do have the opportunity for intimacy with someone you care about, your body may avoid connecting due to fear of rejection or abandonment. Your survival systems might also be so numb and desensitized that it's difficult to perform or stay in tune with yourself and your partner.

This can be extra challenging when your sexual rewards have tapped out and there's a gap between your anticipation and satisfaction.

Your system may get so focused on satisfying your intense pleasure needs that you don't realize the other person is receiving little to no enjoyment in the experience or that you're missing out on a deeper connection.

These issues are often why consent is a difficult topic.

It's pretty common for trauma bonded people to end up in **risky sexual situations**. A numbed out partner with a sexual rewards gap can be more pushy than they realize, and this can easily trigger someone with a trauma history, who becomes frozen and unable to speak up.

As you can imagine, this setup makes it easy for assault victims to blame themselves for not saying anything. And, on the other side, it can be difficult for an offender to realize that they didn't have consent the whole way through the experience.

This is why it's important to understand how other people look and respond when they're feeling distressed and numbed out. And to practice feeling the difference between someone who is moving forward and engaging with you versus pulling away, becoming protective, or shutting down.

Talking about consent without learning to read these signals won't do much to change harmful sexual behaviors.

If you feel like you need support with intimacy skills, **practicing bids for connection can help with building better bonds** with your partner, and with being more in sync with each other. Working to face and heal your stuck emergency networks will also be useful.

These interventions will allow your system to be more regulated, which will help you to be more in tune with each other during coregulation activities like sex and other forms of intimacy.

If needed, you can also seek support from a professional. Sex therapists are experienced with helping individuals and couples to improve intimacy and performance challenges.

And if you have been a victim of uncomfortable, non-consensual, or abusive sexual experiences, it can be helpful to work with a trauma-trained professional and/or victim advocate. There are many ways to reorganize these networks so that they are easier to tolerate and so that you can find safe ways to be intimate again. And, if needed, an advocate can walk you through the process of reporting sexual crimes.

You are not responsible for protecting someone who does not understand sexual consent. Even if they do need their own mental health support or trauma healing, that is something that *they* need to be responsible for. Although honesty may feel like a betrayal, it is actually an opportunity for that person to take accountability for their problems and get help or be required to get help.

Telling the truth about shameful or scary things is so hard. Some people may not believe you, which might make you doubt yourself or make you feel like you're making too big a deal of it all.

Sadly, when you finally say something, it's common for others to get awkward or critical because they feel helpless and aren't sure how to help you. Their own survival responses may come up, and they might avoid the conversation or gaslight you about your experience, especially when they don't know what to do. But these responses are about their fear and not you.

So do your best to find someone who will hear you and believe you if you are ready to be honest about your experience.

Further Study Recommendations:

Abused Boys: The Neglected Victims of Sexual Abuse by Mic Hunter. This book can help you understand more about the impact of sexual abuse on children. Although the author focuses more on abuse toward boys, the information is relevant for any victim of sexual abuse.

Come As You Are: Revised and Updated: The Surprising New Science That Will Transform Your Sex Life by Emily Nagoski, PhD. This book is mainly for women and gives basic information about sex and how to attend to your specific needs and body to improve intimacy.

Life, Reinvented: A Guide to Healing from Sexual Trauma for Survivors and Loved Ones by Erin Carpenter, LCSW. This book can help you work through traumas specifically related to sexual abuse.

Unwanted: How Sexual Brokenness Reveals Our Way to Healing by Jay Stringer. This book talks about unwanted sexual addictions or behaviors and how they are related to sexual traumas, shame, and insecure attachment. It can be a really helpful resource for overcoming shame to get out of the addiction cycle. Although it has a Christian perspective, the advice and information are useful for almost anyone and mainly relate to letting go of shame that is rooted in unforgiving religious beliefs.

Your Brain on Porn: Internet Pornography and the Emerging Science of Addiction by Gary Wilson. This book is for someone who is dealing with unwanted porn and masturbation habits and/or struggling with performance issues. This book is from a non-religious perspective and offers support and ideas for reducing use of quick-fix porn and masturbation habits to enhance long-term sexual satisfaction and performance.

CHAPTER 48 – RESHAPE

You're probably starting to realize that your system didn't get a chance to learn how to live before it had to survive. It can be hard to know how to move forward when you don't know what healthy connection feels like or even looks like.

You know all the things that haven't worked. You have a good idea of what you shouldn't do. But what do you actually work on? How do you know what's healthy or functional? How do you figure out any of this without a model? And you still might even have to figure out who you are to know any of this.

This is why moving forward and healing will likely include learning how to reparent yourself.

Reparenting is the process of **going back to the survival networks from your childhood and helping the younger versions of yourself reset your original emergency responses**.

Sometimes when things have gone pretty far off track, it can be helpful to go back to the beginning and reset.

This can be hard. As you're looking to change your survival patterns, it's easy to get stuck or overwhelmed.

Because of this, reparenting often works best with a trusted and competent professional who can help guide you through these networks.

But if you don't feel ready to get help in this process, there are still some ways that you can address this by yourself.

To prepare for doing this work, it can be important to learn about parenting techniques that support secure attachment. The Bonus Upgrade section has a chapter on parenting with quite a few book recommendations. There are also social media accounts and videos with parenting skills that model what these behaviors might look like.

These tools can help you to learn new patterns that you can bring to your networks.

As your cortex is learning how to listen, rest, be mindful, interrupt, reduce quick fixes, and even titrate, you are increasing your capacity to face these stuck networks and stay in control of your system. And, although this may take a long time, these skills, along with secure parenting techniques, can help you finally start to reshape and shift your survival responses.

To move on to this process, it's important that you have felt comfortable and safe while you have been practicing titration. You'll want to feel confident that you can experience the full impact of an emergency network without getting stuck in the memory or too overloaded by the feelings.

Once you have these pieces in place, you can actually learn how to **step into your stuck networks to support and guide the younger versions of yourself** through the emergencies that they are facing.

Although this might sound a little sci-fi, it's an amazingly effective way to help yourself reshape stuck networks.

Remember how stressful experiences are not traumatic if you are able to make it through all the steps of an emergency cycle? And that children can feel safe when an adult is around to protect them and guide them through these moments?

Well, this process can help you to bring this knowledge and your healthy boss skills to the younger versions of yourself that are stuck in your survival networks.

Depending on the situation, you can do a lot of different things to reshape old networks, but **coregulation will usually be an important focus** in these exercises.

You can actually take the regulation that you've built in one neural network and use that safe network to coregulate the survival network that is still stuck as your traumatized younger self.

This is another reason that practicing mindfulness is so powerful. You're creating regulated networks that can become strong enough to rescue and guide other networks through their trauma.

For situations of neglect or abandonment, you may just need to go back and **imagine holding yourself and letting the younger version of you know that everything is going to be okay and that they're not alone now.**

Show them that you're grown up and that you're strong enough to be with them and protect them.

Having the adult version of you care for and coregulate with your inner child is a great way to teach a stuck emergency network how to regulate for itself.

In memories where there was actually something dangerous or threatening present, **you might have to protect your younger self by standing up for them or helping them get away.**

Trying to figure out where they get stuck in the emergency plan can help you know what they missed. That way you can help them to complete the emergency response in a new way so the network can be filed away and regulated.

And sometimes **your wounded inner child might just need someone to listen and validate** that things have been hard.

Feeling seen and known and loved can sometimes be enough to reshape a stuck network.

Although this process can be extremely rewarding, it's definitely not easy.

Parenting is a tough job, even if it's for yourself. You might get overwhelmed at times and sucked into a time portal without warning. This can often be difficult to manage, so, if you keep getting hijacked, you can add interruptions and/or movement to help you stay anchored in the present and keep your cortex online.

As you interrupt the networks and face them, you are **encouraging your system to pull the stuck networks out of muscle memory and reshape them.**

When the network is no longer signaling and responding the way that it always has, your system will have the chance to take a second look at it.

This means that when the survival network moves out of muscle memory it will go back up to your working, or short-term, memory, where your cortex can weigh in on the situation. And this will allow the network to be filed away by the hippocampus in a new way.

If you remember, the hippocampus is like the assistant to your cortex, and it's in charge of saving long-term memories.

So, if your cortex is using healthy parenting techniques to reshape and resolve the experience, then your amygdala and your emergency networks will get the support and modeling they need to handle the experience and complete the stress cycle. Which means that your hippocampus and your muscle memory can sort out the files that have been left hanging.

This allows the feelings and sensations from your trauma to become a very small echo of what they used to be, and the network doesn't have to be stuck in your emotions and body anymore.

And, if there are parts of the memory that are important to keep in your survival networks, then your hippocampus and amygdala will sort out the difference, leave the real danger matches, and file away everything else.

After years of survival and so much energy, it can feel really amazing to bring your inner children back into your life and let some of the pain and fear dissolve away. Getting through every network will still take a while, but this is the part where you can usually feel that there's a light at the end of the tunnel.

I'm hoping you can stick with it until you get there. And if you can't, consider reaching out for help.

Further Study Recommendations:

Homecoming: Reclaiming and Championing Your Inner Child by John Bradshaw. This book has mindful activities to walk you through interacting with your inner child and repairing the relationship. This book was published in 1990 and the author uses some traditional language around family and gender, and discusses spirituality from a Christian view. Overall the tone is inclusive and may be useful even if it doesn't fully align with your values.

Inner Child Journaling Guide by Nate Postlethwait. https://natewrites.com/inner-child-journaling-guide. This guide can help you to become more aware of your inner children and offers ideas and activities for reconnecting with them.

Reconciliation: Healing the Inner Child by Thich Nhat Hanh. This book can also walk you through connecting with and repairing with your inner child. This book is from a Buddhist and mindfulness approach.

CHAPTER 49 – SECURE

Okay. As usual, go ahead and check in with yourself and see how you're doing with all of this.

Before we repeat our healthy boss activities, I want to walk you through a new activity.

Since it can be helpful to have a bit more support as you work toward the reparenting process, we're going to create a **Calm, Secure Space.**

This will be similar to Calm, Safe Space, but this place is going to be for the younger versions of you who are still stuck. This way your inner children can feel a bit more protected and stable until you're able to figure out how to reparent them.

Depending on how many times your inner child has been stuck or hurt, you might have many ages and versions of your younger self to work with. This might feel overwhelming.

So if it feels like you have quite a few of these wounded inner children, try not to focus too much on the individual kids. Just try to keep a general idea of them as a group. Feel free to keep them blurred out in your mind or have them wait out of sight until you finish setting everything up.

At this point, we're creating this space so that they can find connection and support with some ideal caregivers and give your system another break. This will also make it easier to work with them one at a time and not get overwhelmed as you are intentionally doing reparenting work.

So, to start off, I want you to think of a place that would be safe and enjoyable for children ages 0–12.

You'll probably want a place that allows the kids to be indoors and outdoors.

So let's start to think about what you would add to the indoor space so that it feels secure and calm for these kids.

Make sure that there are plenty of snacks, access to toilets, safe corners to hide in, water to drink, and activities to do.

Try to sense what your inner children might want to do in this space. Again, you can feel this out while they are just out of sight or blurry. Do they want a library, action figures, games, art supplies, stuffed animals, trains, etc?

Now think about the outdoor space. What would it look like? Would it be a fantasy place with talking animals or super powers? Would it be a forest, a desert, a city, a mountain, or outer space?

What kinds of activities would you add to this area? Are there games, bonfires, tree houses, pony rides, or a water park?

If it feels right, add some security to help everyone feel safe. You can create a giant force field or web to protect the space. Or place toys or animals or magic spells around the edges so they can keep guard.

Spend a few minutes putting everything into place and see how it feels. Once it feels good enough (not perfect) let's talk about caregivers.

I want you to start thinking about some people who you could trust to be in this space with your younger selves.

Do you have a grandparent or an ancestor who feels safe enough to take care of these kids and coregulate with them? Do you have an old teacher, babysitter, or mentor who can help these kids build trust? What about any of your friends or their families, or people from church, or someone from your kid's daycare?

As you decide who to invite, go ahead and bring these caregivers into the space and see how it feels to have them there.

If you weren't able to think of any safe adults in your personal life or you would like to add a few more adults in the space, then go ahead and see if there are other people who you might trust.

These can be celebrities like Dolly Parton, LeVar Burton, The Rock, or Mr. Rogers. They can be feel-good influencers on social media like Elyse Myers, Mychal Threets, Mercury Stardust, or Your Korean Dad. They could also be fictional characters like The Black Panther, Samwise Gamgee, Molly Weasley, The Muppets, Totoro, or Bluey's parents. For some of you, this could be spiritual support like a guardian angel, an animal guide, the Virgin Mary, or Mother Nature.

You can even invite a healed future version of yourself to help out if it's difficult to find anyone else you trust.

See how many caregivers you can find who you trust to invite into this Calm, Secure Space with your little ones.

Make sure that the caregivers understand that they will have to work on building trust with these children.

Ask them to crouch down to talk to the littles instead of towering over them. And let them know that it's not okay for the caregivers to get impatient or demanding with the children. Tell them that the kids are allowed to feel however they want and that they can express these feelings whenever and however they want to as long as they don't hurt themselves or others.

If you realize a caregiver doesn't fit or feel safe after a while, that's okay. You can uninvite them or send them somewhere else.

Start to notice where the different caregivers end up in the space. Make sure that there's enough help for all the ages. Create clones of your favorite helpers if you can't think of enough people who feel safe.

Try to find one or two caregivers who can be in charge of the baby areas. Put in bottles, diapers, cribs, and changing tables if you need to.

Identify which caregivers are going to make sure that everyone gets fed. See which caregivers will notice and sit by the kids who are struggling with big feelings or pain. Figure out who can listen to and be patient with the kids who have a lot of questions and want to talk. And have them regularly remind the kids that they can get food and water or go to the bathroom whenever they need to. And that they can ask a caregiver for help at any time.

If you feel like anything is missing, go ahead and add it in, or see if you can find a caregiver who can handle it.

Now, if you've been keeping the children out of sight, let the caregivers know that you are getting ready to leave the Calm, Secure Space and that they will be in charge now.

When you feel ready, come back to the space around you.

Once you feel all the way removed, go ahead and have the caregivers invite the kids to join them in the Calm, Secure Space. Check in with your body and see how you feel as this happens. If there's any stress, let the caregivers know that they can create or adjust anything to keep things safe and secure.

If it feels okay to check in once in a while, go ahead and observe things from a distance. How are the younger versions of yourself settling in? Does it take some of the weight off your shoulders or do you feel skeptical it will stay safe? Do you sense some excitement from your littles or do you feel stressed now that you are more aware of them?

If you're feeling a bit unsettled after this activity, it might help to imagine that this space is in its own universe or far away and that you can only get there by going through a specific door or portal. That way, the space might feel a bit more contained until you're ready to check in again.

Since your littles are being taken care of, it shouldn't be a problem to take a break from each other for a bit.

If you are still worried, you can set up a notification system in case the children need to get your attention or help. Try to make the signals gentle and not overwhelming. Maybe there are buttons that the kids can push to play different song clips in your head, or a remote where they can change the colors of the LED lights in your mind, or give them a phone that only sends memes to show how they are feeling.

That way you can know if something goes off while you're away. And if it does, you can just go through this same process to sort things out. Uninvite anyone who has become unsafe and keep adding or removing things from the space until it feels secure again.

Now, if this activity didn't seem to work for you, that's okay. The next upgrade will go through more tools to help settle your younger selves.

Either way, let's follow all this up with one of *your* mindful activities like Calm, Safe Space, Peaceful Flow, belly breathing, etc. Take a moment and see which one feels like a good fit for what you're feeling right now.

Then, as you begin your activity, notice how your system feels while you're working on this mindfulness and your littles are safely contained in their Calm, Secure Space.

Take as much time as you need and come back to the book when you're ready.

UPGRADE 7.0
RESTORING THE SYSTEM

CHAPTER 50 – PARTS

If you've made it this far in the book, you should be really proud of yourself.

We've gone over a lot and it can feel overwhelming to take it all in.

It might also be changing the way you see everything. Which can be hard too.

For all the relief and answers, there might be even more questions.

Hopefully, this final upgrade will bring it all together and give you some idea of what to expect along your healing journey.

Now that you know about all the different players and processes, we're going to look at the big picture again and discuss how you can reconnect and repair with your different players and networks.

Remember how your cortex and amygdala can end up working against each other? Or how survival networks can take over your system and throw you into time portals? Or how your brain can escape or distract you so you can cope with being overwhelmed?

Well, these processes are all part of something called dissociation.

Dissociation literally means that things are disconnected or not associated.

In this sense, we've been talking about dissociation all along. This is the word we use to explain when **different parts of your system become out of sync and struggle to communicate.**

As we've already talked about, **everyone will dissociate in their lifetime.** Quite a lot actually.

It's really normal.

It's like the times when you drive home from work and forget to pick up milk because you're on autopilot. Or when you yell at your sister even though you didn't think you were mad. Or when you binge 6 episodes of *The Office* instead of 1. Or when you mindlessly buy a donut at the gas station even though you had planned to go home and eat dinner.

These situations happen because your brain and body go through moments where the different networks aren't connecting or associating. This can be from autopilot or when your emergency teams or reward system take over, but it can also just be when your cortex needs a rest. So it takes a break from coordinating everything.

Everyone has moments where they run out of energy, lose focus, or flip into autopilot. There's nothing wrong with dissociating. It's just a normal part of being human.

But, as usual, **trauma and survival systems can make dissociation a lot more challenging**.

When someone goes through trauma and/or insecure attachment as a child, their nerve networks don't get much practice communicating and cooperating with each other. Their system is too focused on survival to work on big-picture coordination or organization.

And remember how the connection with your caregivers shapes and builds your networks and experiences? Well, if your family is outright dangerous or your caregivers are not doing a good enough job of protecting you, then your cortex doesn't get the training to bring it all together. And your nerve networks are kind of left hanging, and they don't get a lot of guidance on how to integrate and communicate with each other properly.

In these survival conditions, **your networks continue to grow and learn and survive, but they don't learn how to work together** very well.

Let's go to our school analogy to help explain this.

If the principal was still really new and the trainers weren't showing up when she needed help, then she would have a hard time knowing how to direct or organize anything. And she'll start guessing how to handle issues and making up rules as she goes.

As for the rest of the staff, they would just work on the things that they are assigned to do and focus on their own stuff. Some staff members might try to improve communication by forming groups or committees to get some things done, but it would still be very disjointed. Everyone would step on each other's toes, redo the same tasks, or try to avoid each other. Some staff might even try to boss other teams around or take over other people's jobs.

In the end, this disjointed system still might get stuff done and function okay because each person or team will just handle their roles and ignore everything else. But overall, this would still be hard to deal with since no one has enough of the big picture to be on the same page.

This is often what widespread dissociation looks like in the body and brain. Your system will learn to function by having **different networks and players handle specific issues instead of cooperating as a whole system**.

You've already learned a lot about how this dissociation works in the previous Upgrades as you've learned about your survival networks, reward system, and muscle memory.

These networks jump in whenever they're activated by certain triggers. And then they pull back when it's over. Since these networks don't have a big picture view and are only meant to handle something specific, these parts can have a hard time working together as a whole without a healthy connection with the cortex.

Sadly, though, dissociation and poor communication can also become an issue *within* your cortex. And this will make it even harder for your cortex to help all these parts work together.

Remember how the cortex takes many years to be fully formed? Well, the process of growing your cortex into one giant nerve center takes a long time and can be impacted by the things you go through in childhood.

In fact, although we have been comparing your cortex to the role of a principal, it's probably a better analogy if we compare your cortex to the whole admin team of a school.

A principal is not the only person who's responsible for the big picture and running the school every day. Most schools have assistant principals and deans and other admin staff that help the principal to keep everything and everyone on the same page.

When an admin team is working really well together, you may not notice how much each person is getting done in the background. You'll probably just see a principal who's getting credit for the efforts of a whole team.

Your cortex is similar. It's made up of a lot of different networks that work together to make up your big picture and on-purpose activity.

When you get good enough caregiving as a child and you feel protected, then all the networks that form your cortex will steadily grow as you go through different experiences and get regular guidance. In this situation, these different parts will work together as they grow to create one big nerve center that we call your cortex.

But, if you grow up in survival, then all the parts that create **your cortex will struggle to grow into one big, unified network.**

All the individual parts of your cortex will grow at different speeds and struggle to communicate because of all the survival interruptions, the lack of regular guidance, and having to handle situations that you don't really understand yet. This will make it hard for your cortex to function as a coordinated team.

Back in our school, if a new principal doesn't understand what her job is supposed to look like, then she will have a hard time organizing or directing anything.

Since the school still has to function and try to deal with big-picture stuff, members of the admin team will begin to step up and handle situations as they emerge.

In this setup, the admin team covers most of the principal and admin duties, but no one really holds all of the big picture and coordinates everything together.

The same setup can happen in your system if you went through ongoing or complex trauma as a child.

Your cortex will still be made up of all the same nerve networks (and may look normal on a brain scan), but the networks that have formed won't connect and coordinate with each other in the same way that they would in a less compartmentalized brain.

Since all these individual networks handle different things, **it's still possible for your system to function without coordination between the parts.** But this means that **your system may have to work harder to keep things together** since every task and thought and feeling is separated from each other and doesn't have access to the overall picture.

For some people, being divided into parts like this might present as masking.

Masking is what you do to **fit into the situations and people around you.** It's like putting on a different face or image depending on your environment.

To some extent, everyone masks like this at one time or another. Your body and brain learn how to act and behave in the different roles you have in your life. You will likely behave differently when you're at work versus when you are at home. Or between church and a sporting event.

Your body will have different modes for being with your spouse, your sister, your dad, your mom, your boss, or your friend. Even though you're still the same person, your system can adjust between different settings and people.

In a more integrated system, this will be more about adjusting your tone or your energy to match those around you. Like being more quiet and still at a funeral or more excited and talkative with friends. It won't really include changing your interests or personality from place to place.

But when your cortex has learned to survive by having different parts handle different situations, then your system might use masking to function. Your system will pull up the nerve network that has kept you safe in the past and that matches the setting. And, of course, this masking will turn into autopilot. So whichever network gets used to handling certain situations will be the one to always handle it.

Although this allows your system to intuitively cope with different situations, it can make it difficult to be aware of your own needs and experiences, especially when your system turns on autopilot to be whoever your system thinks you need to be to survive that moment. Staying connected with yourself can be challenging when you're always more aware of what's going on outside of you than what's inside of you.

When this is the only way you know how to function, then it's going to be hard to know who you are as a whole person. You might find that you're masking and compartmentalizing even when you're by yourself and in your safe relationships.

In other situations, dissociation can also lead to **challenges with executive functioning.**

This could look like having a lot of creativity and intelligence while also struggling to keep your system focused and coordinated. You might find yourself fixating on random things, doing 32 projects at once, being constantly late, procrastinating, feeling over or understimulated, having trouble following through, etc. And you can also struggle to notice basic things in your body that need attention like when you're feeling hungry, sick, or going through hormonal changes.

Since your system doesn't have a great handle on the cooperation between the different parts, your activities and actions can be really disjointed and disconnected, even though your parts are functional and talented in their separate areas.

In this way, your system still figures out how to thrive, even if it's a struggle to keep all your parts coordinated together. (If you're interested, Chapter F in the Bonus Upgrade can offer more information on how survival and neurodivergence often go hand in hand.)

At the most acute level, this lack of big-picture organization can show up as **dissociative identity disorder** or DID. This is when someone has such compartmentalized networks that they show up as **multiple personalities.**

When the neural networks in your system grow very separately and with very little communication, they learn to fully function on their own.

This usually happens when a young child goes through pretty tough trauma. Their networks seem to stay dissociated and out of contact so that the entire experience of the trauma never has to be felt all together. And, although these networks will continue to grow and develop, many of them will more or less stay completely separate and dissociated from each other.

Over time, these separate networks develop enough to become their own individual personalities and usually have names. Many people refer to these as parts or alters. Each part can often take control of the body and the mind when they want to. And all together the different parts organize and manage the system by handling their specific roles.

Sometimes this means that there is a main network or personality who takes on the role of being a host to the outside world. (This is kind of like the principal, even though other parts are handling a lot of big picture stuff too). This hosting network is often referred to as the apparently normal part or ANP.

But sometimes having multiple personalities means that you have many different parts who take turns (or hijack) to lead the system. In these cases, you don't end up with one consistent host.

In the mental health world, this **hosting, or taking over control of the body and mind** is usually called **fronting**.

DID experiences are different from person to person. Some parts might be aware of the other parts, and some might not.

Many people with DID can lose track of time or have blank spots in their memories during the times when different parts or personalities are fronting. They may be surprised when their friends tell them about something that happened and they don't remember. They can also feel confused when the dishes are done or their book has moved and they don't remember doing it. Since this is the way their system has always worked, it may not feel that concerning or unusual.

Believe it or not, **it's possible to live a very functional life this way,** and you may not find out you've been living with separate parts until something comes along to throw your system out of balance.

There are a lot of different ways that disconnection and dissociation can exist. This is why **there can be such a wide spectrum of how parts can show up** from person to person.

It's so dependent on how you grew up, the trauma you experienced, how helpful your caregivers were in training your system, how connected you were to others, and lots of other factors.

Now, whether you experience masking, executive functioning challenges, DID, or something different, dissociation is usually the most obvious when you look at yourself in the mirror and feel that something is off.

Some of your parts can get stuck in different ages and timelines, so they often expect to look different than how you do now. It can be confusing to see the image of yourself reflected in the mirror when a part of you expects to see something else.

You might seem too old, too young, too edgy, or too boring. You might feel surprised by your gender or body shape. And you may even feel hatred or loathing as you catch sight of yourself.

With a lot of different networks doing their own thing and taking over the system randomly, it's possible to end up feeling pretty fragmented, even if you don't have DID.

In fact, it's hard for many people to feel organized with the way that we live life in our modern world. With millions of choices and options, and thousands of things to care about, and living life at top speed, it's a wonder that most body systems are functioning as well as they do.

Most people experience dissociation at some level because of how fragmented everyday life can be. But it's much more pronounced when you've been through ongoing trauma. It's hard to be associated with yourself when your system had to develop during survival.

Further Study Recommendations:

Dissociation Made Simple: A Stigma-Free Guide to Embracing Your Dissociative Mind and Navigating Daily Life by Jamie Marich, PhD. This book is a great resource to understanding the ways that people can experience dissociation and offers suggestions on how to approach working with dissociation in your system.

System Speak, Podcast by Emma Sunshaw, Emily Christensen, PhD, et al. This podcast is the personal experience of a woman who is diagnosed with DID and is also a licensed clinical counselor. The podcast offers the first-hand experiences of many of her parts as well as many episodes with clinical explanations and interviews. The podcast is run by Emma, a teenage part. Dr. Christensen, her counselor part, makes guest appearances to explain concepts and interview leading mental health experts about dissociation.

CHAPTER 51 – PROTECTORS

Now that you understand more about dissociation, we're going to talk about how these compartmentalized networks can become so divided and defensive that they get in the way of healing and changing.

As you've already learned, if one of your survival networks can't resolve a threat and doesn't know how to complete the stress cycle, it will get stuck. And if your body can't find a way to resolve this network, it will have to find other ways to stay safe.

We've already talked a bit about how this might work. Your system might get aggressive and fight when you can't run away. Or you might stay busy when you feel out of control. Or maybe you take care of others when they aren't taking care of you. Or you may think up clever ways to avoid stress or people please so the threats rarely come up. Or you might shut down when you can't stop panicking.

These **backup emergency responses will begin to pop up and try to protect your system when other responses are failing** to help you feel safe and in control.

Many times, this won't be too much of a problem since your body will find a different way to handle the stress. And it can get your system back on track if it helps you figure out how to resolve threats in a new way.

But, of course, this can look much different in a traumatized system.

The more often you have to deal with threats that you can't resolve, the more often you'll have to search for another way to survive. So if you grow up with unsafe adults, or get stuck in stressful experiences over and over, your body will try out a lot of responses and come up with a lot of strategies to try and keep you safe.

And, of course, as these responses and strategies are repeated, they can become strengthened and moved into autopilot. Which means that many of these networks get separated and dissociated from each other and the big picture.

When your body has a ton of survival responses that are disconnected from each other, things can get overwhelming pretty quickly. As **backup emergency networks begin to pile up on each other**, they can **pull your system in many directions**. And they can encourage your body to **respond in inappropriate ways** when they don't have access to the whole picture.

Let's go back to the school to explain this. Imagine that we're back in a school where there has been a lot of danger, and the staff and students are struggling to communicate as a whole. With everyone feeling on edge and struggling to trust that they're safe, it will be hard to get the whole school on the same page when threats keep popping up.

The security team, the principal, the admin staff, the teachers, and the students might all have their own ideas about what will keep them all safe. And many people will start to tune out the directions from the emergency teams or other leaders since these plans have failed in the past.

So when a situation comes up, it's possible that every team or classroom decides to handle the situation a different way. You may have a school full of people running, shouting directions, hiding, evacuating, fighting, or even going on with class as they pretend everything is fine.

Although everyone feels that their reaction is the right thing to do in the moment, nothing is really going to help much if the whole system isn't on board with the same plan. And the school will never really get a handle on staying safe if there isn't enough trust and communication to work together on anything.

The same thing can happen in your system.

Your body and brain can develop dozens of survival responses that take over during different situations depending on what's going on. Sometimes your system will get taken over by one extreme plan, only to be pulled in a totally different direction soon after.

As we discussed in the last chapter this can show up as masking, compartmentalizing, and/or forming different identities.

And many times these divisions can cause your system to get pulled in so many directions at once that your body freezes up or shuts down when the signals get too chaotic.

Let's look at how this may happen.

Let's say that you got bullied in the 3rd grade. Instinctively, your system feels like finding a protector would keep you safe, so you ask your teacher for help. But instead of offering protection or guidance, your teacher doesn't take your fear seriously and they tell you to figure it out.

This means that your system now has to find another strategy for protecting you. As a result, the next time the bully comes around, another survival network hijacks your system and pushes you to fight. But instead of being able to protect yourself, you get a black eye and detention.

And now two different emergency responses have gotten stuck because the situation hasn't been resolved yet. The bully is still harassing you, the adults aren't protecting you, and fighting just made it worse. But it's hard to find other ways to protect yourself when you're 9 years old. So you keep trying to run away, or go back to fighting when you have to.

But now you're worried about fighting because you don't want to disappoint the adults who are helping you survive. So a part of your cortex might start criticizing you for fighting, hoping it'll shut down your anger to protect you from getting in trouble again. And then another survival part might jump in to numb out your find a protector response since that plan failed and the adults now see you as aggressive.

Eventually another part might try and protect you by getting sick every morning to keep you from going to school where you're not safe. It might also be a strategy to get the attention of your caregivers so that they can see you're having a hard time.

Now you have protective responses coming from your cortex, amygdala, reward system, and muscle memory that all get triggered by the same situations, feelings, and memories.

Many years later, you might find yourself being pulled back and forth by these same survival responses, even though your bully is long gone and these reactions are making life harder.

Maybe you have to throw up before a stressful work presentation. Or you get sick whenever you're feeling neglected by your family or friends. Maybe you have an inner critic that constantly shames you about your anger. You could also have a part that pushes you to shut down every time you think about asking for help. And it may not be obvious these responses became so strong because of being bullied in grade school.

Again, whether this shows up as masking, compartmentalizing, or different identities, **your system gets so piled up with these protections that it loses sight of the original experiences** that got everything stuck to begin with. And the more these responses pile up, the harder it is to break through and track down how it all started.

But going back to the beginning is a really important step because there is an inner child at the heart of these original traumas who is still lost and left behind. And although your protector parts pile up because they're trying to defend these inner children, they can also be part of the reason these wounds are getting worse.

Your protector parts had to make hard choices to survive. Maybe they learned to bury and neglect your inner children to keep from being a bother to adults. Other protectors may have been convinced that the only way to save you was through discipline, control, and criticism. And some protectors may have learned to overthink and avoid everything to keep from triggering these wounds.

Since these are not perfect protections, your system also had to develop other protectors to keep things in balance. Maybe these protectors got angry so you didn't die from having your needs neglected. Other parts may have procrastinated doing chores so you didn't drain your already exhausted body. And other parts may have shut down your system to lie in bed all week when your body got too overloaded with anxiety.

Now these protective parts constantly battle each other trying to protect the system.

So your protector parts go around pulling your system back and forth between avoidance and anger, or perfection and procrastination, or anxiety and depression.

The challenge now is that **these parts can also get in the way as you're trying to heal**. They have been piled up around the original memories for so long that they get activated and protective the second you try to reconnect with your past. And it's hard to track down your inner children and get to the roots of all your experiences if these protective networks are constantly on the defensive and drawing attention away from your wounds.

If you keep finding yourself in these kinds of tug-of-wars, then **your healing process might include working with these protector parts to get past the defenses** so that you can reconnect with and reparent your inner children.

Since you've already been taking steps to be a healthier boss by listening to your system and being more in tune, working with these protective networks won't be as difficult as it might seem.

As we discussed before in our school analogy, a healthy principal will get to know her teams and learn about their unique strengths and challenges and their roles in the organization. As she understands their view, she can meet people where they are at to help them see the bigger picture. That way she can figure out ways that they can better fit into the system, work alongside others, and feel more satisfied with their roles.

You can use this same process to work with the parts of you that feel piled up and out of sync.

In most cases, these networks are more open to reconnect than you might realize. Especially if you're trying to listen instead of direct. They will often be able to adjust their protections and reactions as you engage with them. This becomes another way to work with and reset your stuck survival networks.

If you **take the time to understand what they are protecting and help them reconnect to the bigger picture**, you can figure out more effective ways for them to support the system moving forward.

To start this process, you can use the following mindfulness activity called **Get to Know Your Protectors:**

Think of a part that feels like it's been getting in the way lately.

Maybe it's your inner critic, a resentful part, a perfectionist, a blaming part, or your show-off. It could also be a part that zones out or scrolls social media all day.

As you connect with this part, try to imagine what it might look like or feel like. It could be a color, a shape, a person, a character, an animal, or whatever comes to your mind.

Once you have an idea of what it seems like, try to figure out how you feel toward it.

If you notice any uncomfortable feelings toward this part, ask those feelings to step aside for a moment.

In fact, these are likely other protector parts that are in a tug-of-war or pileup with the one you're trying to tune in to. So, it might be helpful to write down a few words about the feeling that you are asking to step away. That way you can keep track of the parts that are stepping aside in case you want to repeat this process and connect with them later.

Keep repeating this process until all the uncomfortable feelings have stepped away and you've written them down. Then go back to the part you started with and see how you're feeling about them. If you keep finding uncomfortable feelings, just keep asking those parts to step aside and write them down.

Once you feel more comfortable with and connected to the original part, then you can start a conversation by asking them how they are trying to protect you.

If you don't get an answer, that's okay. See if you can feel anything about them. If they don't trust you, acknowledge that. If they aren't ready to talk, let them know you're willing to be patient.

You can start with easier questions as a way to start building connection and trust. Ask them how old they are. Ask them about their interests or what's important to them. Ask them about their favorite snacks, movies, or books.

You might want to tell them that you know things have been messy and you're trying to become a better boss. Let them know you're around if they want to offer any info or feedback. You can even offer them a gift or their own Calm, Safe Space if that feels like something they would appreciate.

If they do have something to share but don't know how, see if they can send it in images, feelings, or memories. If they feel young, you might want to sit down with a real-life sketchbook or coloring book and see if they want to share some things through art.

Do your best to stay present by using your mindfulness skills. Since the info may be difficult to sit with, it may help to play these shared feelings or messages as if they are on a black and white TV screen. You can also turn down the volume of the emotions or do some simple movements as these messages are shared. This can help you feel less overwhelmed during this process.

Now, if you *do* get an answer, and it feels okay to keep going, ask them why they started protecting you this way and how long ago. Keep using images, feelings or memories to communicate the answers if that's needed.

Ask them if they know how old you are right now. If not, how old do they think you are? This answer might surprise you.

As you listen, try to stay regulated in your body. See if you can accept the answers and information you receive without arguing or getting defensive. If that does start happening, try to find out which parts are getting defensive or protective and ask them to step aside again. You can let them know that you have been making a list of each part and you'll be coming to check in with them soon.

Once things feel settled again, go back to your original conversation.

If it feels possible, offer some validation or gratitude that this part has really been working hard to protect you. And if it seems genuine, you may want to apologize for not recognizing or appreciating what this part has been doing all these years.

If it feels okay for both of you, let the part know that you're trying to reorganize things in a way that's functional and peaceful for the whole system. Ask the part if they want to do something different or if they need a break.

From this point, the part can decide if they're ready to look at new options, and you can both figure out what that looks like. (It's okay if they're not ready right away and need some time to think.)

Maybe they always feel pressured to take care of friends and family, and now they realize that they would rather go to the Calm, Secure Space and help take care of you and your younger parts. Or maybe instead of always criticizing, they want to take a break in their own safe space in the mountains or on a beach. Or maybe your rescuer part wants to stick around and be a support for you as you get to know the other parts in your system.

If the part isn't sure what they want to do yet, see if they need a snack, or a nap, or some encouraging words in the meantime. Let them know that they can tell you when they're ready to decide. They might need some time to let go or recognize that things need to be updated.

Once you feel like the part is more settled, check in with your body and do any calming activities you might need. This process can be more draining than it seems. Getting different networks to work together takes a *lot* of energy.

When you have energy again, you can repeat this process with any other parts that are ready. Keeping a list of the uncomfortable feelings that come up is a great way to keep track of all the parts that are trying to protect you.

Try to go through the list slowly. Use the one-thing-at-a-time method to keep from getting ahead of yourself.

You might find that some **parts need to make peace with each other** and may need help to see that they have the same goals, just with different ideas on how to get there.

As you are able to do this process with more of your protective parts, you may find that a few things fall into place and you **develop a natural curiosity** about these parts. You can also find that you **feel more compassionate or connected** with these parts and get a sense of what it feels like to **work together** and be a little more whole.

You might even be surprised to realize that some of your protector parts aren't that new to you. It's totally possible for parts to develop real voices and take shape in your senses. So you might discover that your intrusive thoughts and feelings have actually been communications from your parts all along.

It may feel kind of silly or weird at first to work with these parts or networks as if you're talking with other people. But it can be surprising how natural it feels once you get started.

Being able to do this doesn't always mean that you need a DID diagnosis. It's just how bodies work. We're all made up of parts. We all have cortexes, reward systems, and amygdalas that have very different priorities and manage different networks. They're bound to disagree about what you need from time to time. And survival only adds to these divisions and disconnections.

Not to mention that your nerve networks hold emotions, memories, senses, body responses, and thoughts. So each of **these networks make up a small piece of your overall story and identity**. And they all have a very real individual experience while also being part of who you are as a whole.

Your system is just like a school that is one organization made up of a lot of teams. It's important to know if the math department has been covering all the English classes or if the school nurses have been filling in as the deans. Even if it works okay, it's easier for everyone when they are working in a situation where they feel qualified and comfortable.

Now, **if you do have DID, this process can also work for you.** Each alter or personality can learn that they are part of a system (if they don't already know). And they will usually want to help make the system more organized. The difficulty here is that it may be tough to connect with the parts that have become fully dissociated from the rest of the system.

If it's helpful, there are **apps and journals** that are built to allow parts to write things down so that they can share more about themselves with the whole system even when they're disconnected from each other.

Another thing to be aware of in this process is that there can be some protectors who feel really aggressive or scary. Sometimes these are called **persecutor parts** because they **take on the roles of past abusers and their toxic behaviors**. Even these parts think they're helping you because that was how "protection" and "care" were modeled to you. But it can be pretty hard to face these parts because they can feel extremely threatening.

Since many of these parts develop when you are young, they can be a direct mirror of abusive and harmful behaviors. Although they will feel scary or shameful, even these parts can let go of the old patterns and find peace as your system learns how to work together again.

Now, hopefully it's obvious that these processes will be much easier and feel a lot safer with a trusted professional. It's pretty complicated to do all this on your own. Chapter 56 and the Appendix can offer ideas for finding support and the types of care you might want to look for if you are feeling ready.

Further Study Recommendations:

Easy Ego State Interventions: Strategies for Working with Parts by Robin Shapiro. Although this book is written for therapists, it can be helpful to understand more about your parts and how to work with them.

No Bad Parts: How the Internal Family Systems Model Changes Everything by Richard Schwartz, PhD. This book is written by the creator of Internal Family Systems (IFS) and has more info and support to help you get to know your protector parts and begin understanding your inner system.

Shadow Work journals may also be helpful if you need more guidance and structure as you get to know your parts. You can easily find these in app or book form through an online search.

CHAPTER 52 – UNRAVEL

Now that you understand how deep these protections and defenses can be and how far back they might go, I want you to know that the process of healing can feel a lot like **unraveling**.

As you slowly start to **pull things apart and explore your stuck networks**, you're going to find that this journey isn't all that straightforward. It often feels worse before it gets better.

If we go back to our school we can imagine that the principal of a disjointed system will want to find out what's been going wrong and repair the issues. She will have to work past all the drama and defensiveness to figure out what's at the root of the chaos.

The principal will usually have to listen to and sit with a lot of feedback before she can even get to the original problems. And then she has to make sure that she's keeping in touch with everyone as things adjust so the different teams are getting their needs met and aren't getting lost again in the big picture.

Unless everyone is on board, it will be hard to make changes without ongoing fights and resistance. And it can take even longer for everyone to trust that the reorganization is working well and benefiting them.

The same thing is true with your brain and body.

In order to heal your system, you will have to be open to hearing from all your parts and sitting with the discomfort, pain, anger, and distress of all their experiences.

Although this is difficult, you can **help each part to unlearn and unravel the survival responses that are no longer working** for them and help them to find a better sense of belonging in your system. Lowering these protections and defenses will also make it easier to **reconnect with your wounded inner children** and allow you to reparent them in a more settled environment.

This process can take a lot of time and effort. It will push you to explore your identity, relationships, expectations, ideals, and fantasies. You'll also have to face the truth about abuse, pain, losses, betrayal, failures, and your limits. It can get pretty overwhelming pretty quickly.

Plus, until you improve the connection with your protective networks, they will keep defending and distracting you from this process, especially when things get scary or difficult.

Even if your body feels miserable most days, your parts have still gotten used to the way things are. So your system is going to feel nervous about shaking things up.

Facing the truth of how things really are (and always have been) might feel relieving in some ways, but it can also feel really overwhelming in other ways. Especially after many years of numbing and avoidance.

This is why grieving will be a big part of your healing process.

Grief is the feeling you experience when you lose something or someone that has been important to you. And everything you've learned in this book has been preparing you to be able to sit with and face your grief.

Death is usually the most obvious form of loss, but you can grieve the loss of all sorts of things. Grief can come from breakups, divorce, getting fired, becoming disabled, losing a pet, and many other experiences.

As you work to unravel your protections and heal your wounded inner parts, many things will rise to the surface that will remind you of what you have lost or missed out on over the years. And since your system didn't know how to handle these losses when they first came up, your protective parts stepped in to disconnect and distract from the pain.

So part of the process of **healing your networks will require you to face the losses** you've experienced from survival as well as **the grief and pain at the heart of your original wounds.**

You may have to face the grief of being abandoned, betrayed, or rejected. Grief might come up when you realize how much you and your family have lost because of trauma. Maybe you have to sit with the disappointment of failures, missed opportunities, never getting what you want, realizing you have limits, or all your broken relationships. You can feel upset about not being who you thought you were or about the things you never had.

When you think about how neurons work, grief of any kind shows us that there is a real, physical unraveling in your system as you go through loss.

Since you build networks in your body that grow and connect in really specific ways, **your body will literally have to undo and reshape nerve connections** as things change.

So when you begin to work on reorganizing your parts and undoing stuck patterns in your life, this will cause your nerves and neurons to begin unraveling too. Some of your networks will weaken and may even die off from suddenly not being activated in the same ways.

There can be a lot of confusion and pain that surfaces as your networks unravel and as you face the traumas and losses that you've been burying all this time.

It's probably obvious that **the unraveling process can also activate your survival systems**. Your networks will be left with uncertainty and stress as you let go of the behaviors, thoughts, and feelings that have been on autopilot and have helped your life to feel predictable.

Mirror neurons can make this hard too, since many of your networks can become attached to people and patterns outside of you. So an unexpected loss from abandonment, divorce, or the death of a loved one or a pet can sometimes begin the unraveling process before you really feel ready to face everything.

If a lot of your safety files have been tied to these relationships, **your networks can struggle to stay regulated** when these individuals are suddenly not in your life anymore.

Many of your muscle memories will be interrupted because something is missing that used to be there. And simple, everyday tasks will make it painfully obvious that their part in your network is missing.

It makes so much sense that you feel like parts of you are dying when you lose someone. They are. Major networks will start to unravel and fall apart as everything changes. This can be true even if your feelings were complicated towards each other when you were together.

Grief like this is so difficult because most people do not want to let go of the things or people they have loved or depended on. They do not want these memories to fade or die off, so they will continue to activate the memories to try to keep those feelings alive. Most people would much rather sit with grief than give up the memories. And there is nothing wrong with this.

But this is also one of the reasons why you might go back to the same bad relationships or quick fixes that you keep trying to leave. When things fall apart, it's hard to keep your system from going back to something that used to feel regulating or rewarding, even if it's toxic or painful now.

Unfortunately, you will often have the same feelings as your system unravels. **The way things have always been is often more familiar and comfortable.** Your old survival patterns are easier to predict and trust than a wide open future you haven't experienced yet.

So it might be confusing when it's hard to let go of patterns that have been harming you.

The grieving process can also feel difficult because you don't know where things are headed. It will feel scary and overwhelming to watch your system unravel and not be sure that you'll have anything left to rebuild with. And when you haven't had a lot of experience with things working out in the past, your system will struggle to feel confident that it's all for the best.

Think about our school again. If the principal decides to make some major changes to the school, it's going to look messy at first. Roles might be changed, departments might be reworked, schedules might adjust, and it's not going to feel comfortable right away.

Some teams might forget the new processes and go back to old habits. Some adjustments might fail and need to be reworked again. And it might take the whole school a while to be coordinated and functional.

Your system is similar.

As you go through these changes, it's going to look sloppy at first. You're going to be undoing networks that got stuck when you were 4, or 13, or 21. And you might feel embarrassed that you have to go back and unlearn and relearn basic things that you missed back then.

You will probably be really bad at some things for a while. Just because you know that losing your temper isn't helping anything, it doesn't mean that you automatically know better ways to communicate. It will take a lot of trial and error to rebuild new networks that work for you.

And actually, this process will be exhausting.

Although many people will start to feel better as things become unraveled and reset, they are also surprised by how raw and tired they feel.

When you get to the roots of the pain and the trauma, it will probably be relieving but also a little scary and uncomfortable to feel so exposed. It also takes a lot of energy to grieve and sit with all the pain.

In fact, remember how muscle memory is one of the ways that your body manages energy? Since your old networks run on autopilot, they don't take too much energy or effort.

So when you're in this healing process and unraveling a bunch of autopilot networks, the actions and tasks that used to be easy are now going to take a lot more energy. **Everything will require more on-purpose thinking and effort than it used to.** You won't be able to fall back on old habits as much as you did before.

It might surprise you how many regular, everyday tasks are impacted by reorganizing some of the stuck places in your system.

So, it's okay if you're afraid to move forward in this process right now.

The timing can be really important. Some people get there when their life is steadier and they have the support they need. Some people get there when everything has fallen apart and they know that it couldn't get any worse.

Some people get there when the right person comes into their life. This could be someone supportive who helps you to feel safe about revealing your shame and fear. Or it could be someone who treats you so badly that you realize something needs to change.

In some cases, your system doesn't even give you a choice. When things get bad enough, your body and brain will fall apart anyway. As terrible as this feels, sometimes it's the way that your system forces you to face your limits and get help.

You might be unable to get out of bed or leave your house, or maybe you have to be put on suicide watch, or you could even be stealing from your family to get drugs.

The people around you might see these signs as weaknesses or flaws. But they are clearly signs that survival has overtaken you and your system. *And* that your family and community support systems have had inadequate resources and/or limited capacity to meet your needs.

In a weird way, these moments also protect you. At a certain point, you can't keep burying everything or pretending that you're okay when you're not. And falling apart is the way that your system exposes your limits and the limits of your support network.

The truth is that this process never looks exactly the same for anyone. You're the only one who can know if it's time. And it's important to trust those feelings and signals. Your system has been protecting you for all these years. It actually has a pretty good handle on what you're ready for, even when it feels fully dysfunctional.

Your system doesn't want to suffer, and it *does* want to heal. The more you can work with yourself and not against yourself, the less exhausting this will be in the long run.

Further Study Recommendations:

Moving On Doesn't Mean Letting Go by Gina Moffa, LCSW. This book can help you navigate the process of grief no matter what you're grieving for.

When Things Fall Apart: Heart Advice for Difficult Times by Pema Chödrön. This book uses a Buddhist approach to discuss the experience of falling apart and helps you to feel more confident about sitting with and facing the difficult feelings of this process.

CHAPTER 53 – BOUNDARIES

One of the hard parts about unraveling is that you don't always have the space and time to do this. Most people have jobs and families and lives that make it hard to find the room to pull things apart and reset.

So one of the tasks of healing that can be really important is learning boundaries.

Creating boundaries for yourself can give you some of the space and protection you need to unravel and heal. They can also help you to limit your energy and keep you from becoming drained.

Many people think boundaries are the demands that you make for other people to do certain things.

That's not really so much what boundaries are about.

Boundaries are **protections that you create for yourself**. Boundaries are the way that you can make things safe and predictable for you and your relationships.

Unfortunately, many people get walls and boundaries confused.

Walls, in relationships, are really just protections that keep people out. They never really help people know how to feel invited and safely connect, which doesn't really create any change.

Let's go back to the school analogy to understand this.

If a school wants to have visitors but has had a lot of experience with people coming in and being threatening, then they will have to create boundaries.

To do this, they will post a sign outside of the gates that tells visitors what rules they have to follow to be welcome on the property. Generally, these rules will be about safety. Usually they will identify that weapons are not allowed inside the gates or that threatening behaviors will not be tolerated.

This sign will also explain what happens if these rules are broken. Most of the time breaking these rules will get you removed from the building and the property.

Boundaries for humans are a lot like this.

In your relationships, it will be important to know how you want to be treated. And this will include your relationship with yourself.

By having boundaries, you make it clear to yourself and others what things you will and will not tolerate.

But sometimes this is a tricky process. Before you can know how to set up boundaries with others, you need to have a **clear idea of what your limits are**.

It's hard to build a fence and post a boundary sign when you don't even know the property lines.

When you grow up with messy relationships and insecure attachments, your system can actually be confused about where you end and other people begin.

For example, you might still believe that it's your job to make other people happy. Or you might think it's other people's job to make *you* happy. Or you might expect other people to always agree with you. Or you might feel like your needs are much less important than other people's needs.

Honestly, these are difficult lines to figure out sometimes. If this is how you've always lived, it's going to be hard to know how to see things any differently.

It's not like you can go to the county office and request a map.

Part of the unraveling process can begin to teach you where your boundaries need to be.

Your protective parts are often picking up the slack for your lack of boundaries. When you aren't being mindful of your limits and communicating your needs, your protective parts are forced to take over when things get out of hand.

This means that getting to know your protective networks will help you to recognize what your limits are and what needs haven't been getting met. That way you can figure out how to intentionally protect and take care of yourself before your survival systems have to do it for you.

Figuring out how to say "no" will often go a long way toward protecting yourself and your parts. Especially as you need time and space to unravel and focus on yourself.

So, **taking the time to recognize your own feelings and needs** will be an important step. This will help you to discover the lay of your own land and help you be more honest with yourself about your limits.

And this knowledge will then give you the clarity to **better identify where you end and others begin.**

There's a very simple mindfulness exercise that might help with this process. It's called **Boundary Flow**.

Remember how we use color, shape, temperature, texture, and other descriptions to explain energy in your body? Well, this same type of exercise can help you imagine the energy of yourself and those around you to get a better idea of what's going on between the borders of you and someone else.

Start with someone who feels safe. Imagine what their energy looks like and feels like. Then imagine your own energy. If the two energies feel kind of similar, try to focus on the details that make their energy different from yours.

Next, notice how both of your energies interact with each other when you imagine being around them. There's no right way for this to look or feel. Every relationship is different.

Now, think of someone who feels kind of challenging for you. Maybe don't start with your worst relationship, though. Think of someone a *little* challenging. Imagine your energy and their energy and how they look when you're next to each other. What happens? Again, there's no right way for this to look or feel.

If you begin to compare these two experiences, you might be able to notice some clear differences about how the energies connect or interact.

With a safer person, you might notice that the energies seem more balanced. Maybe the energies flow equally between both of you. Maybe the energies look and feel like a secure cable that connects you both. Maybe as the energies touch, they become bouncy or more colorful or lighter. If it's a parent or grandparent, maybe it feels like all the energy is directed toward you and filling your body with warmth.

With a challenging person, you might notice that your energy is being drained. Maybe your energy is clearly being sucked away by the other person. Maybe the other person's energy is overbearing and pushy with your energy. Maybe as the energies connect they become heavy, or dark, or change color. Or maybe your energy is clearly being rejected and walled off by the other person.

If you spend some time using this energy practice with people around you, it might give you an idea of your needs and limits. It can tell you when someone is expecting too much of you or you are expecting too much of yourself. It can tell you when parts of you are getting stepped on or forgotten. It might even help you see when you're expecting too much from others or not taking responsibility for your own needs.

Since there's no right way for this to look, you get to decide what this tells you about your limits and boundaries. And what relationships and patterns make your system feel safe and respected.

As you learn what you do and don't prefer, you can start to work on the final part of boundaries which is **helping other people to understand what you need to feel safe** when you're together.

This step can also be challenging.

Sharing your boundaries with others isn't so much about forcing them to do anything. It's **communicating how you would like to be treated and letting them know how *you* will respond** if you are not treated that way during your time with them.

Just telling someone that they can't yell at you or disrespect you isn't a full boundary. The boundary has to include how you will choose to protect yourself when this happens. Usually this will be to disengage or leave the situation.

For example, you can let your sister know that you don't feel that it is fair when she dumps all her problems on you. You can explain that you *do* want a relationship with her and see if there are ways that you can make the relationship more balanced for both of you.

If your sister struggles to understand your feelings and won't respect this request, then you can let her know that you will have to enforce a boundary when she attempts to dump her problems on you the next time. You might tell her that you will politely change the subject or encourage her to talk to a therapist when she starts to vent. If she doesn't stop after you try to redirect her, you might have to tell her that you will hang up or leave the room if she continues.

When you share boundaries with others, you will need to **give clear expectations about how you will take responsibility for yourself** if your boundaries are not respected.

Since the only control you have in a relationship is what *you* choose to do, you have to decide how you will protect yourself when other people can't. It will be hard to enforce boundaries if you are not willing to follow through with what you say you will do.

This is important because other people don't always love boundaries, especially at first. As you ask people to change the way that they interact with you, it can create tension or confusion and even trigger insecurities in other people, who might feel you're abandoning them or judging them.

It might take them a while to see that you're trying to improve the relationship. Although clear boundaries can help relationships become more safe and predictable, it's hard to see this at first.

Unfortunately, this might mean that a relationship has to change to be safer. If the other person isn't able to meet you where you're at, then you might have to keep them at a certain distance so that you feel safe.

You might have to **repeat the expectation many times** before the other person realizes that you're trying to help the connection and not end it. But sometimes you might have to completely disconnect from a relationship if it's threatening or abusive.

This can be so hard when you already struggle with insecure relationships. It might feel terrifying to ask others to treat you differently. As we already discussed, being vulnerable is risky. Setting boundaries is part of that process.

It can take a lot of courage to speak up for yourself or walk away when you're not safe. Remember that it can take time to get there.

Further Study Recommendations:

Drama Free: A Guide to Managing Unhealthy Family Relationships by Nedra Glover Tawwab. This book is an easy-to-use guide to holding boundaries with family. It has very practical advice and example phrases so you don't have to think up the words on your own. I would recommend reading this in book form as the layout is very helpful and may not translate as well over audio.

Set Boundaries, Find Peace: A Guide to Reclaiming Yourself by Nedra Glover Tawwab. This book can help you understand the basic principles of boundaries and how to use them in your healing process.

CHAPTER 54 – REPAIR

In order to heal, a big part of the process will be to learn how to repair.

Although repairing might seem like the same thing as healing, it's actually a little different.

Healing is the natural process that happens over time. Your body and brain are naturally wired to heal after damage. This is true for both your physical cuts and your emotional wounds.

Some damage needs more intervention than others. With some wounds, you might have to keep yourself away from toxic situations and take the time to get some things reset or stitched up. This is the process of repair.

Boundaries are how you protect yourself from other people's choices and behaviors. **Repairing** is the process **of taking accountability for the damages that have been caused** by *your* choices and behaviors. *And* **taking responsibility for the wounds that you still carry.**

Going back to our school analogy, the principal can help to reduce future damage by creating clear expectations and boundaries for each group and staff member as she reorganizes and shifts things around. But the school still won't be able to function well until the damage has been acknowledged and repaired.

Many of these damages can happen within the school and between the staff. Some staff might be super overworked, certain groups may have terrorized each other, and other staff could be owed a lot of backpay.

It's also possible that the school has damaged relationships with other schools. There might be broken contracts with partner schools or disrespectful techniques that were used while the staff trained other schools.

This means that the principal may have to repair the relationships between staff as well as the relationships outside of the school in order for things to get better.

In a similar way, you may also have a lot of damages to deal with as a result of your survival experiences.

You have already started this process with yourself as you work on facing your system and bravely **working with your parts and your memories to repair the connections**.

As you continue to work on healing, you will probably find that there are **also repairs needed in your outside relationships** due to all your years in survival. This process can be incredibly scary, especially if you didn't have great models to show you how to do this.

This is why starting with your own parts is important. It's a lot easier to repair with others when your own wounds aren't as sensitive and easily triggered. Plus, you will get some practice with the repair process as you work with your own parts. That way you will have a better idea of what it feels like before you have to do it with others.

Now, in order to work on **repairing with yourself and others**, you will have to be ready to do a few things.

1. You must recognize and acknowledge that damage was done.

It will be impossible to repair if you can't or won't see when you have been unsafe or harmful toward someone else. This is tricky because your body and brain may use a lot of protections to keep you from seeing the situation clearly and/or taking responsibility.

2. You have to understand how the damage has impacted the other person.

Taking accountability won't do much to close the gap if you can't listen to or consider the other person's point of view long enough to understand how much the damage has impacted them. If you try to repair something without having an accurate view of the harm, then you'll never know how to measure whether it's healing or not.

Many times this will require some effort to put yourself in their shoes or ask questions without getting defensive about their responses. In fact, you may have to be patient for a long time before that person will be ready to let you in again and be honest about their feelings. And unless you listen to and respect their boundaries during this time, you will not be making any progress in gaining their trust.

This is tricky because it's easy for guilt and fear to trigger emergency responses. Trying to sit in these spaces before you're ready can cause your system to flip on the protections. The damage will only get worse if you try to blast through someone's boundaries instead of waiting for them to invite you in. Or if you criticize, minimize, avoid, or blame them as they let their guard down to repair.

This is why professional help can be important as you're working on repairing with yourself or others. Having a mediator around can keep things from getting too out of hand.

3. You have to try your best to take accountability and fix the damage.

Although you cannot always take back the things that you've done and said, you have to take responsibility for addressing and cleaning up the damage. At a minimum, this will almost always require an apology and a clear acknowledgement of your accountability to the other person for what you did. This is just as true for repairing with your own parts as it is with other people.

But in some situations, it may also be important to try and make up for the damage or set it straight.

With your parts, this can look like taking out time to play when you realize that you've been blocking the curiosity of your inner children. It could also look like prioritizing meals when you've been starving yourself. Or it might even be finding ways to catch up on rest when you've been working too hard. In fact, giving your body more rest will likely be a big part of this repairing process.

In your relationships, this might be making monthly payments for things that you broke while you were in a rage. It may be taking over some household chores or the kid's nighttime routines since your partner had to handle everything while you were avoiding family time. These repairs need to feel reasonable to both sides.

The goal is not to be indebted forever. But to demonstrate that you understand your accountability and responsibility in the damage.

In some extreme situations, making amends might be accepting legal responsibility to make restitution to the community. This can be a difficult step to take, especially with severe crimes, but it will often be worth it when you can finally repair and face all your parts without fear or shame.

4. You have to work on changing the damaging actions and communicate how you're working on those changes.

This step is important because things can't be rebuilt or repaired if they keep getting damaged all the time. Even if you get really good at making amends but don't change your harmful behaviors, then things will never get better.

Some of the most toxic people can show a lot of remorse after being violent or dangerous. They may buy gifts or shower someone in praise, but without working on the root of the problem, these amends are just quick fixes that aren't repairing the relationship.

Once you are working on changing, it's also important to communicate how you're doing this. Other people, and even parts, won't realize that you're trying to reset harmful patterns if you're not clearly and directly passing along the info about what you're working on.

5. You will need to stay open to feedback and correction as the relationship heals.

Even though the damage has been acknowledged and you're doing your best to make changes, the healing process will still take time. Just because you're removing what's toxic and trying to stitch things up, it doesn't mean that there is trust.

To build or rebuild a healthy connection, your behaviors will have to become safe and predictable. Which, as we discussed before, can take time.

Luckily, you don't have to be perfect for this to happen.

Like we talked about in Chapter 46, using vulnerability and bids for connection will help to create safety and predictability in your relationships. But you can also be safe and predictable when other people know that you will always try to repair things by taking accountability, apologizing for your mistakes, and doing better.

Although these steps can feel overwhelming at first, they will get easier as you practice.

And the best way to do this is by starting repairs with your own parts.

Many of your parts will need to repair and reset their relationships with each other after years of battling. This might be between your critical and avoidant part. It could also be your extravert and your introvert. Maybe it's your perfectionist and your procrastinator. Maybe it's your adult and child parts. Using these repair steps with your parts can bring a lot of healing when your system is tired of the tug-of-war.

As your parts begin to repair with each other, they will pull back their defenses and allow you to access the original wounds and inner children that have been stuck underneath all the chaos. You will be able to see them more clearly and offer them the support, repair, and guidance that they need to heal and to trust that they belong.

You and your parts will start to see that you are not your wounds, and the shame will slowly fade. In time, all the fears that you've had about being unlovable will start to fade away as you prove that you are worthy of love by taking care of and respecting yourself.

This clearer view of yourself will usually make it easier to repair with other people too.

You will be more able to own your mistakes and take responsibility when you have less shame and feel more worthy of love.

Now, repairing your relationships won't look exactly the same for every situation. Some people and parts may need a lot of time, especially if they feel pretty damaged by your actions and interactions. Some people and parts might be able to quickly repair and forgive right away. But some people may not be willing to repair at all.

It's possible that some people have been so hurt by your behaviors that they feel that their only protection is to disconnect from the relationship.

When people choose not to accept your apology or to repair things with you, it can be really difficult.

It's important to understand that **you have no control over how other people respond to your attempts at repairing** things.

Other people have the right to hold their own boundaries and boundary lines.

Trying to blast or bulldoze through these lines by yelling, complaining, demanding, guilt tripping, etc. will only force other people to create stricter boundaries and maybe even put up walls.

Generally, the most important repairs will be made with your partner and your children.

These relationships come with a lot more vulnerability and connection, so the damage can be much more painful than your other relationships. This is especially true for your children as they depend on you to survive and grow and they don't have the same power to hold boundaries that adults do.

Family or couples therapy can be really helpful in this repair process if everyone is open to it and willing to take accountability for their own part. Many partners and children are on board to forgive and try again when they see your willingness to listen and change harmful patterns.

Now, as an adult child in a family you can sometimes be responsible for the harm that you do to your siblings and parents, but it's important to pay attention to the patterns of your family before you decide what to take accountability for.

Since many children survive by taking on adult roles, it's possible that you're accepting responsibility for harm that isn't yours to carry. Although it can feel safer to help your parents or guardians avoid their responsibility in your family trauma cycles, they won't ever get the chance to find their own healing if they're always relieved of their accountability.

Further Study Recommendations:

A Good Apology: Four Steps to Make Things Right by Molly Howes, PhD. This book can help you better understand and walk you through the process of repairing relationships by taking accountability and making apologies.

CHAPTER 55 – REVIEW

You're here. You've made it to the last repeat of our mindful activities.

There are a couple more chapters about getting help and rebuilding, and a Bonus Upgrade if you're interested, but you've made it through a massive amount of info.

Be so proud of yourself. Even if nothing has changed yet, getting through this much information is extraordinary.

We're going to practice the calming activities one more time.

Hopefully you understand why we've spent so many chapters repeating them.

They will help you listen to your system. They will help you to strengthen and balance your networks. They will help you face and reconnect with all the parts of your system and help you to be more in sync with yourself.

As you choose an activity one final time, see if there are parts that would like to join you and participate.

The caregivers in your Calm, Secure Space can practice some mindfulness activities with your younger selves while you do your own activity. And any protective parts you've connected with can join you in your activity or find their own if that feels better right now.

If your parts are not ready to be together or on the same page, you might see if you can create a *Group* **Calm, Safe Space**.

It should be separate from your original Calm, Safe Space. It can be a large mansion or a college, or a city with many buildings, or a forest or meadow with individual areas and clear boundaries that can create separate spaces for all of you.

You don't even have to create each individual space. Just create a safe place that has room for everyone and makes sense for your system. Let your parts know that they can claim their own area and settle in and make it their own. Let them know they can make their space unique and functional for them. They can also have fences or doors or locks until they feel safe and are ready to connect and repair.

Giving all your parts permission to take some space can be really helpful. And many people find that their parts can feel a lot better with a small gesture that they belong somewhere in the system.

You can also choose to connect this space with your Calm, Secure Space if it makes sense to have your inner children and their caretakers nearby. But do what feels safe for your system and keep them in separate places if that feels right for you.

Eventually, as you do this work, it's possible to bring all your parts into a council or community. To have spaces where everyone belongs together, respects the system, and has a clear role and a voice that they feel satisfied with.

But for now, just try to sit with the fact that you have a complicated system. And that it might take time to resettle everything and be in a healthier place.

On that note, go ahead and **do whichever activities or exercises that feel like a good fit** right now.

Come back to the book when you're ready.

CHAPTER 56 – SUPPORT

As we wrap up this book, I'm going to talk about getting help.

This can be a huge part of healing.

Getting help can sometimes make all the difference in your recovery process, but sometimes it can actually make things harder.

Some of you may have tried to get help and support in the past and found that family, friends, and professionals have made the problem worse.

This might be one of the reasons you avoid trying to find support.

When other people do not understand these systems, they can accidentally set you up to fail.

Have you tried talking to or working with a professional who didn't take the time to build trust? Maybe they didn't consider that you've been betrayed in the past or that their nosey or careless comments put you off.

This can feel extra hard when you need their skill set but you also don't feel safe. It can feel like you have to fake trust to get what you need. But this can be extra triggering if masking, faking, or hiding is how you have survived your trauma. Their knowledge won't matter very much if your system can't feel safe enough to stop being protective and let the information in.

Most people do not heal because they find a medication or coping skill that magically pops everything into place. They get better because someone takes the time to walk with them through the deep process of healing.

This means it is important to try and find a provider or helper who has experience with your kind of symptoms or history, but **it's going to be *most* important that you trust them.**

Remember that trust comes from spending time with someone who is safe and predictable.

Providers have to do the same thing if you're going to trust them.

This does get more challenging when you live in a place without a lot of options, or you have terrible insurance, or you literally just can't afford to see who you want.

These are very real problems. Getting help is not as simple as people like to make it seem.

This is why I want you to know that you can heal with many types of support.

You can look for doctors, mental health therapists, or body workers like massage therapists or acupuncturists. You can also look for spiritual healers, or volunteer programs, or support groups.

There are a lot of places you can start with until you figure out the next steps. Maybe it's taking time to save up for professional support. Maybe it's learning about support programs and getting on waitlists or applying for financial scholarships. Maybe it's searching for local support groups until you find the right one.

Start where you can.

If you can get professional support, it's important to realize that you can ask for what you need.

In my opinion, **the best providers will do three things**. They will listen. They will learn. And they will adapt.

When someone is really trying to understand where you are at, they will **listen**.

And when they don't understand, they will clarify and ask more questions. They will let you know that they are trying to see things from your perspective before they make recommendations or give a lot of advice.

As they spend time listening, it will be clear that they are working to **learn** about you and your needs.

They will be listening well enough to put the information together and build clear ideas of what's going on so they can figure out the best approaches and treatment.

And if they're continuing to listen and learn, they will also be able to **adapt**.

This means that they will keep listening, even after you begin working on treatments or programs. They will be open to feedback about how you're doing and actually adjust when you say it's not working. They will help you to feel comfortable with asking questions and won't get impatient when they have to explain things many times or when you repeat yourself a lot.

And even when they have to be direct about some of your blind spots or harmful behaviors, they will be nonjudgmental and regulated enough to sit with your upset or uncomfortable feelings.

Connection is our first and most powerful system of healing and survival. When you start to feel connected and safe, it will be easier to process the stuck places and help your emergency responses become a little less triggered.

In fact, a lot of healing can happen with a provider just by spending time with them. As they **model safe and regulated behaviors**, they help your body to mirror these feelings, and **your system gets to learn and practice coregulating**.

Sometimes your symptoms and issues will be too complicated for the professional you find. Some professionals are good at having this conversation and helping you find a better fit, but sometimes they make it seem like you're the problem.

If this has happened to you, you are *not* the problem. There are professionals out there who can absolutely help you. They will know how to work with your system and help you feel more whole again.

It might be really hard to keep trying when you feel like giving up on yourself. I'm so sorry if there are helpers or providers who have made you feel this way.

Now that you have more words for the challenges you are facing, you might have an easier time looking for the professionals who know how to help you. You can ask most providers for a free phone meeting to see if they feel like a good fit before you decide to pay them.

If you know that you struggle with boundaries or shame or insecure relationships, you can look for and interview professionals to see if they have experience treating these things. Ask them how they work on building trust. Ask them if they will be frustrated if it takes you a year or more to fully open up.

Most people who have been through survival need a long time before their system can even feel safe and trusting enough to share their feelings, let alone accept help. So this is not a crazy timeline.

In fact, when some professionals try to use fast-paced therapies or quick fixes, it can send the message that you're a problem to be fixed, which might reinforce your shame and negative beliefs.

But, when you have the right support and are given a lot of time and respect, many of the changes that you need to make will actually start to come more naturally. As your system begins to know what it's like to feel safe, you won't have to push yourself to do most things. Your system will naturally want to do what feels healthy and lead you toward better decisions.

Your reward system will be able to go back to long-term goals. Your amygdala will be able to sort out incorrect matches. Your cortex will get more energy again and be able to focus on the big picture.

If you feel that your provider is expecting you to work faster or do more than you can handle, do your best to tell them. I know this is hard. Especially when you haven't been heard in the past, or your feelings have been dismissed before.

Giving feedback to a professional is a great way to see if they are really listening, learning, and adapting.

No professional is perfect. They can't read minds. They might not grasp how bad you feel or how hard you're trying if your system is really shut down. The feelings and pain that you're feeling on the inside might not match what you're expressing on the outside. So if you can tell them when things are off or when you're not satisfied with what's happening, it gives them the chance to show you that they can hear and adjust and learn more about you.

Write it in an email or a letter if you need to. A caring professional will do their best to get on the same page again. And if they don't, you can stop meeting with them and find someone else.

CHAPTER 57 – REASSEMBLE

One of the hardest parts of change can be the rebuilding process. After you go through all the effort to unravel and pull everything apart, it can be difficult to know what to do next.

It might take a while to find out who you are and where you want to go now that you're not being bossed around by survival.

You may have to **go back and give yourself a chance to be a kid again**. Allowing yourself to be playful and curious can help you find and reconnect with the inner children that got hijacked or left behind.

Climb a tree or fly a kite. Buy yourself stickers or coloring books. Try unusual foods. Sit and watch the clouds. Play with your pet. Explore new things and see what sparks your interest.

Your inner children have been desperately waiting for adult protection. And your overworked adult parts will often be grateful for moments to be a kid again. So your parts can often find a lot of comfort by carving out time to play together.

Going back to these moments can also help you to discover who you used to be, and what parts of you never had a chance to grow. You will likely **reawaken joy, passion, gratitude, clarity, faith, hope, excitement, love, and many more feelings** that never got a chance to be safely nurtured and developed.

Try to take it one day at a time.

As you build new networks, it can feel exhausting. But they do eventually move to muscle memory. And bit by bit, it will get easier.

You probably won't feel it changing along the way as you're exhausted and unraveling. It's hard to see progress when it goes slowly. It's like getting taller when you're a kid. You won't notice it each day until you outgrow your shoes or you get measured at a check up.

But on some random day in the future, you'll wake up and realize that things aren't as hard as they used to be.

And you've just arrived at one of those points.

You've made it to the end of this book.

Getting through 57 chapters is a huge win. If you are here, you have already grown quite a bit.

Just learning these concepts will be powerful.

You may need to reread this information many times as you grow. Unraveling can make it difficult to keep all these thoughts together. As you go through that process, you can return to this book at any time and remind yourself of whatever you need to.

Some information might take on new meaning as you grow and heal.

Remember that you're much more complicated and unique than a leaky pipe or a piece of broken furniture.

You are a rich human being with many layers and more value than you know.

One day, I hope you will be able to see just how much your system has been fighting for you. And that you have been on your own side all along.

BONUS UPGRADE

This section has information on some more specific topics that may be helpful if they apply to you.

CHAPTER A – PARENTS AND GUARDIANS

As we talked about in Chapter 48, it can be so hard for parents and guardians to help children learn and grow in ways that you were never taught.

And when you have unresolved issues in your system, you are going to have a hard time not just passing on those same stuck patterns to your children.

The fear and avoidance of **your buried pain and stuck emergency networks can get in the way of really connecting and being in tune with your children**. Although these protections served you in the past, they can be incredibly heartbreaking when they cause you to be defended against your own kids.

If your feelings and behaviors were often criticized and punished as a child, then it can be hard not to get triggered by your kids when they show up with these same feelings and behaviors. When there wasn't room in your childhood for high-energy play, curiosity, and mistakes, then you might see these same patterns in your children as a sign of weakness or badness. You might also get resentful or jealous that they get to be a kid when you didn't.

This is why **your own healing is super important**. For them and for you.

It's important to know that you will never be perfect as a parent or guardian. There will always be more to learn and do. There will always be things that get in the way of a perfect family.

Think about the training school analogy we talked about earlier.

Trainers are going to be overloaded as they have to help other schools to function and stay safe, and guide new principals through their development, all while running their own organization and modeling what it all should look like. And if their own organization is already falling apart or struggling to function, it's going to make an overwhelming job even harder.

This is what it's like to be a parent. You're expected to keep up with an impossible amount of energy, wisdom, and patience.

It's also difficult because children are always developing. So your cortex will have to keep learning new connections to keep up. This means the big picture part of parenting rarely gets to be on autopilot and takes an exhausting amount of energy.

For all your love and sacrifice as a parent, you will fall short, no matter how qualified you are. And that's okay. You will go through amazing and difficult times, and you won't be able to do everything you want for yourself or your kids.

That's normal.

You cannot run your system all day, every day, and be even close to functional when you're also keeping someone else alive and trying to keep up with their emotional, educational, recreational, spiritual, and physical needs on top of your own.

It can be so helpful to find your own support and help through all the years of raising children.

I know this can be hard in many communities though. There may not be many options that fit your needs and family, and/or you may not be able to afford, or find time for, the options that do exist.

This is a very real problem in our modern society. **Raising children without access to family leave, childcare, or community support networks can be isolating and overwhelming**. This is especially true if you have children with disabilities and/or you are a single parent with sole or majority custody, and even harder if you don't get child support.

If you are facing these barriers, it can be useful to **reach out to parent networks** online and even **parenting hotlines** when things become overwhelming.

Here are a few options to start with:

- Crying Baby Hotline: Call 866-243-2229 - This is a 24/7 line for when you feel overwhelmed and possibly unsafe due to a baby who won't stop crying.
- Fussy Baby Warmline: Call 888-431-BABY (2229) or visit erikson.edu/fussy-baby-network/ - This service is available in English and Spanish for parents struggling with fussy infants.
- Parent Stress Line: Call 800-632-8188 or visit parentshelpingparents.org – This is a 24/7 line that offers support for anyone raising a child, especially when you're worried things are getting to be too much and you're heading for a crisis.
- National Parent and Youth Helpline: Call or text 855-427-2736 or visit nationalparentyouthhelpline.org/ - This helpline is available 24/7 for caretakers or youth to get help with family challenges and/or crisis. This service is available in 240 languages.

Carving out time for friends, family, books, groups, and/or therapy can also help you to keep your sanity. If this means your kids get more screen time or bribes, fine. Finding small moments for **your own growth will benefit your children much more in the long run** and allow you to be more patient and present with them in the future.

And, as you learn to help yourself and pay attention to your own needs, you will learn how to be a healthy boss for your own system. And as you learn this, you will have a much easier time teaching your children healthy boss skills, even if all you're doing is modeling it. That's the best way to teach anyway.

Showing your kids that it's okay to be flawed, make mistakes, apologize, repair, and try again will give them such great skills for their own lives and future.

And remember, **the small changes you make can improve your family cycles for generations** to come. You're doing a great job with an impossible situation.

Further Study Recommendations:

The Connected Child: Bring Hope and Healing to Your Adoptive Family by Karyn B Purvis, PhD, David R. Cross, PhD, and Wendy Lyons Sunshine. This book has parenting tools for foster and adoption care and might also be useful for blended families.

Good Inside: A Guide to Becoming the Parent You Want to Be by Dr. Becky Kennedy. This book offers really simple and practical ways of holding boundaries with your children while maintaining connection and trust.

How to Hug a Porcupine: Negotiating the Prickly Points of the Tween Years by Julie A. Ross, MA. This book provides practical tools for parents as they are raising tweens and teens.

No-Drama Discipline: The Whole-Brain Way to Calm the Chaos and Nurture Your Child's Developing Mind by Tina Payne Bryson, PhD, and Daniel J. Siegel, MD. This book gives practical tools for parents as they are raising young children.

Parenting from the Inside Out: How a Deeper Self-Understanding Can Help You Raise Children Who Thrive by Daniel Siegel, MD, and Mary Hartzell, Med. This book can help you through the process of reparenting yourself while you're parenting your children.

Project Parent Coach on Tik Tok (@projectparent) and Instagram (@projectparentcoach) by Dr. Jenny Hwang. This influencer creates short and useful clips to help parents handle their own reactions and their teen's reactions to better communicate and work with each other.

Raising Good Humans: A Mindful Guide to Breaking the Cycle of Reactive Parenting and Raising Kind, Confident Kids by Hunter Clarke-Fields, MSAE. This book can help you understand how your survival systems are impacting your parenting and offers ideas to help yourself stay regulated. This book may be especially helpful if you find that you have a lot of angry or irritated responses with your children.

Reconnecting with Your Estranged Adult Child: Practical Tips and Tools to Heal Your Relationship by Tina Gilbertson, LPC. This book provides tools for parents with estranged adult children and helps them understand ways to work toward reconnection.

CHAPTER B – HELPERS AND PROFESSIONALS

If you're a helping professional like a medical worker, first responder, school employee, social worker, therapist, church leader, volunteer, or any other type of helper, then this chapter is for you.

As you read this book, it might be easy to think about how these systems work for others. But if you're regularly helping others, you might need to consider whether you're stuck in survival too.

Secondary trauma is a real concern for helpers.

Because mirror neurons copy and match the feelings around you, it's possible to end up with survival networks that carry the same grief, pain, and trauma that you work around every day. **Your system can get stuck from hearing about and seeing stuck cycles all around you**. This is especially true after many years of exposure.

Remember that it's possible to get stuck in the 5th step of the stress cycle even if you handle stress well. When there's just too much trauma to digest and integrate, it has nowhere to go and will start to shut you down and numb you out. This is why many professionals can end up feeling bored or resentful toward their patients and clients after many years on the job.

If this is you and you've been starting to feel hopeless about your efforts, you might be burned out on secondary trauma and need to work on your own stuck networks.

It's **hard to give care and support from an overdrawn account**, and it's really hard not to resent others when they start taking more than you have to give. It can also be hard when you don't know how to ask for help and/or don't have the same support that you are offering to others.

So it's really important to consider whether you are facing your own stuck places if you are spending a lot of time serving others.

It's also possible that you are feeling stuck because of your own unhealed wounds or stuck survival systems. Many times **helpers are drawn to service careers** because they went through difficult experiences and want to help others who are suffering in similar ways.

This can be challenging, though, if your wounds are still not healed and you're using caretaking as your own survival response.

If this is the case, then it can be difficult to help others in the way that they need or in a way that's healthy for you.

Your pain or triggers might get in the way of seeing other people's problems clearly. It might make your helping more about you than about them. You might feel like the only way to fit in is if you're rescuing others or solving their problems.

You might not realize that you need to be needed. And if that's the case, it can be hard to hear other people tell you that they don't want your help or that you're not helping in a way that is useful for them.

Sometimes it's difficult to know exactly what's going on when you're always surrounded by survival. So it's okay to take a break and reevaluate what's going on with you. Stepping back and getting help can often give you the reset you need to be a more effective helper in the long run.

Now, if you're ready to implement some of these survival concepts in your helping roles, then **the following guidance may be useful** in your practice and organizations.

First, **environments are a really big deal** when you're working with traumatized people.

Schools, churches, hospitals, emergency vehicles, and professional offices often have a lot of the same sensory clips from place to place.

Hospitals and doctors offices usually look and smell the same from location to location. Emergency vehicles look the same and sound the same. Medical professionals have the same scrubs and masks and gloves. First responders have the same outfits and equipment. Churches and schools often have the same smells, sounds, and images.

This is important to realize because there are many environments that people come into that are already matched into their emergency response systems without having been in that specific place before.

It might take a lot of effort to help someone know they are safe when they have strong danger matches that are telling them they are not. Many children who had early birth problems will likely have danger matches connected to medical clinics that make doctors visits and vaccinations more stressful.

Dentist offices are particularly difficult with this since numbing injections can sometimes activate an adrenaline rush that feels like or actually triggers a panic attack. Not to mention that tooth pain can be extreme and will easily activate survival responses. The increased pain and stress is why dentist offices may feel very threatening for some people.

Church buildings can also hold a lot of danger and safety matches for people who were raised with religion. Regular church attendance for many years creates very powerful matches.

If these experiences were mostly comforting, then these buildings may feel peaceful and protective to you. But if someone was abused while they were at church, or terrified of going to hell, or felt ashamed of not measuring up, then they may struggle to feel safe when they are around the same prayers, paintings, incense, people, or buildings.

Schools are also an important consideration. When a child spends 20–30 hours each week in the same building with the same patterns and with the same people, these matches will become incredibly strong. If a kid experiences success and support, they will create very different matches in their system than kids who experience regular failure and punishment.

This is important for helpers to realize because all these environments might have safe matches for *your* system and even be places that are extra comforting for *you*. It might not occur to you that this could be exactly the opposite for someone else.

Some people feel really safe around police officers or when they hear church choir music or when they walk the halls of their old school.

But these same matches might be extremely threatening to another person who has had bad experiences with these same situations and places.

Second, it's important to **believe people when they tell you that they don't feel safe.**

Even when *you* know that they are safe, their system won't believe you when there are danger matches everywhere. And you will only add to the stress and confusion when you don't listen or take their fear seriously.

In fact, as a helper it can be really good to start learning what different emergency responses can look like. Remember that these may look very different from person to person.

You might save yourself a lot of stress if you can recognize that a child is acting defiant or aggressive because they feel threatened. Or you might learn to recognize when a teen is in a freeze response and help others to see that they're not just having an attitude.

Children behave well if they can. So it's up to adults to help kids figure out what is going on and what's triggering them.

When someone is having intense behaviors that seem confusing to you, it can be really helpful to assume that they are trying to protect themselves. When you believe that someone is not purposefully being hurtful or difficult, you'll have a better chance of figuring out what's wrong.

Bad behaviors are usually a sign that someone needs help. It's an attempt for their system to get attention when they are overwhelmed and not sure what to do or how to help themselves.

Third, in situations where someone is putting up their walls with you, you will want to **figure out what actions you can take to show that you're not a threat** and that you're trying to understand.

This will often take time but will be the only way to get real answers and understand what they need to feel safe.

Check your posture and facial expressions and try to soften your body. Pay attention to the environment and see if you can move them away from anything triggering. Be mindful if you're wearing a weapon or a mask and see if there's a way to safely remove it and put it somewhere else. Notice if you're much bigger or taller than them and see if it's helpful to get at their eye level and back up a bit.

You might encourage people to leave the room if it's busy or invite someone of a different gender into the area to see if that helps them feel safer. You can remove an aggressive animal, or put a coat over your uniform, or take some slow deep breaths to regulate yourself.

In most situations, though, just showing that you are listening and believing someone will go a long way towards cooling things down.

Fourth, even if their thoughts, ideas, or words don't seem reasonable, **the experience and feelings are real to them.**

Unless you're on a jury, it's not your job to decide what's true or not true. When you start really listening to what people are telling you, and your own stress responses are not getting in the way, you'll be amazed at how much easier it is to help others stay calm. You'll be able to give them the time and space they need to open up and work with you.

Even if their words don't make sense, acknowledge and validate the feelings they're displaying. Trying to force someone into "seeing reality" when they are stuck in a survival experience isn't going to magically regulate their system or bring them back to the present.

In fact, this will likely force them to be more protective and resistant to engaging with you. And it might even switch them into fight mode.

Instead, now that you understand these concepts, you can appreciate that they're protecting themselves. Knowing this can help you stay regulated in your own body so that you are better able to listen and help them get through these difficult moments.

In time, this kind of patience and understanding can help them overcome some of their feelings of shame and rejection. And this will make it much easier to get to the root of their pain and find opportunities for healing.

Further Study Recommendation:

Trauma Stewardship: An Everyday Guide to Caring for Self While Caring for Others by Laura van Dernoot Lipsky with Connie Burk. This book can offer some insight to professionals who may struggle with repeating survival cycles in their personal and work life due to their own trauma and the secondary trauma that comes from helping survivors.

We Are All Perfectly Fine: A Memoir of Love, Medicine, and Healing by Jillian Horton, MD. This book is a stylized memoir of the author's experience with her own history of trauma and her secondary trauma due to working as a doctor.

CHAPTER C – TEENS AND YOUTH

Teens and young adults are often more likely to struggle with survival systems because their brains are in a very unique place. This chapter can help you better understand how to support them as they transition into adulthood.

During childhood, the connections in the brain and body have been growing incredibly fast for many years. By about 10 years old, these networks get pretty overgrown. And although your brain likes to know and predict many things, there's a point where too many connections will make it extra difficult to keep everything coordinated and organized.

As children grow, their system starts to decide which connections to keep and which ones to trim. This process starts early on in childhood, but most of **the neuron trimming process gets really active at the beginning of the teen years.**

While this is happening, their brain is also working on something called **myelination** that **helps nerves to send signals faster.**

As their system figures out which connections are most important, they will myelinate these networks to improve speed and efficiency.

It's also important to remember that a lot of these connections are helping to form the cortex and teaching them about logic and big-picture thinking in the world. But the cortex isn't really finished being trimmed and myelinated until about 25 years old.

So, during these years, teens and young adults are trying to understand who they are and learn about the world while **their brain is still in major reconstruction.**

This is why it can be hard for youth to be as prepared as older adults want them to be. Their brain isn't done organizing the basics yet. And just being told how to live and grow doesn't really exercise these networks and put things into place. They need opportunities to explore and learn for themselves so that their cortex can sort out the world around them through personal experience.

During the teen and young adult years, **the reward system is also getting really active** and pushes them to seek new experiences and thrills. Considering that the cortex isn't complete, this makes it hard for young people to have awareness of their own safety and be able to think through their actions and decisions beforehand.

This can be a really frustrating time for parents and guardians who might have forgotten what it was like to feel so impulsive and excited about life. And it might be even harder when parents were judged by their caregivers for their youthful mistakes and they still feel ashamed of these memories.

It can also make things harder when teens and young adults start to pull away from their parents.

Pulling away is an important process for this time of life. As part of building their networks, youth are trying to figure out who they are and what they want for themselves. It can be difficult to discover these things when their family relationships make it hard to see where they end and other people begin.

For many young people, this is why appearance and preferences can become really unique during this time. Hairstyles, piercings, clothing, tattoos, etc. may help teens and young adults feel like they're **forming a distinct identity**, especially when they aren't allowed to make choices or control their life in other ways.

This is also why **friendships start to become a large influence**. Learning more about other people and creating independent relationships help teens and young adults to form their own likes and dislikes and spend time figuring out who they are and what they want in their life.

Having teens pull away and spending more time with friends can sometimes be **stressful for parents or guardians.** You may feel worried about keeping your teen safe, but it may also trigger feelings of abandonment or even cause resentment or grief as you feel unappreciated.

Teens and young adults might pull away even harder if parents are adding guilt or shame to this process. Youth don't often have the skills yet to express that they are trying to find their own identity and, even if they do, they may struggle to share this with parents when they know it might be taken offensively or cause hurt feelings.

This often means that teens and young adults avoid, ignore, and defend themselves from conversations and interactions that bring up this guilt or fear. Their own fears of being a disappointment can bleed into this if adults are telling them that they are being selfish or irresponsible. It's hard for anyone to want to engage in relationships where they're told that their experiences are bad or wrong.

For parents or guardians with teens, this is a really difficult balance. There's no perfect way to keep young people close enough to be safe while also independent enough to feel satisfied.

The reward system is always trying to push that boundary, so no matter how much freedom a teen has, it's likely that they will want more. But, on the other hand, the more restricted their freedom becomes, the more likely they are to break away and fully disconnect. It's a difficult balance for parents to manage.

It can also be confusing for a parent or guardian when a teen demands independence one minute and then falls apart over a video game the next. Or when they say that they can handle school all by themselves but have dozens of missing assignments they forgot about.

It's important to note that **many schools can struggle to support teens in a way that works for their brains**. Since teens are still developing their frontal cortex, they can be set up to fail in schools where they are expected to be as organized as adults.

Without a lot of patience and guidance, teens will often fall short of the expectations created for them by adults, like keeping track of assignments and grades across many months and staying focused for too many hours in a row. Especially when they're dealing with overwhelming passing periods in a sea of a thousand other students, or have limited time for creativity and exploration, and have early starting times that interrupt their naturally late sleep rhythms.

Some adults may not realize that these expectations are out of reach for many students as there will always be a handful of youth with high-level functioning, caretaking, and people-pleasing survival responses that are highly motivated to prove that these things can be achieved. Unfortunately, out-of-reach expectations take a toll on everybody, even the overachievers.

A teen or young adult's mind is still working on the big picture, and they may not realize how much they still have to learn. It's hard to recognize if there are gaps missing, and, sometimes, it's even harder to get an adult to take these concerns seriously.

Now, in survival, this will obviously get more tricky.

Many **teens and young adults who have grown up in survival might actually be much more independent** than the average young person. When they've been facing life-or-death feelings for most of their life, their brain will be forced to develop in a way that protects them.

So children who have gone through severe neglect and/or abuse will often have many adult skills and big-picture perspectives out of necessity to stay alive. This doesn't mean that their brain is fully developed, just that certain networks had to develop more quickly to survive while other networks were left behind.

Many adults can make survival situations worse as they dismiss the feelings and opinions of young people because of their limited experiences or "deviant" survival responses. When older adults don't spend enough time figuring out how to help youth succeed by giving their reward system attainable, bite-sized goals, then quick fixes and emergency responses become the next best option for youth to cope with the overwhelm.

If you are a parent or guardian of a young person, or an adult that works with youth, then it's important to give young people the benefit of the doubt and spend a lot of time listening so you can meet them where they are at. Teens may not realize that they aren't communicating things as well as they think, and a trusted adult can help them to open up and figure out how to organize their thoughts and experiences.

It won't be fair or reasonable to expect young people to have a decent enough handle on their struggles to tell you exactly what's wrong and be clear about what they need from you. These are skills that can even be hard for mature adults some days. So, unless these patterns are modeled really well for a very long time, teens won't be able to do this intuitively. And even if high-achieving youth are able to do this sometimes, it's because of their survival history, and they'll still need help learning how to go back and reclaim the non-survival parts of their life.

Also, when you can, let teens listen to their music. Music is often the one thing they can choose and have control over. It usually helps them to focus and distract their overloaded nerve networks and keep their body regulated. Artistic activities and fidget toys can also help with focus when music isn't an option.

Overall, youth are a pretty truthful group. But they may lie to you if they don't feel safe. When they have learned that adults cannot be trusted, they can be very protective, secretive, and even threatening. Many adults are often suspicious and hostile towards youth, especially when they're playing or having fun, so it's no wonder that many teens develop the same attitudes back.

Try to remember that **a lot of negative behaviors are a sign that a young person is in survival** and needs help.

This can be hard because many abused and neglected teens do not want to tell you about their history or family secrets, even if things are really bad. And for many kids and teens, the only socially acceptable options to survive a difficult household are by shutting down, escaping, caretaking, and telling parents and adults what they want to hear. But because their brain is in major reconstruction, they might also act out a lot as their buried feelings flare up.

And because of all this, or maybe in spite of it, many teens seem to understand that their parents are struggling with their own damage and pain. They often feel protective of them and may not share what's really going on for fear of betraying or disappointing their parents.

It can be easy to forget that teens and young adults will often feel helpless because they are not allowed to be in charge of their own body and their own life. In a toxic home, they are required to fall in line or be a target unless child protective services completely removes and separates them from their family, which often feels like the scarier option.

They are also required to go to school every day, where they usually get a very limited say in their schedule and how they spend their free time. And if they miss too much school, then they might be sent to court. Which rarely does anything to help with household trauma or solve the problems of their overwhelmed or neglectful parents.

Teens and young adults also struggle to have enough money to be independent as the cost of living increases, so they are often stuck living in unsafe homes for longer than they expect. And this can make it hard to stay motivated and functional. They may also jump into risky situations and relationships to have the freedom to live their own way and be their own person.

Although life can get harder as you get older, it doesn't mean that it's okay to dismiss the challenges of youth. It doesn't have to be a competition. **Trying to navigate an adult world as a young person is really hard**, and you may have forgotten what that was like. The teen years feel much easier in hindsight with your fully grown brain and years of practice.

So try your best to cut the young people some slack. The world they're facing today is uncharted. Teens and young adults are trying to navigate a world that most adults still don't have a handle on. They know you're lying to yourself or to them when you tell them it's not that hard to figure out.

Now, **if you are a youth in this age range, the healing processes in this book will also work for you**. But it can be tricky to work toward unraveling your trauma experiences when you are still living with your parents or in a home where you have a history of abuse or neglect. Trying to change your protective responses when you still don't feel safe may be risky and even cause more challenges.

Getting support from trusted people can be a really useful start to your healing process. Having someone who will listen and believe you can help you to learn trust and connection. It's often possible to find one or two trusted adults at school or in the community. And many schools have mental health professionals available if you need them. In some states, minors can even seek mental health treatment on their own and are eligible for free and low-cost programs.

Keep doing your best and try to trust yourself and your body as you go. You've got this.

Further Study Recommendations:

Brainstorm: The Power and Purpose of the Teenage Brain by Daniel Siegel, MD. This book talks about the brain science of teens and young adults and what to expect during these years.

How to Hug a Hedgehog: 12 Keys for Connecting with Teens by Brad Wilcox and Jerrick Robbins. This book can help you understand how to connect with and support teens as they come of age.

Never Enough: When Achievement Culture Becomes Toxic – And What We Can Do About It by Jennifer Breheny Wallace. This book can help parents, caregivers, and teachers better understand the stressors that teens currently face with school and other expectations. And how to more effectively nurture their gifts and help them to grow.

CHAPTER D – JUDGMENT AND DISCRIMINATION

Talking about discrimination is important when we're discussing survival.

It may not seem very related, but so much of the trauma that is experienced in our world has come about because of the judgmental and biased views we hold about each other. And the more we feel dismissed or disposable in our world, the more activated our survival systems become. And the more we justify our own judgments and discriminations.

Now, let's be clear. **Everyone on earth has biases about other people.** It's impossible to grow up without them. This is because putting things in categories is something your amygdala and your cortex are supposed to do.

Your amygdala creates matches for safety and danger, and your cortex likes to file things away in predictable and searchable ways. So, between these two systems, it's really easy for stereotypes to get built into your survival systems as you grow.

Many of these may come from caregivers or community members who went through experiences and world events that created these categories and matches. And these patterns get passed on through the generations by the mirror neurons and the modeling of your caregivers.

Remember that your nerves and networks learn by repeating the patterns of the people around you. In general, these patterns teach you how to keep yourself protected and feeling safe so you can handle the world you live in.

And most of what is modeled to you as a child feels normal since you don't have anything to compare it to. So, without really meaning to, your system can develop muscle memory that makes you feel reactive towards certain people and groups.

It's also possible for these judgments to be transmitted to you by the media and other influencers during stressful times. The lack of stability and increased stress in your day-to-day life will make it easier for your system to accept that certain people or groups are to blame for everything that's wrong and threatening. You might even feel justified in dismissing these groups if you perceive that they first harmed you.

Sadly, your cortex and amygdala will feel resolved when they think they've found something or someone to blame for all the problems. Sorting out these matches and categories will give your system a sense of security that it now has a straightforward idea of where the danger is coming from. Even if this data is mostly wrong, it allows your system to sort out the stress. And the relief of filing it away with a solid danger match just reinforces the feeling that these judgments were right to begin with.

This is why **fear is always at the root of discrimination**. These misfiled matches and categories will not only create emergency responses that flood your body when these topics come up, but your system will also fight like crazy to keep these files in place. Your system doesn't want to let go of biases that help you make sense of the world and make you feel safe, even if it's a false sense of safety.

It can be hard to realize that your stereotypes and judgments are misfiled danger matches and protective parts that are keeping you from seeing the big picture. And it can be hard to reevaluate your biases when you will probably have to face the guilt and regret of holding on to judgments that have hurt yourself and others.

This is why it's so easy for discussions about discrimination to become so tense and stressful so quickly.

This is why it's easier for some people to disown a family member rather than take the time to sit down together and face something new.

This is why some church leaders can become hostile and condemning when they feel helpless to sit with doubts and difficult questions.

This is why doctors and providers may be more believing or empathetic to the pain of one patient over another.

This is why some people may mock or tease those who pray or wear religious clothing or accessories.

This is why certain groups will hurt or kill innocent people with a different skin color or sexual orientation.

This is why political parties struggle to work together on bipartisan changes that benefit everyone.

This is why strangers believe it's their duty to comment on, give advice to, or insult other people's bodies and appearance.

This is why some religious followers feel stubbornly justified for not using or respecting preferred names and pronouns.

Discrimination is a serious issue that affects all of us. Just like the parts of your system, if one part doesn't belong, then the whole system is impacted. When your biases are getting in the way of unity, cooperation, and understanding, then you're hurting yourself and the world you live in more than you probably realize.

If you have found yourself becoming hostile, stubborn, or trying to deflect when someone else is sharing their experience and voice, please consider the situations and patterns that have brought you here.

No amount of anger, disrespect, or control will change someone else's mind or feelings. Being willing to stand divided over someone else's differences or battle against their life choices is really just an attempt to contain things that you cannot handle. Your system is not acting from a logical or reasonable space. It is trying to control and escape your fears around these topics. And these kinds of quick fixes will only keep you stuck.

Although it can take a lot of work to unravel some of these emergency responses, it can be very rewarding when you learn how to be free of these fears and stay connected with others, even when you still disagree.

Much of this work will come naturally if you are working through the healing process and facing stuck networks. Many of the judgments that you carry are going to be related to the places where you feel insecure and judgmental of yourself. Without constant survival mode, you'll be able to see the world with less fear, and you won't need to rely on blaming or controlling others to feel safe anymore.

If you are ready to work on and face your judgments or stereotypes more directly, working on mindfulness is a great way to start.

Mindfulness activities help your body and brain to stay present as you face challenging feelings and triggers. This means that **you can use mindfulness to face the fears that come up when you are exposed to or reminded of the people, ideas, or groups that cause you discomfort.**

You don't have to go in planning to agree or see eye-to-eye. The goal is to try and stay mindful instead of getting flipped into stress responses. Without a sense of safety in your system, your protective responses will just take over. And it will be impossible to let yourself listen to or understand anything without fear getting in the way and warping your perspective.

Finding ways to stay present and be mindful with these topics will allow you to hear and understand other perspectives. And it can even help you really discover what you feel and believe instead of just going along with what you've always "known" or been taught.

Again, you're not doing this just to agree. You're trying to reset any survival networks that are getting activated so that you can be more intentional about your perspective rather than reactive.

An easier place to start facing these stereotypes is through **learning more about the history of the people or groups you're judging**. This may help you to see more about what you have in common rather than only focusing on what's different. And it can often give you empathy for the difficult things that others have been through.

Seeking out videos, blogs, and social media accounts of different people can also be an easy way to see into someone else's experience and try to understand their point of view.

Further Study Recommendations:

Becoming Kin: An Indigenous Call to Unforgetting the Past and Reimagining Our Future by Patty Krawec. This book can help you to better understand the traumatic experiences of native and indigenous people. It also offers guidance on connecting more with diverse communities to increase your knowledge and awareness.

Biased: Uncovering the Hidden Prejudice That Shapes What We See, Think, and Do by Jennifer L. Eberhardt, PhD. This book explores the statistics related to prejudice and racism, especially toward black individuals. But it is also useful for recognizing how our fears fuel our biases and can lead to discrimination.

Invisible Women: Data Bias in a World Designed for Men by Caroline Criado Perez. This book discusses the challenges with gender bias and the difficulties that everyone experiences in societies where there is inequitable gender representation.

My Grandmother's Hands: Racialized Trauma and the Pathway to Mending Our Hearts and Bodies by Resmaa Menakem. This book can help you understand how biases and discrimination contribute to social and generational trauma.

Permission to Come Home: Reclaiming Mental Health as Asian Americans by Jenny T. Wang, PhD. This book can offer some insight into the history and experience of Asian Americans and the assumptions and prejudices that impact them.

Poverty, By America by Matthew Desmond. This book explains how financial insecurity and caste can lead to communities living in survival and create fear and bias toward minorities.

Radical Belonging: How to Survive and Thrive in an Unjust World (While Transforming It for the Better) by Lindo Bacon, PhD. This book discusses how discrimination can be traumatizing and why learning to be more tolerant and compassionate can improve the world around us. This book includes discussions around body shaming, homophobia, transphobia, racism, sexism, ableism, ageism, and religious intolerance.

Tattoos on the Heart: The Power of Boundless Compassion and *Barking to the Choir: The Power of Radical Kinship* by Gregory Boyle. These can be useful books for learning more about and increasing compassion towards the challenges of gang members and those who grow up in poverty. The author is a Jesuit priest who uses his spiritual beliefs to advocate for community care.

What It Takes to Heal: How Transforming Ourselves Can Change the World by Prentis Hemphill. This book offers insight and support in healing from discrimination as well as guidance on addressing your own prejudice and fears.

CHAPTER E – DETERIORATION AND DYING

As you age, your body is not able to keep up with the energy required to keep your system running in the same way it always has. This means that **your system starts to prioritize where it sends energy and materials**.

When your energy levels decrease and you can't keep up the same pace, your body will reduce your cortex function and rely more on muscle memory, emergency responses, your reward system, and the body functions that keep you alive.

For many people, this may begin in midlife as your **hormone levels drop or shift** and force your system to rely more on survival functioning. These changes can be due to perimenopause, menopause, or low testosterone and are known to impact mood regulation, concentration, muscle and joint pain, weight gain, sleep, and much more.

Many times these hormone shifts can be treated by a knowledgeable provider using hormone replacement or lifestyle changes. In many cases, this can improve your mood and functioning since your energy isn't being spent trying to make up for the low supply. And your body isn't left drained and having to use your survival systems to function every day.

These same patterns can also show up with untreatable aging issues like **degenerative or terminal diseases**. Managing survival systems can be difficult since your body is struggling to repair itself and won't have the energy and resources to keep up with regular functioning.

As these situations progress, you may start to feel more confused or disorganized as you **lose cortex function and the ability to put new memories into long-term storage**. You might also lose the ability to move or speak and struggle to stay present long before you pass away.

This is why you might remember complicated dances or songs in your muscle memory but not be able to access much from your long-term memory. Your muscle memories will stay intact much longer than your cortex.

As your cortex loses priority, your **amygdala and emergency systems will have to take control more often**, and they can start to **bring old emergency responses to the surface**.

This can be frustrating because survival memories and feelings will be much harder to manage without your big-picture functioning. This is why it might be getting difficult to handle your feelings and stop yourself from freaking out, blowing up, or shutting down all the time.

If this is your situation, it's actually **still possible to get help with managing these survival systems**. An experienced professional can help your system to process and organize many of your old and stuck survival networks, even if your memory isn't what it used to be or it's hard to move or speak.

Although this won't cure aging or disease, it can often help your final years to be more peaceful for you and your family.

It can also be useful to look for ways to express and honor the grief that comes with losing these pieces of you. Finding support through groups, professionals, family, friends, and spiritual leaders may allow your body to find some peace during this time.

Further Study Recommendations:

The Art of Dying Well: A Practical Guide to a Good End of Life by Katy Butler. This book provides a helpful overview of the aging and dying process and offers practical and specific information about preparing for death. It offers guidance for those who are facing death as well as their caretakers.

The New Menopause: Navigating Your Path Through Hormonal Changes with Purpose, Power, and Facts by Mary Clair Haver, MD. This book provides information about the different stages of menopause and how to support your body through these changes.

CHAPTER F – NEURODIVERGENCE AND SCHIZOPHRENIA

Many people are born with or develop **neural differences or neurodivergence** in their system. This means that **your brain connects and signals in a way that's different from the average person.**

In fact, in some ways everyone is neurodivergent since no two body systems will grow with the exact same combination of neural networks. But some neurodivergent situations like autism, sensory processing differences, and schizophrenia can make it more difficult to manage survival responses.

Generally, if you are neurodivergent, it means that the connections in your brain and body process information differently than others, especially when it comes to your senses. These differences aren't naturally a problem or bad, but they can become challenging when you have to live in a world that wasn't designed for the way your system works.

In our school analogy, these kinds of differences might look like the hallway loudspeakers being twice as loud as the average speaker, or having 100 security camera feeds instead of 10, or having radios that echo a lot. These differences don't make the school any better or worse than others, but it might affect the way the system operates.

If you have neuro differences, you might find that sensory experiences in your day-to-day life are really difficult to understand and are even completely overwhelming at times.

You might have a hard time coping with senses like sounds, touch, body sensations, emotions, smells, tastes, or images. You might have a hard time tuning into people's faces or emotions. Or you might have a hard time speaking or noticing the signals that are coming from your own body.

Since your survival systems mainly use your senses and perceptions to decide if something is safe or dangerous, **you might have a harder time managing stress or triggers** if your feeds are overloaded all day by the things that everyone else finds to be low effort.

Imagine how much more difficult your survival responses might be if it felt like your clothes were always scratching or cutting you. What if the sound of a fan at work felt as loud as a helicopter? What if eye contact felt like a police interrogation? What if it took all your energy just to take in every shape and color in the room? What if being hugged felt like being poked with pins? What if your brain couldn't recognize your own voice?

These kinds of differences mean that it could feel pretty stressful for someone with neurodivergence to live in a family or culture where eye contact, casual conversations, and shaking hands are part of the norm. Even though one of these things might be totally fine to prepare for and handle on its own, having to deal with these situations every day can easily put your system on overload.

This is why it can be easy for one small change in your day to completely derail your system and flip on your emergency networks. It's hard to handle any situation when your system is at full capacity from handling sensory overload and you don't have any energy or focus left to deal with anything else.

On the other hand, neurodivergence can also make it difficult to use your connection and safety networks to be soothed when the stimulations around you are so big and overwhelming that it's hard to notice someone holding you or caring for you or offering you something calm. It's even harder when your sensory signals make touch, connection, or affection feel repulsive or painful.

This is why neurodivergent folks can have a hard time managing their feelings, behaviors, and expressions, especially when they are already overwhelmed.

What's interesting about these differences is that, in some situations, it's hard to know which differences are something you're genetically born with and which ones are created by (or made worse by) your environment or trauma.

Many people have found that their processing differences might actually be related to early traumas that shaped their systems as they were growing.

For example, a baby in the NICU might become overly sensitive to sounds after being treated for heart problems. Being exposed to the alarms and beeping of medical monitors, the pain of her own body, and the stress around her can easily cause her system to match loud noises with chest pain and stress.

And because her tiny body is starting to put nerve connections together, her system might overly develop her hearing in order to be extra sensitive to the beeps and alarms that signal threats. This might cause her system to focus so much on building her hearing that sounds end up twice as loud for her as someone else. Clearly these changes in her nerves will make it really easy for her to be overstimulated by everyday noises.

Also, an overly strong emergency network like this at the beginning of her life can add up to a lot of overstimulated survival networks as she grows. Even if her heart problems are treated and fixed, the pain and dysfunction from these early memories can create nerve networks that cause tension in her chest every time she hears certain sounds. Which may lead to chronic chest pain and feeling overly distressed by certain noises throughout her life.

This type of situation is more likely to lead to a diagnosis of a sensory processing difference.

A **sensory processing difference or disorder** is a diagnosis given to people who struggle to function in everyday environments because their **senses can be more activated than the average person**.

Studies show that these sensitivities can develop because they are passed on through genetics, but it's also possible to have these sensitivities formed during early life stressors and/or get worse because of trauma.

ADHD or attention deficit hyperactivity disorder is also a form of neurodivergence.

Although there are genetic markers related to ADHD, it seems that trauma and insecure attachment play a big part in activating these markers and developing dissociated networks.

Folks with ADHD will often struggle to manage impulses, stay organized, focus, be on time, and pay attention. They can also be easily distracted, inattentive, and/or hyperactive.

For the most part, these are all skills that are handled by your cortex. So it makes sense that ADHD can also develop from or be activated and intensified by being raised in survival environments.

When families and caregivers are always functioning out of survival, a child's cortex will get less training and modeling, and they may miss out on learning certain big-picture skills. Without a lot of time with organized and secure adults, it will be difficult for a child to learn how to regulate and manage their system in a big-picture way.

In addition, folks with symptoms of hyperactivity are likely struggling with overactive go-mode, and those with symptoms of inattention may be dealing with slow-mode. These survival reactions can make it hard for your system to prioritize organization and focus in general.

Now, just to be clear, this doesn't mean that people with ADHD are less intelligent or that their system is less developed than others. Just that the cortex part of their system didn't develop in the same way as others or in the way that everyone expects.

Bodies and brains develop in many different ways, and they will keep growing however they can. As we discussed before with dissociation, your system can learn to thrive even when it's more compartmentalized.

Differences in function or development like this will often encourage your system to find out-of-the-box ways to live. Your system might have developed in more creative and emotional ways that have helped you to understand the natural world and patterns around you.

Even if your focus challenges made school hard, you might have a really strong grasp of physics, gardening, bodywork, computers, art, animals, spirituality, etc. just from exploring the world around you. Many people have found a lot more joy in their lives as they acknowledge and honor these differences and use them to benefit themselves and others.

Now, if you have ADHD and you feel like you're struggling with your symptoms, you can improve some of the challenges in your system by doing the work in this book to face stuck networks and improve regulation. This can help your system to reduce the amount of survival responses that are hijacking you. In most cases, this will allow you to have more energy to learn and practice the skills that can help you become more organized (if that feels like something you want).

But it's also important to recognize that learning organizational skills won't just make your differences disappear and switch you to "normal." You'll just be learning how to work with these differences in a way that supports you and your life.

You might also consider looking for careers, social groups, partners, or activities where you feel like your differences are accepted rather than spending all your energy trying to fit in.

Autism is another diagnosis that is part of this type of neurodivergence and is also called **Autism Spectrum Disorder or ASD**. Autism can be difficult to understand since it can show up really differently from person to person. For some people, autism symptoms can make it difficult or impossible to communicate or even be in control of your body. For other people, it can be very similar to a sensory processing diagnosis and may not be as obvious to others.

Autism is usually diagnosed in early childhood and is passed on through genetics. Based on what scientists know so far, it seems unlikely that these differences are created by the environment or a trauma.

This diagnosis can be particularly difficult because there are many theories about what causes autism that can make this diagnosis feel like something to "fix." Some families will go to great lengths to push someone into therapies, nutrition plans, or rigid routines to "cure" their symptoms.

Although this can be helpful with some common symptoms like stomach issues, anxiety, or self-harming behavior, these supports can also feel hurtful if it implies that the person isn't good enough to belong as they are, especially when their differences don't change.

This is a tricky situation because people with autism begin receiving support from their parents when they are children and don't really have a say in their treatment or know how they feel about their diagnosis until they're older.

And, even then, not all people with autism feel the same way about their diagnosis or treatment.

Some people feel like they don't need to be fixed or changed at all and that their differences make them unique and important. Other people wish they could live without their differences. And more people fall somewhere in between.

This is also hard because autism includes such a wide range of people and symptoms that it's hard to expect everyone to be on the same page about what's best.

Hopefully future research and study will help us understand these diagnoses better. But, in the meantime, understanding survival systems can be quite useful if you are diagnosed with autism and feel like you're looking to relieve some of the difficulties that come up from sensory differences and the stress of navigating a neurotypical world.

Emergency responses are usually more difficult to manage with sensory overload and/or body limitations. This might be why many people with ASD can have such intense fixations and/or stimming behaviors. When their system gets overwhelmed and they find it hard to be calmed or soothed by others, they will usually find ways to manage this by themselves as much as they can.

Another neuro difference that can be really hard on your survival systems are diagnoses like **schizophrenia**. Schizophrenia, and other **hallucination and delusion-based disorders**, also seem to change how senses come through the live feed and complicate your survival systems.

These kinds of diagnoses make it hard for you to understand the difference between what's real and not real and to keep your thoughts organized and logical.

Schizophrenia and delusion-based disorders seem to come from a combination of genetics and environment. It's possible that these diagnoses come from changes in the brain because of ongoing trauma from childhood. And it's also possible that differences in the brain make things more traumatizing.

So all together, it might be tricky to know what's more likely to cause these differences. It is also a little different from other neuro differences because it may not surface until your late teens or early adulthood.

Some research shows that schizophrenia might affect the ability for the brain to recognize itself and/or that neuron signals in the body get interrupted while they're trying to send messages. Other research shows that dopamine (a reward hormone) might get so activated that it creates intense hallucinations during stressful situations.

These differences would clearly make it hard to handle everyday activities like everyone else. And, of course, it would cause your survival systems to be on edge and easily triggered when it's hard to sort out incomplete signals and vivid hallucinations.

There are many **other types of neurodivergence** that we can't possibly cover in this book. Some of these include neuro differences that come up because of illnesses or accidents like strokes, traumatic brain injuries, mold or heavy metal poisoning, seizure disorders, etc. And even complex trauma and living in survival can create neuro differences that make life more challenging.

Luckily, in most instances of neurodivergence, **facing and healing survival networks can really help to improve your system**. Even if nothing changes about your neuro differences (or you don't want to change anything about them) it's almost always relieving to reduce your survival overload. And navigating a world that isn't built for your brain and body is stressful enough.

By working on your survival networks, you will have a lot more focus and energy on navigating the world with your differences and not be drained by an overloaded system.

If you have neuro differences, it's easy to feel frustrated or overwhelmed by your survival system. In most cases your neuro differences will escalate your emergency networks (especially sensory differences since they're more likely to overstimulate your system). By learning more about your triggers and getting help with addressing old traumas or stuck networks, you might find that your neuro differences become easier to navigate.

It can also be helpful to **work on building a lifestyle that supports your neuro differences**. You, your friends, and your family can often help you to find ways to reduce overstimulation in your day-to-day life. And knowing more about your limits and setting boundaries can also help with this, especially if you need a lot of support from others due to some of your differences.

In this case, most of the treatments that will be more successful will likely use nerve feedback to train and balance your brain signals. See the Appendix to review treatment options that might be useful with these differences.

As always, a professional who is really good at listening, learning, and adapting can be helpful, even if it's to listen long enough to refer you to more qualified programs or people.

And if your differences make it hard to stay present or you feel disconnected from reality a lot, it's important to find someone who doesn't dismiss or judge you for this and who does their best to understand where you're coming from, even if they can't always make sense of it right away.

Further Study Recommendations:

ADHD 2.0: New Science and Essential Strategies for Thriving with Distraction – from Childhood Through Adulthood by Edward M. Hallowel, MD, and John J. Ratey, MD. This book can help you to understand some of the information and skills that can help you to improve your experience with ADHD.

Connecting with the Autism Spectrum: How to Talk, How to Listen, and Why You Shouldn't Call It High-Functioning by Casey "Remrov" Vormer. This book is a short read that can help you understand some basic ways to interact with and connect with someone on the autism spectrum.

Differently Wired: Raising an Exceptional Child in a Conventional World by Deborah Reber. This book can help parents understand how to balance allowing your neurodivergent children to be themselves while also helping to manage some of the experiences that are challenging for you and your child.

"Hearing Voices Network USA" at www.hearingvoicesusa.org/. This online community is non-judgmental place to get support for those who experience auditory hallucinations.

NeuroTribes: The Legacy of Autism and the Future of Neurodiversity by Steven Silberman. This book can help you understand the overall picture of how ASD became more widely known and how different individuals and families experience this diagnosis.

The Out-Of-Sync Child: Recognizing and Coping with Sensory Processing Differences by Carol Stock Kranowitz, MA. This book can introduce you to the different ways that sensory processing differences can show up in children and provide some basic interventions to help these kids better connect and engage, especially in school environments.

Sincerely, Your Autistic Child: What People on the Autism Spectrum Wish Their Parents Knew About Growing up, Acceptance, and Identity by Emily Paige Ballou, Sharon daVanport, and Morénike Giwa Onaiwu. This book offers some thoughts from people who are diagnosed with autism and what they wish other people understood. These experiences are mostly from females and non-binary individuals.

Surviving Schizophrenia, 7th Edition: A Family Manual by E. Fuller Torrey, MD. This book is mostly written for families to help you manage and navigate schizophrenia treatment as it can be difficult to handle all by yourself.

CHAPTER G – EPIGENETICS AND METHYLATION

There is a process in your body called *methylation* that might be adding to some of your survival challenges. This word is pronounced meth-uh-lay-shun.

Methylation is a little complicated, and we don't have time to fully explain it here, but it has to do with your DNA and epigenetic markers that we talked about in Chapter 44. Methylation is one of the ways that your epigenetic markers switch the codes in your system.

So if your methylation system is having issues, **it can shift the way that your DNA is functioning in your body** and create other problems that will lead to disorganized survival systems.

Whether your body is **undermethylated** or **overmethylated**, your body can struggle to process reward hormones properly, which can make it difficult to balance your mood and keep your survival systems from taking over.

It's amazing that this seemingly small problem can be so hard on your body. But it really can be.

In the research, these imbalances seem to be responsible for a lot of pain and inflammation, especially in the digestive system. They can make it hard to focus or sleep (even when you're exhausted). And they make it hard for your body to keep the right balance of reward hormones to manage your pain and moods. Some research even suggests that these issues may be at the root of many fibromyalgia cases.

Now, if that wasn't enough, methylation issues **can also make it hard for some mental health meds to work properly**. And in some cases the medication can throw off the balance even more. It can feel devastating to finally try medications only to have things get worse.

If you want to see if you have methylation issues or if you've had bad experiences with mental health meds in the past, it can be helpful to find a doctor, practitioner, or nutritionist to test for and treat methylation issues. These providers can work with you to find the right balance of supplements, diet, and/or med changes based on your tests and situation.

An important side note with this is that folic acid and folates supplements (or vitamin B9) can make some methylation problems worse. And the U.S. has required folic acid to be added to wheat products since 1998 to prevent birth defects. This practice has continued in many other countries now, but this additive may be contributing to increased challenges with methylation and mental health.

So it's possible that some of the folks who feel better on a gluten-free diet may have methylation issues they don't know about.

Further Study Recommendations:

Nutrient Power: Heal Your Biochemistry and Heal Your Brain by William Walsh, PhD. This book is written by the scientist who discovered methylation patterns. The book is a little dense but can help you learn more about the power of nutrients on your mental health.

The Walsh Institute website also has simpler explanations of this research on their website: www.walshinstitute.org/biochemical-individuality--nutrition.html.

Appendix

TREATMENTS AND MODALITIES

Because there are many treatments and methods that can help you through this journey, and there are more being created all the time, there's no possible way to list every single one. Here are some more common treatments and what they target.

It's possible that many professionals are trained in more than one method and will use a few different approaches to fit the needs of their clients.

Bodywork can be a great way to work on healing. Many bodywork methods focus on improving the mind/body connection and can help you in your healing process. These options might include things like cranial sacral massage, acupuncture, yoga, chiropractics, energy work, etc. Some bodywork providers may also use natural herbs, medicines, or other treatments to work on balancing and healing the body.

Many professionals in these fields are trauma informed and can help you heal survival networks using titration with your body. This option can be especially helpful when your high-functioning or caretaking stress responses cause you to be overly defensive or too compliant in talk therapy. This can also be useful when working on preverbal trauma experiences.

Brainspotting uses the feedback and communication from your eyes to identify, process, and resolve stuck emergency responses. This is usually used along with other treatment methods.

Cognitive Behavioral Therapy (CBT) is a therapy that is used to help with negative beliefs and intrusive thoughts. This approach can be helpful to reduce the obsessive thoughts that drive compulsive behaviors. This method is most effective when it's used alongside more holistic treatments.

Couples/Family Therapy is an option for doing work with relationships. For couples work, methods like emotionally focused therapy (EFT) and the Gottman approach can be helpful to get to the root of the hurt and disconnect.

Cultural and Spiritual Healing Practices can include some of the bodywork options we discussed like acupuncture and yoga practices, but they can also include sacred ceremonies that increase safety and balance in the body.

Prayer circles, singing and music rituals, and psychedelic healing ceremonies have all been shown to help in the healing process. This is especially true when these practices focus on decreasing shame and increasing your sense of belonging to yourself, your community, the universe, your ancestors, and/or a higher power.

Developmental Needs Meeting Strategy (DNMS) is a type of ego states therapy to help with finding, protecting, and reconnecting with parts that have been abandoned and/or traumatized.

Dialectical Behavioral Therapy (DBT) is a therapy that teaches you skills to help tolerate and regulate overwhelming emotions and improve communication skills. This approach can give you more ways to cope with facing stuck networks, and it can also help you in the rebuilding process as you are retraining your networks and reparenting your inner children.

Ego State Therapy is a parts work therapy approach that can help you to find and get to know different parts of yourself so that you can protect and reparent the parts that need healing and support.

The Emotional Freedom Technique (also EFT) uses tapping movements on your body's acupressure points to reduce stress and increase feedback and communication between your body and brain. This is usually a method used alongside other approaches.

Exposure and Response Prevention (ERP) is a therapy that can help with OCD and compulsive thoughts and behaviors. It helps you to sit with and manage the fears and intrusive thoughts that push you to quick fix with compulsive behaviors.

Eye Movement Desensitization and Reprocessing (or EMDR) is a psychotherapy that uses back and forth, left and right body movements to interrupt, titrate, and reorganize trauma memories until they are integrated into long-term memory and no longer feel painful or overwhelming. This approach can also be used to address preverbal traumas.

Flashforward is a technique within EMDR that can help with obsessive compulsive behaviors and phobias.

Flash Technique is an intervention that can be used to quickly reduce and titrate the pain and stress related to an overwhelming or painful trauma memory. This usually works best with trauma experiences that only happened once or twice and were not repeated throughout your life.

Inner Child Work is an approach that helps you to connect with the younger parts of yourself that feel abandoned or lost. In this approach, you learn to get in touch with your inner children and repair with and/or reparent them.

Internal Family Systems (or IFS) is a therapy that works with your protective parts to improve communication and help the parts to find common ground to work together. This helps your system to prepare for the process of repairing with and reparenting your inner children (or exiles as they are called in the IFS model).

Journaling and **Sketching** are activities that you can do on your own to process through survival feelings and experiences. But you can find guided workbooks, journals, and sketchbooks that can help to organize feelings and thoughts. There are also ones specifically for DID to help sort out and get to know your different parts.

Medication Assisted Therapy uses medications to reduce intense symptoms from your survival networks in order to help you work on reorganizing your system. Medications can range from anti-anxiety and anti-depression meds all the way to ketamine or psychedelic treatments.

Medication interventions generally seem to work best when they're paired with trauma work and guided support. Hallucinogenic or psychedelic interventions also seem to be most effective when they are guided by safe providers or spiritual healers.

Genetic Testing may help you to better identify which mental health medications can be more effective based on your genes. Although this is not a perfect science right now, it seems to help some patients better identify which medications will work best for their system. See Chapter G in the Bonus Upgrade to learn more about how this relates to methylation issues.

Narrative Therapy is a therapy that invites you to tell your story and learn how to bring more information and different perspectives into that story. This can allow you to integrate your traumas and reconnect with parts to start seeing the bigger picture again.

Neurofeedback is a type of treatment that uses technology to improve feedback and communication in your brain. This approach uses machines that measure your brain activity and sends signals, through your senses, that interrupt, strengthen, and rebalance your system. This approach can be useful in addressing preverbal trauma as it helps to adjust muscle memory without having to bring up direct thoughts or memories.

In more complex cases, it is recommended that you combine this with other treatments for best effect.

Neurofeedback may also be good for folks with neuro differences who struggle with human interaction. Although this still might be difficult if the person would feel overstimulated with electrodes on their head or body.

Nutrition Therapy can sometimes be helpful if your body is responding to foods or nutrients that are causing allergic reactions or that are hard on your organs as they digest. Food intolerances can often make your emergency responses more sensitive and easily triggered.

Getting allergy food tests, checking blood sugar, checking iron levels, and/or getting tested for mold and heavy metal poisoning can sometimes help you get treatments or make changes that help your body to reduce survival reactions and make it a bit easier to face the deeper trauma work.

Some diet changes may also improve methylation issues if you have been diagnosed with this. See Chapter G.

Occupational Therapy (OT) can be helpful with neuro differences and preverbal trauma. Through body movements and exercises, these professionals help the brain and body titrate and reconnect to improve cooperation and feedback in your whole system. OT can often help to retrain missing developmental stages in your body that are keeping your parts and networks stuck.

Sensorimotor Psychotherapy and **Somatic Experiencing Therapy** are psychotherapy treatments that work with your body to rerun and reshape stuck networks until they have resolved and successfully made it through all the steps of an emergency cycle. The goal of this treatment is to help your body slowly and naturally return to its intuition and balance through movement and expression. These approaches can often be used to address preverbal trauma.

Sensory Management Tools are another option for supporting neuro differences or managing trigger sensitivity.

Sound-reducing ear plugs like Loop or Flare can help manage overstimulation in loud situations.

Weighted blankets and squeeze machines can be physically soothing when someone doesn't want to be touched.

Fidget toys, texture strips, vibration bracelets, and other similar tools can help increase focus, and/or help you get through overwhelming situations.

Shadow Work is an approach from Jungian psychology that helps you to get in touch with the hidden or unconscious parts of yourself and learn how to work together.

Sound Therapy, Sound Baths, and **Binaural Beats** can be effective support or treatment for someone with neuro differences like sensory processing or autism. These treatments play different sound frequencies to adjust brain waves. This increases feedback in the brain that can help to reconnect and repair stuck networks. It can also balance some of the sensory overload and increase communication inside the brain and body.

There are groups that meet together to work on healing with these interventions. But you can also do them alone. The sound doesn't have to be loud, and it can often be used at home. Since this is such a gentle way to work with someone and doesn't require too close of contact with other people, this can be a useful treatment for someone who is very overstimulated by others.

Transcranial Magnetic Stimulation (TMS) is a procedure that uses magnetic fields to stimulate the brain and adjust frequency and communication within the body system. It has shown to be helpful with reducing shutdown, OCD, and some addictive behaviors.

BIBLIOGRAPHY

Preface

American Psychiatric Association. "Americans' Overall Level of Anxiety about Health, Safety and Finances Remain High." *Psychiatry.org*. Published March 19, 2019. www.psychiatry.org/newsroom/news-releases/americans-overall-level-of-anxiety-about-health-safety-and-finances-remain-high.

Chudler, Eric. "History of Neuroscience." University of Washington, last updated September 9, 2024. faculty.washington.edu/chudler/hist.html.

Kecmanovic, Jelena. "Could Our Efforts to Avoid Anxiety Only Be Making It Worse?" *The Washington Post*, July 9, 2019. www.washingtonpost.com/lifestyle/wellness/could-our-efforts-to-avoid-anxiety-only-be-making-it-worse/2019/07/09/df031504-91f5-11e9-aadb-74e6b2b46f6a_story.html.

Upgrade 1.0

Bear, Mark, Barry Connors, and Michale A. Paradiso. *Neuroscience: Exploring the Brain, Enhanced Edition*. Jones & Bartlett Learning, 2020.

Goodman, Whitney. *Toxic Positivity: Keeping It Real in a World Obsessed with Being Happy*. TarcherPerigee, 2022.

Kandel, Eric R. *The Disordered Mind: What Unusual Brains Tells Us About Ourselves*. Farrar, Straus and Giroux, 2018.

Pittman, Catherine M., and Elizabeth M. Karle. *Rewire Your Anxious Brain: How to Use the Neuroscience of Fear to End Anxiety, Panic, & Worry.* New Harbinger Publications, 2015.

Ratey, John J. *A User's Guide to the Brain: Perception, Attention and the Four Theaters of the Brain.* Vintage Books, 2002.

Upgrade 2.0

Amen, Daniel G., and Lisa C. Routh. *Healing Anxiety and Depression: Based on Cutting-Edge Brain-Imaging Science.* Berkley Books, 2004.

Cleveland Clinic. "Cortisol: What It Is, Function, Symptoms & Levels." Last reviewed Dec 10, 2021. my.clevelandclinic.org/health/articles/22187-cortisol.

Dana, Deb. *The Polyvagal Theory in Therapy: Engaging the Rhythm of Regulation.* W.W. Norton & Company, 2018.

Dance, Amber. "Making and Breaking Connections in the Brain." *Knowable Magazine*, August 18, 2020. https://doi.org/10.1146/knowable-081720-3.

Edwardes, Dan. "Why Extreme Sports Aren't Extreme." *Dan Edwardes*, Published May 1, 2016. danedwardes.com/2016/05/01/why-extreme-sports-arent-extreme/.

Figueiro, Mariana G. "Individually Tailored Light Intervention Through Closed Eyelids to Promote Circadian Alignment and Sleep Health." *Sleep Health* 1, no. 1 (2014): 75-82. http://dx.doi.org/10.1016/j.sleh.2014.12.009.

Foo, Stephanie. *What My Bones Know: A Memoir of Healing from Complex Trauma.* Allen & Unwin, 2022.

Gruber, June, Christopher Oveis, and Dacher Keltner. "Risk for Mania and Positive Emotional Responding: Too Much of a Good Thing?" *Emotion* 8, no. 1 (2008): 23–33, https://doi.org/10.1037/1528-3542.8.1.23.

Hersey, Tricia. *Rest Is Resistance: A Manifesto*. Little, Brown Spark, 2022.

Ironside, Maria, Michael Browning, Tahereh L. Ansari, et al. "Effect of Prefrontal Cortex Stimulation on Regulation of Amygdala Response to Threat in Individuals with Trait Anxiety." *JAMA Psychiatry*: 76, no. 1 (2019): 71-78.

Kozlowska, Kasia, Peter Walker, Loyola McLean, and Pascal Carrive. "Fear and the Defense Cascade: Clinical Implications and Management." *Harvard Review of Psychiatry* 23, no. 4 (2015): 263–287. https://doi.org/10.1097/hrp.0000000000000065.

Lancel, Marike, Hein J. F. van Marle, Maaike M. van Veen, and Annette M. van Schagen. "Disturbed Sleep in PTSD: Thinking Beyond Nightmares." *Frontiers in Psychiatry* 12, no. 1 (2021). https://doi.org/10.3389/fpsyt.2021.767760.

Price, Devon. *Laziness Does Not Exist*. Simon and Schuster Audio, 2022.

Porges, Stephen W. *The Pocket Guide to Polyvagal Theory: The Transformative Power of Feeling Safe*. W.W. Norton & Company, 2017

Porges, Stephen W., and Deb Dana. *Clinical Applications of the Polyvagal Theory: The Emergence of Polyvagal-Informed Therapies*. W. W. Norton & Company, 2018.

Roy, Holly Ann, and Alexander L. Green. "The Central Autonomic Network and Regulation of Bladder Function." *Frontiers in Neuroscience* 13, (2019). https://doi.org/10.3389/fnins.2019.00535.

Schwartz, Arielle. *The Complex PTSD Treatment Manual: An Integrative, Mind-Body Approach to Trauma Recovery*. Pesi Publishing, 2021.

van der Kolk, Bessel. *The Body Keeps the Score: Brain, Mind, and Body in the Healing of Trauma*. Penguin Books, 2014.

Walker, Matthew P. *Why We Sleep: The New Science of Sleep and Dreams*. Penguin Books, 2017.

Walker, Pete. *Complex PTSD: From Surviving to Thriving: A Guide and Map for Recovering from Childhood Trauma*. Azure Coyote, 2013.

Weekes, Claire. *Hope and Help for Your Nerves: End Anxiety Now*. Berkeley, 2020.

Upgrade 3.0

Axmacher, Nikolai, Christian E. Elger, and Juergen Fell. "Working Memory-Related Hippocampal Deactivation Interferes with Long-Term Memory Formation." *Journal of Neuroscience* 29, no. 4 (2009): 1052–60. https://doi.org/10.1523/jneurosci.5277-08.2009.

Boisgontier, Matthieu P., and Stephan P Swinnen. "Proprioception in the Cerebellum." *Frontiers in Human Neuroscience* 8 (2014): 14301–14306. https://doi.org/10.3389/fnhum.2014.00212.

Bostan, Andreea C., Richard P. Dum, and Peter. L. Strick. "The Basal Ganglia Communicate with the Cerebellum." *Proceedings of the National Academy of Sciences* 107, no 18 (2010): 8452–56. https://doi.org/10.1073/pnas.1000496107.

Cerritelli, Francesco, Martin G. Frasch, Marta C. Antonelli, et al. "A Review on the Vagus Nerve and Autonomic Nervous System during Fetal Development: Searching for Critical Windows." *Frontiers in Neuroscience* 15 (2021): 721605. https://doi.org/10.3389/fnins.2021.721605.

De Couck, Marijke, Ralf Caers, Liza Musch, Johanna Fliegauf, Antonio Giangreco, and Yori Gidron. "How breathing can help you make better decisions: Two studies on the effects of breathing patterns on heart rate variability and decision-making in business cases." *International Journal of Psychophysiology* 139 (2019): 1–9. https://doi.org/10.1016/j.ijpsycho.2019.02.011.

Gómez, Rebecca L., and Jamie O. Edgin. "The Extended Trajectory of Hippocampal Development: Implications for Early Memory Development and Disorder." *Developmental Cognitive Neuroscience* 18 (2016): 57–69. https://doi.org/10.1016/j.dcn.2015.08.009.

Graybiel, Ann M., and Scott T. Grafton. "The Striatum: Where Skills and Habits Meet." *Cold Spring Harbor Perspectives in Biology* 7, no. 8 (2015): a021691. https://doi.org/10.1101/cshperspect.a021691.

Greenberg, Jonathan, Victoria L. Romero, Seth Elkin-Frankston, et al. "Reduced Interference in Working Memory Following Mindfulness Training Is Associated with Increases in Hippocampal Volume." *Brain Imaging and Behavior* 13, no. 2 (2018): 366–76. https://doi.org/10.1007/s11682-018-9858-4.

Harrison, Olivia K., Laura Köchli, Stephanie Marino, et al. "Interoception of Breathing and Its Relationship with Anxiety." *Neuron*, 109, no. 25 (2021): 4080–4093. https://doi.org/10.1016/j.neuron.2021.09.045.

Lagercrantz, Hugo. "The Birth of Consciousness." *Early Human Development* 85, no. 10 (2009): S57–58. https://doi.org/10.1016/j.earlhumdev.2009.08.017.

Leszczynski, Marcin. "How Does Hippocampus Contribute to Working Memory Processing?" *Frontiers in Human Neuroscience* 5 (2011). https://doi.org/10.3389/fnhum.2011.00168.

Nakano, Tamami, and Shigeru Kitazawa. "Development of Long-Term Event Memory in Preverbal Infants: An Eye-Tracking Study." *Scientific Reports* 7, no. 1, (2017): 44086. https://doi.org/10.1038/srep44086.

Perry, Bruce D., and Oprah Winfrey. *What Happened to You?: Conversations on Trauma, Resilience, and Healing*. Flatiron Books, 2021.

Porges, Stephen W., and Senta A. Furman. "The Early Development of the Autonomic Nervous System Provides a Neural Platform for Social Behaviour: A Polyvagal Perspective." *Infant and Child*

Development 20, no. 1, (2010): 106–18. https://doi.org/10.1002/icd.688.

Schapiro, Anna C., Allison G. Reid, Alexandra Morgan, Dara S. Manoach, Mieke Verfaellie, and Robert Stickgold. "The Hippocampus Is Necessary for the Consolidation of a Task That Does Not Require the Hippocampus for Initial Learning." *Hippocampus* 29, no. 11, (2019): 1091–1100. https://doi.org/10.1002/hipo.23101.

Solan, Matthew. "Ease Anxiety and Stress: Take a (Belly) Breather." *Harvard Health*, May 10, 2022. www.health.harvard.edu/blog/ease-anxiety-and-stress-take-a-belly-breather-2019042616521.

The Guardian. "Is it possible to remember being born?" *Notes & Queries: The Body Beautiful.* https://www.theguardian.com/notesandqueries/query/0,5753,-2899,00.html.

van der Kolk, Bessel. "Posttraumatic stress disorder and the nature of trauma." *Dialogues in Clinical Neuroscience* 2, no. 1 (2000): 7–22. https://www.ncbi.nlm.nih.gov/pmc/articles/PMC3181584/.

Yonelinas, Andrew. P. "The hippocampus supports high-resolution binding in the service of perception, working memory and long-term memory." *Behavioural Brain Research* 254, (2013): 34–44. https://doi.org/10.1016/j.bbr.2013.05.030.

Yu, Wilson, and Esther Krook-Magnuson. "Cognitive Collaborations: Bidirectional Functional Connectivity between the Cerebellum and the Hippocampus." *Frontiers in Systems Neuroscience* 9, (2015). https://doi.org/10.3389/fnsys.2015.00177.

Upgrade 4.0

Bacon, Linda [now Lindo]. *Health at Every Size: The Surprising Truth About Your Weight.* Benbella Books, 2010.

Bacon, Linda [now Lindo], and Aphramor, Lucy. *Body Respect: What Conventional Health Books Get Wrong, Leave Out, and Just Plain Fail to Understand about Weight.* Benbella Books, 2014.

Burke Harris, Nadine. "How Childhood Trauma Affects Health across a Lifetime." TED Talk, September 2014. Video, 15 min., 49 sec. https://www.ted.com/talks/nadine_burke_harris_how_childhood_trauma_affects_health_across_a_lifetime?subtitle=en.

Chen, Cheng, Almut G. Winterstein, Roger B. Fillingim, and Yu-Jung Wei. "Body Weight, Frailty, and Chronic Pain in Older Adults: A Cross-Sectional Study." *BMC Geriatrics* 19, no. 1 (2019). https://doi.org/10.1186/s12877-019-1149-4.

D'Agnelli, Simona, Lars Arendt-Nielsen, Maria C. Gerra, et al. "Fibromyalgia: Genetics and Epigenetics Insights May Provide the Basis for the Development of Diagnostic Biomarkers." *Molecular Pain* 15 (2018). https://doi.org/10.1177/1744806918819944.

Dahlin, Dondi. *The Five Elements: Understand Yourself and Enhance Your Relationships with the Wisdom of the World's Oldest Personality Type System.* TarcherPerigee, 2016.

Davis, KC. *How to Keep House While Drowning: A Gentle Approach to Cleaning and Organizing.* Simon Element, 2022.

Duncan, Alaine D. *Tao of Trauma: A Practitioner's Guide for Integrating Five Element Theory and Trauma Treatment.* North Atlantic Books, 2019.

Edwards, Scott. "Nightmares and the Brain." *On The Brain*, Autumn 2015. hms.harvard.edu/news-events/publications-archive/brain/nightmares-brain.

Fagelson, Marc. "Tinnitus and Traumatic Memory." *Brain Sciences* 12, no. 11 (2022): 1585. https://doi.org/10.3390/brainsci12111585.

Fayyaz, Humaira, Shazadi Ambreen, Hammad Raziq, and Azmat Hayyat. "Comparison of Cortisol Levels in Patients with Vasovagal Syncope and Postural Tachycardia Syndrome." *Pakistan Journal of Medical Sciences* 38, no. 1 (2021). https://doi.org/10.12669/pjms.38.1.4122.

Ho, Emma, Kwan-Yee, Lingxiao, Chen, Milena Simic, et al. "Psychological Interventions for Chronic, Non-Specific Low Back

Pain: Systematic Review with Network Meta-Analysis." *British Medical Journal* 376 (2022): e067718. https://doi.org/10.1136/bmj-2021-067718.

Isohookana, Reetta, Mauri Marttunen, Helinä Hakko, Pirkko Riipenen, and Kaisa Riala. "The Impact of Adverse Childhood Experiences on Obesity and Unhealthy Weight Control Behaviors among Adolescents." *Comprehensive Psychiatry* 71 (2016): 17–24. https://doi.org/10.1016/j.comppsych.2016.08.002.

Khan, Zainab A., C. Whittal, S. Mansol, and Lisa A. Osborne. "Effect of Depression and Anxiety on the Success of Pelvic Floor Muscle Training for Pelvic Floor Dysfunction." *Journal of Obstetrics and Gynaecology* 33, no. 7 (2013): 710–14. https://doi.org/10.3109/01443615.2013.813913.

Kolacz, Jacek, and Stephen W. Porges. "Chronic Diffuse Pain and Functional Gastrointestinal Disorders after Traumatic Stress: Pathophysiology through a Polyvagal Perspective." *Frontiers in Medicine* 5 (2018). https://doi.org/10.3389/fmed.2018.00145.

Kubzansky, Laura D., Paula Bordelois, Hee Jin Jun, et al. "The Weight of Traumatic Stress." *JAMA Psychiatry* 71, no. 1 (2014): 44-51. https://doi.org/10.1001/jamapsychiatry.2013.2798.

Levine, Peter A. *Healing Trauma: Restoring the Wisdom of the Body*. Sounds True, 2012.

Levine, Peter A. *In an Unspoken Voice: How the Body Releases Trauma and Restores Goodness*. North Atlantic Books, 2010.

Maté, Gabor. *When the Body Says No: The Cost of Hidden Stress*. Vermilion, 2019.

Maté, Gabor, and Daniel Maté. *The Myth of Normal: Trauma, Illness, and Healing in a Toxic Culture*. Penguin Publishing Group, 2022.

Nagoski, Emily, and Amelia Nagoski. *Burnout: The Secret to Unlocking the Stress Cycle*. Ballantine Books, 2020.

Ogden, Pat. *The Pocket Guide to Sensorimotor Psychotherapy in Context.* W.W. Norton & Company, 2021.

Pavlov, Valentin A., and Kevin J. Tracey. "The Vagus Nerve and the Inflammatory Reflex—Linking Immunity and Metabolism." *Nature Reviews Endocrinology* 8, no. 12, (2012): 743–54. https://doi.org/10.1038/nrendo.2012.189.

Payne, Peter, Peter A. Levine, and Mardi A. Crane-Godreau. "Somatic experiencing: using interoception and proprioception as core elements of trauma therapy." *Frontiers in Psychology* 6, no. 93, (2015): doi.10.3389/fpsyg.2015.00093.

Pollack, Lauren O., and Kelsie T. Forbush. "Why Do Eating Disorders and Obsessive–Compulsive Disorder Co-Occur?" *Eating Behaviors* 14, no. 2, (2013): 211–15. https://doi.org/10.1016/j.eatbeh.2013.01.004.

Rosenberg, Stanley. *Accessing the Healing Power of the Vagus Nerve: Self-Help Exercises for Anxiety, Depression, Trauma, and Autism.* North Atlantic Books, 2017.

Sapolsky, Robert. *Why Zebras Don't Get Ulcers: The Acclaimed Guide to Stress, Stress-Related Diseases, and Coping.* Holt, 2004.

Schlauch, Karen A., Robert W. Read, Stephanie M. Koning, Iva Neveux, and Joseph J. Grzymski. "Using phenome-wide association studies and the SF-12 quality of life metric to identify profound consequences of adverse childhood experiences on adult mental and physical health in a Northern Nevadan population." *Frontiers in Psychiatry* 13 (2022). doi.org/10.3389/fpsyt.2022.984366.

Shapiro, Livia. *The Somatic Therapy Workbook: Stress-Relieving Exercises for Strengthening the Mind-Body Connection and Sparking Emotional and Physical Healing.* Ulysses Press, 2020.

Taylor, Sonya Renee. *The Body Is Not an Apology: The Power of Radical Self-Love.* Berrett-Koehler Publishers, Inc., 2018.

Tinkham, Pamela. *Healing Trauma from the Inside Out: Practices from the East and West.* CreateSpace Independent Publishing Platform. 2017.

Zhang, Ming, Yuqi Zhang, and Yazhuo Kong. "Interaction between Social Pain and Physical Pain." *Brain Science Advances* 5, no. 4 (2019): 265–73. https://doi.org/10.26599/bsa.2019.9050023.

Upgrade 5.0

After Skool. "How Childhood Trauma Leads to Addiction - Gabor Maté." January 19, 2021. YouTube, 9 min., 09 sec. https://www.youtube.com/watch?v=BVg2bfqblGI.

Alcoholics Anonymous. *Twelve Steps and Twelve Traditions.* Alcoholics Anonymous World Services, 2009.

Bär, Karl-Jürgen, Marco Herbsleb, Andy Schumann, Feliberto de la Cruz, Holger W. Gabriel, and Gerd Wagner. "Hippocampal-Brainstem Connectivity Associated with Vagal Modulation after an Intense Exercise Intervention in Healthy Men." *Frontiers in Neuroscience* 10 (2016). https://doi.org/10.3389/fnins.2016.00145.

Belujon, Pauline, and Anthony A. Grace. "Regulation of Dopamine System Responsivity and Its Adaptive and Pathological Response to Stress." *Proceedings of the Royal Society B: Biological Sciences* 282, no. 1805 (2015): 20142516, https://doi.org/10.1098/rspb.2014.2516.

Brand, Russell. *Recovery: Freedom from Our Addictions.* Henry Holt and Company, 2017.

DeMare, Sheila R. *Tourette Syndrome: Stop Your Tics by Learning What Triggers Them.* Association for Comprehensive Neurotherapy, 2017.

Edmondson, Amanda J., Cathy A. Brennan, and Allan O. House. "Non-Suicidal Reasons for Self-Harm: A Systematic Review of Self-Reported Accounts." *Journal of Affective Disorders* 191 (2016): 109–117. https://doi.org/10.1016/j.jad.2015.11.043.

Flores, Philip J. *Addiction as an Attachment Disorder.* Rowman & Littlefield, 2004.

Fotuhi Majid, David Do, and Clifford Jack. "Modifiable factors that alter the size of the hippocampus with ageing." *Nature*

Reviews Neurology 8, no.4 (2012):189-202. doi: 10.1038/nrneurol.2012.27.

Gage, Suzanne H., and Harry R. Sumnall. "Rat Park: How a Rat Paradise Changed the Narrative of Addiction." *Addiction* 114, no. 5 (2018): 917–22. https://doi.org/10.1111/add.14481.

Godier, Lauren R., and Rebecca J. Park. "Does Compulsive Behavior in Anorexia Nervosa Resemble an Addiction? A Qualitative Investigation." *Frontiers in Psychology* 6, (2015). https://doi.org/10.3389/fpsyg.2015.01608.

Grayson, Jonathan. *Freedom from Obsessive-Compulsive Disorder: A Personalized Recovery Program for Living with Uncertainty*. Berkley Books, 2014.

Hoffman, Jonathan, Dee Franklin, Ciana Mickolus, and Myriam Padron. "International OCD Foundation | Are Eating Disorders Obsessive Compulsive Disorder? Let Us Discuss." *International OCD Foundation*, Winter 2022. iocdf.org/expert-opinions/are-eating-disorders-ocd/.

Kar, Ayesha, Archana Adikey, Jennifer Wells, and Anita Kablinger. "Obsessive-Compulsive Disorder Driven by Aspects of Ritual Addiction: A Case Report and Review of Literature." *Psychopharmacology Bulletin* 51, no. 2 (2021): 65–68. www.ncbi.nlm.nih.gov/pmc/articles/PMC8146564/.

Koob, George F., and Nora D. Volkow. "Neurobiology of Addiction: A Neurocircuitry Analysis." *The Lancet Psychiatry* 3, no. 8 (2016): 760–73. https://doi.org/10.1016/s2215-0366(16)00104-8.

Krishnan, Seetha, Chad Heer, Chery Cherian, and Mark E.J. Sheffield. "Reward Expectation Extinction Restructures and Degrades CA1 Spatial Maps through Loss of a Dopaminergic Reward Proximity Signal." *Nature Communications* 13, (2022): 6662. https://doi.org/10.1038/s41467-022-34465-5.

Lai, Vicky T., Jos van Berkum, and Peter Hagoortet. "Negative affect increases reanalysis of conflicts between discourse context and world knowledge." *Frontiers in Communication* 7 (2022). doi.org/10.3389/fcomm.2022.910482.

Marich, Jamie. *Trauma and the 12 Steps: An Inclusive Guide to Enhancing Recovery*. Berkeley, California: North Atlantic Books, 2020.

Mate, Gabor. *In the Realm of Hungry Ghosts: Close Encounters with Addiction*. Ebury Digital, 2019.

McCauley, Kevin. "Pleasure Unwoven: An Explanation of the Brain Disease of Addiction." The Institute for Addiction Study, 2009. Video. 1 hr., 10 min.

Mental Health America. "What Are Endorphins?" www.mhanational.org/what-are-endorphins.

Nehme, Coralie. "The Effect of Post Traumatic Stress Disorder on the Ability to Recognize Facial Expressions." *Applied Psychology Opus*, 2016. https://wp.nyu.edu/steinhardt-appsych_opus/the-effect-of-post-traumatic-stress-disorder-on-the-ability-to-recognize-facial-expressions/.

Rai, Dev, T.S. Jaisoorya, Janardhanan C. Narayanaswamyet, Shyam Sundar Arumugham, Y.C. Janardhan Reddy. "Behavioural Addictions in Obsessive Compulsive Disorder – Prevalence and Clinical Correlates." *Psychiatry Research Communications* 2, no. 1 (2022): 100016. https://doi.org/10.1016/j.psycom.2021.100016.

Sacks, Oliver. *Hallucinations*. Pan Macmillan, 2013.

Sacks, Oliver. *The Man Who Mistook His Wife for a Hat: And Other Clinical Tales*. Simon & Schuster, 1985.

Schultz, Colin. "There's a Scientific Reason Why Self-Harm Makes Some People Feel Better." Smithsonian Magazine, October 16, 2014. www.smithsonianmag.com/smart-news/theres-scientific-reason-why-self-harm-makes-some-people-feel-better-180953062/.

Selby, Edward A., Amy Kranzler, Janne Lindqvist, et al. "The Dynamics of Pain during Nonsuicidal Self-Injury." *Clinical Psychological Science* 7, no. 2, (2018): 302–20. https://doi.org/10.1177/2167702618807147.

Sternberg, Eliezer J. *NeuroLogic: The Brain's Hidden Rationale Behind Our Irrational Behavior.* Pantheon, 2016.

Nam, Seok Hyun, Juhyun Park, and Tae Won Park. "Clinical Aspects of Premonitory Urges in Patients with Tourette's Disorder." *Journal of Korean Academic Child Adolescent Psychiatry* 30, no. 2, (2019): 50–56. https://doi.org/10.5765/jkacap.180025.

Szalavitz, Maia. *Unbroken Brain: A Revolutionary New Way of Understanding Addiction.* Macmillan, 2016.

Tan, Oguz. "Is Obsessive–Compulsive Disorder Preventive against Addiction?" *The Journal of Neurobehavioral Sciences* 8, no. 3, (2021): 251-261. https://doi.org/10.4103/jnbs.jnbs_15_21.

Varma, Vijay R., Yi-Fang Chuang, Gregory C. Harris, Erwin J. Tan, and Michelle C. Carlson. "Low-intensity daily walking activity is associated with hippocampal volume in older adults." *Hippocampus* 25, no. 5 (2015):605-15. doi: 10.1002/hipo.22397.

Volkow, Nora D., Gene-Jack Wang, Joanna S. Fowler, Dardo Tomasi, Frank Telang, and Ruben Baler. "Addiction: Decreased Reward Sensitivity and Increased Expectation Sensitivity Conspire to Overwhelm the Brain's Control Circuit." *BioEssays* 32, no. 9 (2010): 748–55. https://doi.org/10.1002/bies.201000042.

Yang, Yihong, Hui Zhou, Tiantian Hong, et al. "Glutamate Concentration of Medial Prefrontal Cortex Is Inversely Associated with Addictive Behaviors: A Translational Study." *Research Square*, (2024). https://doi.org/10.21203/rs.3.rs-3685426/v1.

Upgrade 6.0

Adams, Kenneth. *Silently Seduced, Revised and Updated: When Parents Make Their Children Partners.* Health Communications, Incorporated, 2011.

Bellis, Mark A., Katie Hardcastle, Kat Ford, et al. "Does Continuous Trusted Adult Support in Childhood Impart Life-Course Resilience against Adverse Childhood Experiences - a Retrospective Study on

Adult Health-Harming Behaviours and Mental Well-Being." *BMC Psychiatry* 17, no. 1 (2017). https://doi.org/10.1186/s12888-017-1260-z.

Boyle, Greg. *Barking to the Choir: The Power of Radical Kinship.* Simon & Schuster Paperbacks, 2018.

Boyle, Greg. *Tattoos on the Heart: The Power of Boundless Compassion.* Free Press, 2011.

Bradshaw, John. *Home Coming: Reclaiming and Championing Your Inner Child.* Piatkus, 1990.

Brown, Brené. *Braving the Wilderness: The Quest for True Belonging and the Courage to Stand Alone.* Random House, 2017.

Brown, Brené. *Daring Greatly: How the Courage to Be Vulnerable Transforms the Way We Live, Love, Parent, and Lead.* Penguin Random House Audio Publishing Group, 2012.

Brownlee, Brooke. "Couples' Attunement & Coregulation: Why It's Important." *Modern Intimacy*, February 11, 2023. www.modernintimacy.com/couples-attunement-coregulation-why-its-important/.

Buqué, Mariel. *Break the Cycle: A Guide to Healing Intergenerational Trauma.* New York: Dutton, 2024.

Butler, Oisin, Gerd Willmund, Tobias Gleich, et al. "Hippocampal Gray Matter Increases Following Multimodal Psychological Treatment for Combat-Related Post-Traumatic Stress Disorder." *Brain and Behavior* 8, no. 5 (2018): e00956, https://doi.org/10.1002/brb3.956.

Carpenter, Erin. *Life, Reinvented: A Guide to Healing from Sexual Trauma for Survivors and Loved Ones.* Quantum Publishing Group, 2014.

Cerritelli, Francesco, Martin G. Frasch, Marta C. Antonelli, et al. "A Review on the Vagus Nerve and Autonomic Nervous System during Fetal Development: Searching for Critical Windows."

Frontiers in Neuroscience 15 (2021): 721605. https://doi.org/10.3389/fnins.2021.721605.

Cortes Viniegra, Cristina, and Marie F. Aumeunier-Gizard. "Facilitating Integrated Mental, Emotional, and Physical States in Children Who Have Suffered Early Abandonment Trauma." *European Journal of Trauma & Dissociation* 5, no. 4 (2021): 100214. https://doi.org/10.1016/j.ejtd.2021.100214.

Cundy, Linda. *Anxiously Attached: Understanding and Working with Preoccupied Attachment.* Routledge, 2019.

Cundy, Linda. *Attachment and the Defence Against Intimacy: Understanding and Working with Avoidant Attachment, Self-Hatred, and Shame.* Routledge, 2019.

Dana, Deb. *The Polyvagal Theory in Therapy: Engaging the Rhythm of Regulation.* W.W. Norton & Company, 2018.

Debiec, Jacek, and Regina M. Sullivan. "Intergenerational Transmission of Emotional Trauma through Amygdala-Dependent Mother-To-Infant Transfer of Specific Fear." *Proceedings of the National Academy of Sciences* 111, no. 33 (2014): 12222–27. https://doi.org/10.1073/pnas.1316740111.

Dixon, Holly C., Lisa M. Reynolds, and Nathan S. Consedine. "Containing Attachment Concerns: Does Trait Mindfulness Buffer the Links between Attachment Insecurity and Maladaptive Sexual Motivations?" *The Journal of Sex Research* 60, no. 8 (2022): 1126–1137. https://doi.org/10.1080/00224499.2022.2043229.

Feeney, Judith. "Attachment and Perceived Rejection: Findings from Studies of Hurt Feelings and the Adoption Experience." *E-Journal of Applied Psychology*. 1, no. 1 (2005): 41–49. https://doi.org/10.7790/ejap.v1i1.8.

Field, Tiffany, and Miguel Diego. "Vagal Activity, Early Growth and Emotional Development." *Infant Behavior and Development* 31, no. 3 (2008): 361–73. https://doi.org/10.1016/j.infbeh.2007.12.008.

Foo, Stephanie. *What My Bones Know: A Memoir of Healing from Complex Trauma.* Allen & Unwin, 2022.

Fox, Daniel J. *Borderline Personality Disorder Workbook: An Integrative Program to Understand and Manage Your BPD.* New Harbinger, 2020.

Gibson, Lindsay C. *Adult Children of Emotionally Immature Parents: How to Deal with Distant, Rejecting or Self-Involved Parents.* New Harbinger Publications, 2015.

Gibson, Lindsay C. *Recovering from Emotionally Immature Parents: Practical Tools to Establish Boundaries & Reclaim Your Emotional Autonomy.* New Harbinger Publications, 2019.

Golombok, Susan, Jennifer Readings, Lucy Blake, Polly Casey, Alex Marks and Vasanti Jadva. "Families Created through Surrogacy: Mother–Child Relationships and Children's Psychological Adjustment at Age 7." *Developmental Psychology* 47, no. 6 (2011): 1579–88. https://doi.org/10.1037/a0025292.

Gottman, John, and Joan DeClaire. *The Relationship Cure: A Five-Step Guide to Strengthening Your Marriage, Family, and Friendships.* Three Rivers Press, 2002.

Hampton, Debbie. "How Trauma Can Damage the Brain for Generations and Can Be Reversed." *The Best Brain Possible*, January 28, 2018. thebestbrainpossible.com/epigenetics-trauma-brain-reversed-mental-health/?fbclid=IwAR1vagAwNO2ea2JqS713ncxhXxHJa0y-CsVQHsEBbD1ispEVXdM6Jlyi-IM.

Heller, Diane Poole. *Healing Your Attachment Wounds: How to Create Deep and Lasting Intimate Relationships.* Sounds True, 2017.

Heller, Diane Poole. *The Power of Attachment: How to Create Deep and Lasting Intimate Relationships.* Sounds True, 2019.

Heller, Laurence, and Brad J. Kammer. *The Practical Guide for Healing Developmental Trauma.* North Atlantic Books, 2022.

Hunter, Mic. *Abused Boys: The Neglected Victims of Sexual Abuse.* Fawcett Columbine, 1991.

Jackman, Robert. *Healing Your Lost Inner Child: How to Stop Impulsive Reactions, Set Healthy Boundaries and Embrace an Authentic Life*. Practical Wisdom Press, 2020.

Jeon, Hyeonjin, and Seung-Hwan Lee. "From Neurons to Social Beings: Short Review of the Mirror Neuron System Research and Its Socio-Psychological and Psychiatric Implications." *Clinical Psychopharmacology and Neuroscience* 16, no. 1 (2018): 18–31. https://doi.org/10.9758/cpn.2018.16.1.18.

Johnson, Sue. *Hold Me Tight: Seven Conversations for a Lifetime of Love*. Little Brown & Co, 2011.

Johnson, Sue. *Love Sense: The Revolutionary New Science of Romantic Relationships*. Little, Brown and Company, 2013.

Kaneshiro, Kiyomi Raye, Thea A. Egelhofer, Andreas Rechtsteiner, Chad Cockrum, and Susan Strome. "Sperm-Inherited H3K27me3 Epialleles Are Transmitted Transgenerationally in Cis." *Proceedings of the National Academy of Sciences* 119, no. 40 (2022). https://doi.org/10.1073/pnas.2209471119.

Lawson, Christine Ann. *Understanding the Borderline Mother: Helping Her Children Transcend the Intense, Unpredictable, and Volatile Relationship*. Rowman & Littlefield, 2004.

Lorenz, Tierney A., Christopher B. Harte, Lisa Dawn Hamilton, and Cindy M. Meston. "Evidence for a Curvilinear Relationship between Sympathetic Nervous System Activation and Women's Physiological Sexual Arousal." *Psychophysiology* 49, no. 1 (2011): 111–17. https://doi.org/10.1111/j.1469-8986.2011.01285.x.

Marriot, Sue. and Ann Kelly, hosts, Therapist Uncensored, episode 96. "TU96: Treating Attachment & Self-Protective Strategies with Guest Patricia Crittenden (Part 1)." May 15, 2019. therapistuncensored.com/episodes/tu96-treating-attachment-self-protective-strategies-with-guest-patricia-crittenden-part-1/.

Menakem, Resmaa. *My Grandmother's Hands: Racialized Trauma and the Pathway to Mending Our Hearts and Bodies*. Central Recovery Press, 2017.

Menanno, Julie. *Secure Love: Create a Relationship That Lasts a Lifetime*. CORUK, 2024.

Nagoski, Emily. *Come As You Are: The Surprising New Science That Will Transform Your Sex Life*. Simon & Schuster, 2021.

Nhat Hanh, Thích. *Reconciliation: Healing the Inner Child*. Parallax Press, 2011.

O'Connor, Mary-Frances. *The Grieving Brain: The Surprising Science of How We Learn from Love and Loss*. HarperCollins, 2022.

Olivera, Lisa. *Already Enough: A Path to Self-Acceptance*. Simon and Schuster, 2023.

PeaceHealth. "Dolls Help NICU Babies Use Sense of Smell to Bond with Parents," January 22, 2020. www.peacehealth.org/everyday-moments/dolls-help-nicu-babies-use-sense-smell-bond-parents.

Perry, Bruce D., and Maia Szalavitz. *The Boy Who Was Raised as a Dog: And Other Stories from a Child Psychiatrist's Notebook: What Traumatized Children Can Teach Us about Loss, Love, and Healing*. Basic Books, 2017.

Pfaltz, Monique C., Sandra Passardi, Bianca Auschra, Natalia E. Fares-Otero, Ulrich Schnyder, and Peter Peyk. "Are You Angry at Me? Negative Interpretations of Neutral Facial Expressions Are Linked to Child Maltreatment but Not to Posttraumatic Stress Disorder." *European Journal of Psychotraumatology* 10, no. 1 (2019): 1682929. https://doi.org/10.1080/20008198.2019.1682929.

Postlethwait, Nate. "Inner Child Journaling Guide." https://natewrites.com/inner-child-journaling-guide/.

Rand, Katherine, and Amir Lahav. "Maternal Sounds Elicit Lower Heart Rate in Preterm Newborns in the First Month of Life." *Early Human Development* 90, no. 10 (2014): 679–83. https://doi.org/10.1016/j.earlhumdev.2014.07.016.

Rodkey, Elissa N., and Rebecca Pillai Riddell. "The Infancy of Infant Pain Research: The Experimental Origins of Infant Pain

Denial." *The Journal of Pain* 14, no. 4 (2013): 338–50. https://doi.org/10.1016/j.jpain.2012.12.017.

Rogol, Alan David. "Emotional Deprivation in Children: Growth Faltering and Reversible Hypopituitarism." *Frontiers in Endocrinology (Pediatric Endocrinology)* 11, (2020) https://www.frontiersin.org/articles/10.3389/fendo.2020.596144/full.

Schwartz, Arielle. *The Complex PTSD Treatment Manual: An Integrative, Mind-Body Approach to Trauma Recovery*. Pesi Publishing, 2021.

Schore, Allan N. "Effects of A Secure Attachment Relationship on Right Brain Development, Affect Regulation, and Infant Mental Health." *Infant Mental Health Journal* 22, no. 1-2 (2001): 7–66. https://doi.org/10.1002/1097-0355(200101/04)22:1%3C7::AID-IMHJ2%3E3.0.CO;2-N.

Seiler, Annina, Roland von Känel, and George M. Slavich. "The Psychobiology of Bereavement and Health: A Conceptual Review from the Perspective of Social Signal Transduction Theory of Depression." *Frontiers in Psychiatry* 11, (2020): 565239. doi: 10.3389/fpsyt.2020.565239.

Simpson, Elizabeth A., Lynne Murray, Annika Paukner, and Pier F. Ferrari. "The Mirror Neuron System as Revealed through Neonatal Imitation: Presence from Birth, Predictive Power and Evidence of Plasticity." *Philosophical Transactions of the Royal Society B: Biological Sciences* 369, no. 1644, (2014): 20130289. https://doi.org/10.1098/rstb.2013.0289.

Stanton, Amelia M., Carey S. Pulverman, and Cindy M. Meston. "Vagal Activity During Physiological Sexual Arousal in Women with and Without Sexual Dysfunction." *Journal of Sex & Marital Therapy*, 43, no. 1 (2016): 78-89. doi: 10.1080/0092623X.2015.1115793.

Stiles, Joan, and Terry L. Jernigan. "The Basics of Brain Development." *Neuropsychology Review* 20, no. 4, (2010): 327–48. https://doi.org/10.1007/s11065-010-9148-4.

Stringer, Jay. *Unwanted: How Sexual Brokenness Reveals Our Way to Healing*. NavPress, 2018.

Strunz, Sandra, Constanze Schermuck, Sarah Ballerstein, Christoph J. Ahlers, Isabel Dziobek, and Stefan Roepke. "Romantic Relationships and Relationship Satisfaction among Adults with Asperger Syndrome and High-Functioning Autism." *Journal of Clinical Psychology* 73, no. 1 (2016): 113–125. https://doi.org/10.1002/jclp.22319.

Tatkin, Stan. *We Do: Saying Yes to a Relationship of Depth, True Connection, and Enduring Love.* Tantor Audio, 2018.

Tatkin, Stan. *Wired for Dating: How Understanding Neurobiology and Attachment Style Can Help You Find Your Ideal Mate.* New Harbinger Publications, 2016.

Tatkin, Stan. *Wired for Love: How Understanding Your Partner's Brain and Attachment Style Can Help You Defuse Conflict and Build a Secure Relationship.* New Harbinger Publications, 2012.

Ustun, Beyza, Nadja Reissland, Judith Covey, Benoist Schaal, and Jacqueline Blissett. "Flavor Sensing in Utero and Emerging Discriminative Behaviors in the Human Fetus." *Psychological Science* 33, no. 10 (2022). https://doi.org/10.1177/09567976221105460.

Voorendonk, Eline M., Ad De Jongh, Linda Rozendaal, and Agnes van Minnen. "Trauma-focused treatment outcome for complex PTSD patients: results of an intensive treatment programme." *European Journal of Psychotraumatology* 11, no. 1 (2020): 1783955. doi: 10.1080/20008198.2020.1783955.

Walker, Pete. *Complex PTSD: From Surviving to Thriving: A Guide and Map for Recovering from Childhood Trauma.* Azure Coyote, 2013.

Weiss, Karen G. "Too Ashamed to Report: Deconstructing the Shame of Sexual Victimization." *Feminist Criminology* 5, no. 3 (2010): 286–310. https://doi.org/10.1177/1557085110376343.

Weiss, Karen G. "'You Just Don't Report That Kind of Stuff': Investigating Teens' Ambivalence toward Peer-Perpetrated, Unwanted Sexual Incidents." *Violence and Victims* 28, no. 2 (2013): 288–302. https://doi.org/10.1891/0886-6708.11-061.

Wilson, Gary. *Your Brain on Porn: Internet Pornography and the Emerging Science of Addiction.* Commonwealth Publishing, 2014.

Wolynn, Mark. *It Didn't Start with You: How Inherited Family Trauma Shapes Who We Are and How to End the Cycle.* Penguin Books, 2017.

Yehuda, Rachel. "How Parents' Trauma Leaves Biological Traces in Children." *Scientific American,* July 1, 2022. https://www.scientificamerican.com/article/how-parents-rsquo-trauma-leaves-biological-traces-in-children/.

Zhang, Shiyan, and Chunmei He. "Effect of the Sound of the Mother's Heartbeat Combined with White Noise on Heart Rate, Weight, and Sleep in Premature Infants: A Retrospective Comparative Cohort Study." *Annals of Palliative Medicine* 12, no. 1 (2023). https://doi.org/10.21037/apm-22-1269.

Upgrade 7.0

Anderson, Frank G., Martha Sweezy, and Richard C Schwartz. *Internal Family Systems Skills Training Manual: Trauma-Informed Treatment for Anxiety, Depression, PTSD & Substance Abuse.* Pesi Publishing & Media, 2017.

Ardito, Rita B., and Daniela Rabellino. "Therapeutic Alliance and Outcome of Psychotherapy: Historical Excursus, Measurements, and Prospects for Research." *Frontiers in Psychology* 2, no. 270 (2011). https://doi.org/10.3389/fpsyg.2011.00270.

Chalavi, Sima, Eline M. Vissia, Mechteld E. Giesen, et al. "Abnormal Hippocampal Morphology in Dissociative Identity Disorder and Post-Traumatic Stress Disorder Correlates with Childhood Trauma and Dissociative Symptoms." *Human Brain Mapping* 36, no. 5 (2014): 1692–1704. https://doi.org/10.1002/hbm.22730.

Chödrön, Pema. *When Things Fall Apart: Heart Advice for Difficult Times.* Shambhala, 2016.

DeAngelis, Tori. "Better Relationships with Patients Lead to Better Outcomes." *Monitor on Psychology* 50, no. 10 (2019): 38. www.apa.org/monitor/2019/11/ce-corner-relationships.

Devendorf, Andrew R., Ruba Rum, Todd B. Kashdan, and Jonathan Rottenberg. "Optimal Well-Being after Psychopathology: Prevalence and Correlates." *Clinical Psychological Science* 10, no. 5 (2022). https://doi.org/10.1177/21677026221078872.

Devine, Megan. *It's Ok That You're Not Ok: Meeting Grief and Loss in a Culture That Doesn't Understand*. Sounds True, 2018.

Gnaulati, Enrico. *Saving Talk Therapy: How Health Insurers, Big Pharma, and Slanted Science Are Ruining Good Mental Health Care*. Beacon Press, 2018.

Howes, Molly. *A Good Apology: Four Steps to Make Things Right*. Grand Central Publishing, 2020.

Hiser, Jaryd, and Michael Koenigs. "The Multifaceted Role of the Ventromedial Prefrontal Cortex in Emotion, Decision Making, Social Cognition, and Psychopathology." *Biological Psychiatry* 83, no. 8 (2018): 638–47. https://doi.org/10.1016/j.biopsych.2017.10.030.

Lebois, Lauren A. M., Nathaniel G. Harnett, Sanne J.H. van Rooij, et al. "Persistent Dissociation and Its Neural Correlates in Predicting Outcomes after Trauma Exposure." The *American Journal of Psychiatry* 179, no. 9 (2022): 661–72. https://doi.org/10.1176/appi.ajp.21090911.

Lebois, Lauren A. M., Poornima Kumar, Cori A. Palermo, et al. "Deconstructing Dissociation: A Triple Network Model of Trauma-Related Dissociation and Its Subtypes." *Neuropsychopharmacology* 47, no. 13 (2022): 2261–70. https://doi.org/10.1038/s41386-022-01468-1.

Marich, Jamie. *Dissociation Made Simple: A Stigma-Free Guide to Embracing Your Dissociative Mind and Navigating Daily Life*. North Atlantic Books, 2023.

Mills, Kim, Speaking of Psychology, episode 184, "Speaking of Psychology: How Grieving Changes the Brain, with Mary-Frances O'Connor, PhD." American Psychological Association, February 2022. www.apa.org/news/podcasts/speaking-of-psychology/grieving-changes-brain.

Moffa, Gina. *Moving on Doesn't Mean Letting Go.* Balance, 2023.

Schlumpf, Yolanda R., Ellert R.S. Nijenhuis, Sima Chalavi, et al. "Dissociative part-dependent biopsychosocial reactions to backward masked angry and neutral faces: An fMRI study of dissociative identity disorder." *NeuroImage Clinical* 3, (2013): 54-64. doi:10.1016/j.nicl.2013.07.002.

Schlumpf, Yolanda R., Antje A. T. S. Reinders, Ellert R. S. Nijenhuis, Roger Luechinger, Matthias J. P. van Osch, and Lutz Jncke. "Dissociative Part-Dependent Resting-State Activity in Dissociative Identity Disorder: A Controlled FMRI Perfusion Study." *PLoS ONE* 9, no. 6 (2014): e98795. https://doi.org/10.1371/journal.pone.0098795.

Schwartz, Richard C. *Greater Than the Sum of Our Parts: Discovering Your True Self Through Internal Family Systems Therapy.* Sounds True, 2018.

Schwartz, Richard C. *No Bad Parts: How the Internal Family Systems Model Changes Everything.* Sounds True, 2021.

Schwartz, Richard. *You Are the One You've Been Waiting For: Applying Internal Family Systems to Intimate Relationships.* Random House, 2023.

Shapiro, Robin. *Easy Ego State Interventions: Strategies for Working with Parts.* W.W. Norton & Company, 2016.

Sunshaw, Emma. "System Speak - Podcast Archive." Systemspeakcommunity.com. systemspeakcommunity.com/podcast-archive/.

Tawwab, Nedra Glover. *Drama Free: A Guide to Managing Unhealthy Family Relationships.* Penguin Books, 2023.

Tawwab, Nedra Glover. *Set Boundaries, Find Peace: A Guide to Reclaiming Yourself.* Penguin Publishing Group, 2021.

University of Aberdeen. "Brain Changes Linked to Emotion Discovered in Mysterious 'Broken Heart Syndrome.'" *Neuroscience News*, June 9, 2022. www.neurosciencenews.com/emotion-broken-heart-syndrome-20793/.

University of California - Los Angeles. "Putting Feelings into Words Produces Therapeutic Effects in the Brain." *ScienceDaily*, June 22, 2007. www.sciencedaily.com/releases/2007/06/070622090727.htm.

Vermetten, Eric, Christian Schmahl, Sanneke Linder, Richard J. Loewenstein, and J. Douglas Bremner. "Hippocampal and Amygdalar Volumes in Dissociative Identity Disorder." *American Journal of Psychiatry* 163, no. 4 (2006): 630, https://doi.org/10.1176/appi.ajp.163.4.630.

Yup, Kayla. "'How People Fall Apart': Yale Faculty Discuss the Impact of Burnout on the Brain." *Yale Daily News*, March 29, 2022. yaledailynews.com/blog/2022/03/29/how-people-fall-apart-yale-faculty-discuss-the-impact-of-burnout-on-the-brain/.

Zoet, Harmen A., Anouk Wagenmans, Agnes van Minnen, et al. "Presence of the dissociative subtype of PTSD does not moderate the outcome of intensive trauma-focused treatment for PTSD." *European Journal of Psychotraumatology* 9, no. 1 (2018). doi: 10.1080/20008198.2018.1468707.

Bonus Upgrade

Chapter A

Clarke-Fields, Hunter. *Raising Good Humans: A Mindful Guide to Breaking the Cycle of Reactive Parenting and Raising Kind, Confident Kids.* New Harbinger Publications, 2019.

Gilbertson, Tina. *Reconnecting with Your Estranged Adult Child: Practical Tips and Tools to Heal Your Relationship.* New World Library, 2020.

Greene, Ross W. *The Explosive Child: A New Approach for Understanding and Parenting Easily Frustrated, Chronically Inflexible Children.* HarperCollins, 2021.

Kennedy, Becky. *Good Inside: A Guide to Becoming the Parent You Want to Be.* Harper Thorsons, 2022.

Purvis, Karyn B., David R. Cross, and Wendy Lyons Sunshine. *The Connected Child: Bring Hope and Healing to Your Adoptive Family.* McGraw Hill Professional, 2007.

Ross, Julie A. *How to Hug a Porcupine: Negotiating the Prickly Points of the Tween Years.* Mcgraw Hill, 2008.

Siegel, Daniel J., and Tina Payne Bryson. *No-Drama Discipline: The Whole-Brain Way to Calm the Chaos and Nurture Your Child's Developing Mind.* Bantam Books, 2016.

Siegel, Daniel J., and Tina Payne Bryson. *The Whole-Brain Child: 12 Revolutionary Strategies to Nurture Your Child's Developing Mind.* Bantam Books, 2012.

Siegel, Daniel J., and Mary Hartzell. *Parenting from the Inside Out: How a Deeper Self-Understanding Can Help You Raise Children Who Thrive.* TarcherPerigee, 2014.

Chapter B

DeAngelis, Tori. "Better Relationships with Patients Lead to Better Outcomes." *Monitor on Psychology* 50, no. 10 (2019): 38. www.apa.org/monitor/2019/11/ce-corner-relationships.

Hoffman, Kent, Glen Cooper, and Bert Powell. *Raising a Secure Child: How Circle of Security Parenting Can Help You Nurture Your Child's Attachment, Emotional Resilience, and Freedom to Explore.* Guilford Press, 2017.

Horton, Jillian. *We Are All Perfectly Fine: A Memoir of Love, Medicine, and Healing.* HarperCollins, 2021.

van Dernoot Lipsky, Laura, and Connie Burk. *Trauma Stewardship: An Everyday Guide to Caring for Self While Caring for Others.* Oakland, Ca: Berrett-Koehler Publishers, 2009.

<u>Chapter C</u>

Arain, Mariam, Maliha Haque, Lina Johal, et al. "Maturation of the Adolescent Brain." *Neuropsychiatric Disease and Treatment* 9, no. 9 (2013): 449–61. https://doi.org/10.2147/ndt.s39776.

Chen, Li. "Influence of music on the hearing and mental health of adolescents and countermeasures." *Frontiers in Neuroscience* 17, (2023). https://doi.org/10.3389/fnins.2023.1236638.

Siegel, Daniel J. *Brainstorm: The Power and Purpose of the Teenage Brain.* TarcherPerigee, 2014.

Sparks, Sarah D. "The Teen Brain: How Schools Can Help Students Manage Emotions and Make Better Decisions." *Education Week*, Oct. 9, 2018. www.edweek.org/leadership/the-teen-brain-how-schools-can-help-students-manage-emotions-and-make-better-decisions/2018/10?utm_source=fb&utm_medium=soc&utm_campaign=edit.

Spear, Linda Patia. "Adolescent Neurodevelopment." *Journal of Adolescent Health* 52, no. 2 (2013): S7–13. https://doi.org/10.1016/j.jadohealth.2012.05.006.

Wallace, Jennifer Breheny. *Never Enough: When Achievement Culture Becomes Toxic—and What We Can Do About It.* Penguin, 2023.

Wilcox, Brad, and Jerrick Robbins. *How to Hug a Hedgehog: 12 Keys for Connecting with Teens.* Familius, 2014.

Chapter D

Bacon, Lindo. *Radical Belonging: How to Survive and Thrive in an Unjust World (While Transforming It for the Better)*. BenBella Books, 2020.

Criado Perez, Caroline. *Invisible Women: Exposing Data Bias in a World Designed for Men*. London: Vintage, 2019.

Desmond, Matthew. *Poverty, by America*. Crown Publishing Group, 2023.

Eberhardt, Jennifer L. *Biased: Uncovering the Hidden Prejudice That Shapes What We See, Think, and Do*. Penguin Books, 2020.

Krawec, Patty. *Becoming Kin: An Indigenous Call to Unforgetting the Past and Reimagining Our Future*. Broadleaf Books, 2022.

Menakem, Resmaa. *My Grandmother's Hands: Racialized Trauma and the Pathway to Mending Our Hearts and Bodies*. Central Recovery Press, 2017.

Wang, Jenny T. *Permission to Come Home: Reclaiming Mental Health as Asian Americans*. Balance, 2024.

Chapter E

Behrman, Sophie, and Clair Crockett. "Severe Mental Illness and the Perimenopause." *BJPsych Bulletin* (2023): 1-7. doi: 10.1192/bjb.2023.89.

Butler, Katy. *The Art of Dying Well: A Practical Guide to a Good End of Life*. Scribner, 2020.

Elia, M., P. Ritz, and R. Stubbs. "Total Energy Expenditure in the Elderly." *European Journal of Clinical Nutrition* 54, no. S3 (2000): S92–S103. https://doi.org/10.1038/sj.ejcn.1601030.

Fricker, Michael, Aviva M. Tolkovsky, Vilmante Borutaite, Michael Coleman, and Guy C. Brown. "Neuronal Cell Death." *Physiological Reviews* 98, no. 2 (2018):813–80. https://doi.org/10.1152/physrev.00011.2017.

Haver, Mary Claire. *The New Menopause: Navigating Your Path Through Hormonal Changes with Purpose, Power, and Facts.* Randomhouse Publishing Group, 2024.

Vlahos, Hadley. *The In-Between: Unforgettable Encounters During Life's Final.* Random House Audio, 2023.

Chapter F

Ballou, Emily P., Sharon daVanport, and Morénike Giwa Onaiwu. *Sincerely, Your Autistic Child: What People on the Autism Spectrum Wish Their Parents Knew About Growing up, Acceptance, and Identity.* Beacon Press, 2021.

Crenshaw, Wes, and Jordan Mayfield. "The Relationship between PTSD and ADHD: Symptoms, Diagnosis, Treatment." *ADDitude*, February 5, 2024. www.additudemag.com/ptsd-symptoms-adhd-diagnosis-difficult/.

Gandal, Michael J., Jillian R. Haney, Brie Wamsley, et al. "Broad Transcriptomic Dysregulation Occurs across the Cerebral Cortex in ASD." *Nature* 611, (2022): 532–539. https://doi.org/10.1038/s41586-022-05377-7.

Hallowell, Edward M., and John J. Ratey. *ADHD 2.0: New Science and Essential Strategies for Thriving with Distraction–from Childhood through Adulthood.* Ballantine Books, 2021.

Kandel, Eric R. *The Disordered Mind: What Unusual Brains Tells Us About Ourselves.* Farrar, Straus and Giroux, 2018.

Kranowitz, Carol, and Lucy Jane Miller. *The Out-Of-Sync Child, Third Edition: Recognizing and Coping with Sensory Processing Differences.* Penguin Publishing Group, 2022.

Nerenberg, Jenara. *Divergent Mind: Thriving in a World That Wasn't Designed for You*. HarperOne, 2021.

Reber, Deborah. *Differently Wired: Raising an Exceptional Child in a Conventional World*. Workman Publishing Company, 2018.

Ruiz, Rebecca. "How Childhood Trauma Could Be Mistaken for ADHD." *The Atlantic*, July 7, 2014. www.theatlantic.com/health/archive/2014/07/how-childhood-trauma-could-be-mistaken-for-adhd/373328/.

Silberman, Steve. *NeuroTribes: The Legacy of Autism and the Future of Neurodiversity*. Avery, 2016.

Thapar, Anita. "Discoveries on the Genetics of ADHD in the 21st Century: New Findings and Their Implications." *American Journal of Psychiatry* 175, no. 10 (2018): 943–50. https://doi.org/10.1176/appi.ajp.2018.18040383.

Torrey, E. Fuller. *Surviving Schizophrenia, 7th Edition*. Harper Collins, 2019.

Vormer, Casey. *Connecting with the Autism Spectrum: How to Talk, How to Listen, and Why You Shouldn't Call It High-Functioning*. Rockridge Press, 2020.

Zhang, Yi, Hui-xin Hu, Ling-ling Wang, et al. "Altered Neural Mechanism of Social Reward Anticipation in Individuals with Schizophrenia and Social Anhedonia." *European Archives of Psychiatry and Clinical Neuroscience* 273, (2023): 1029–1039, https://doi.org/10.1007/s00406-022-01505-6.

Chapter G

D'Agnelli, Simona, Lars Arendt-Nielsen, Maria C. Gerra, et al. "Fibromyalgia: Genetics and Epigenetics Insights May Provide the Basis for the Development of Diagnostic Biomarkers." *Molecular Pain* 15 (2018). https://doi.org/10.1177/1744806918819944.

Gerra, Maria C., Davide Carnevali, Paolo Ossala, et al. "DNA Methylation Changes in Fibromyalgia Suggest the Role of the

Immune-Inflammatory Response and Central Sensitization." *Journal of Clinical Medicine* 10, no. 21 (2021): 4992. doi: https://doi.org/10.3390/jcm10214992.

Greden, John F., Sagar V. Parikh, Anthony J. Rothschildet, et al. "Impact of Pharmacogenomics on Clinical Outcomes in Major Depressive Disorder in the GUIDED Trial: A Large, Patient- and Rater-Blinded, Randomized, Controlled Study." *Journal of Psychiatric Research* 111 (2019): 59–67. https://doi.org/10.1016/j.jpsychires.2019.01.003.

Gustafson, Craig. "William Walsh, PhD: Epigenetics as a Source of Mental Health Dysfunction and the Nutrient-Based Solution." *Advances* 28, no. 2 (2014): 26-32. www.walshinstitute.org/uploads/1/7/9/9/17997321/epigenetics_source_of_mental_dysfunction_and_the_nutrient-based_solution_william_walsh_phd.pdf.

Howell, Kate Joanne, Judith Kraiczy, Komal M. Nayak, et al. "DNA Methylation and Transcription Patterns in Intestinal Epithelial Cells from Pediatric Patients with Inflammatory Bowel Diseases Differentiate Disease Subtypes and Associate with Outcome." *Gastroenterology* 154, no. 3 (2018): 585–98. https://doi.org/10.1053/j.gastro.2017.10.007.

Kamenov, Kaloyan, Conal, Twomey, Maria Cabello, Matthew Prina, and J. L. Ayuso-Mateos. "The Efficacy of Psychotherapy, Pharmacotherapy and Their Combination on Functioning and Quality of Life in Depression: A Meta-Analysis." *Psychological Medicine* 47, no. 3 (2017): 414–25. https://doi.org/10.1017/S0033291716002774.

Kim, Ji Woon, Anita E. Autry, Elisa S. Na, et al. "Sustained Effects of Rapidly Acting Antidepressants Require BDNF-Dependent MeCP2 Phosphorylation." *Nature Neuroscience* 24, no. 8 (2021): 1100–9. https://doi.org/10.1038/s41593-021-00868-8.

Matosin, Natalie, Cristiana Cruceanu, and Elisabeth B. Binder. "Preclinical and Clinical Evidence of DNA Methylation Changes in Response to Trauma and Chronic Stress." *Chronic Stress* 1 (2017). https://doi.org/10.1177/2470547017710764.

Murphy, Michaela E., and Cara J. Westmark. "Folic Acid Fortification and Neural Tube Defect Risk: Analysis of the Food Fortification Initiative Dataset." *Nutrients* 12, no. 1 (2020): 247. https://doi.org/10.3390/nu12010247.

Walsh, William. "Biochemical Individuality & Nutrition." Walsh Research Institute, www.walshinstitute.org/biochemical-individuality--nutrition.html.

Walsh, William. *Nutrient Power: Heal Your Biochemistry and Heal Your Brain*. Skyhorse Publishing, 2014.

Winkelman, Gil. "How Methylation Therapy Can Help Your Depression." Dr. Gil Winkelman ND, askdrgil.com/methylation-therapy/.

Winkelman, Gil. "The Colossal Mistake of All People Taking Methylated Folate." Dr. Gil Winkelman ND, Jun 9, 2017. askdrgil.com/colossal-mistake-everyone-taking-folic-acid/.

Winkelman, Gil. "What You Need to Know about Using Methylated Folate." Dr. Gil Winkelman ND, https://askdrgil.com/need-know-using-methylated-folate/.

Young, Calvin, and Danielle MacDougall. "An Overview of Pharmacogenomic Testing for Psychiatric Disorders: CADTH Horizon Scan." *Canadian Agency for Drugs and Technologies in Health*, 2023. www.ncbi.nlm.nih.gov/books/NBK595332/.

www.ingramcontent.com/pod-product-compliance
Lightning Source LLC
Chambersburg PA
CBHW070125080526
44586CB00015B/1559